D0712606

WITHDRAWN
UTSA Libraries

RENEWALS 458-4574

The Trouble with Ed Schools

The Trouble with Ed Schools

David F. Labaree

Yale University Press

New Haven and London

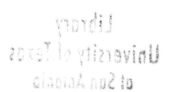

Library
University of Texas
at San Antonio

Copyright © 2004 by Yale University. All rights reserved. This book may not be reproduced, in whole or in part, including illustrations, in any form (beyond that copying
permitted by Sections 107 and 108 of the U.S. Copyright Law and except by reviewers
for the public press), without written permission from the publishers.

Set in Adobe Garamond type by The Composing Room of Michigan, Inc.
Printed in the United States of America.

Library of Congress Cataloging-in-Publication Data

Labaree, David F., 1947–
    The trouble with ed schools / David F. Labaree.
        p.   cm.
    Includes bibliographical references and index.
    ISBN 0-300-10350-6 (cloth : alk. paper)
    1. Teachers colleges—United States.   2. Teachers—Training of—United States.
3. Teacher educators—United States.   I. Title.
    LB1811.L33 2004
    370′.71′1—dc22

                                                                                2004001184

A catalogue record for this book is available from the British Library.

The paper in this book meets the guidelines for permanence and durability of the
Committee on Production Guidelines for Book Longevity of the Council on
Library Resources.

10 9 8 7 6 5 4 3 2 1

Library
University of Texas
at San Antonio

To Carole Ames, Steve Koziol, and my former colleagues and students in the College of Education at Michigan State University, who have taught me what an ed school can aspire to become.

Contents

Acknowledgments

As suggested in the dedication, this book arose in large part from my eighteen years as a faculty member in the College of Education at Michigan State University. I am enormously grateful to my colleagues and students there, who taught me much of what I know about education schools. Like many successful forms of education, this learning experience was the result of a collective instructional effort involving a large number of people over a long stretch of time. The MSU ed school is a remarkable institution, which has sought to position itself in such a way as to bridge many of the polarities of orientation that divide American ed schools and undermine their effectiveness—between practice and theory, between school and university, and between teacher preparation and educational research. In particular, I want to give thanks to Carole Ames, for being a wonderfully supportive dean, colleague, and friend, and to Steve Koziol, for being a wonderfully supportive department chair, colleague, and friend.

I am grateful to Tom Popkewitz and Barbara Beatty, who read a draft of this book for Yale University Press and provided me with feedback that was both deeply sympathetic and insightfully critical. I am also grateful to an array of colleagues, at a variety of institutions, who read early versions of papers that became part of this book and who gave me comments that have helped shape the book's argument: Tom Bird, Lynn Fendler, Bill Firestone, Andrew Gitlin, Ivor Goodson, Andy Hargreaves, E. D. Hirsch, Jeff Mirel, Aaron Pallas, Penelope Peterson, and Diane Ravitch. I presented material from this book in a number of settings in which the participants provided helpful comments, including annual meetings of the American Educational Research Association, the History of Education Society, and the International Standing Conference for the History of Education, and conferences or seminars organized by the PACT group (Professional Actions and Cultures of Teaching), the Brookings Institution, the Social Science Research Council, and the National Research Council. I also received remarkably constructive, if challenging, advice from anonymous reviewers at two academic journals, *Educational Researcher* and *American Educational Research Journal.* Three individuals at Yale University Press were very helpful in working with me on this manuscript, Susan Arellano and Erin Carter, the successive editors for the project, and Marie Blanchard, the manuscript editor. In addition, there are many friends and colleagues who provided the kind of ongoing support and stimulation without which the book would not have been possible: Cleo Cherryholmes, Mary Conn, Bob Floden, Susan Melnick, Michael Sedlak, Steve Weiland, and Suzanne Wilson. Finally, I want to thank my parents, Benjamin Labaree and Jean Ridgley Labaree, who gave me a terrific education and taught me the value of learning, and my wife, Diane Churchill, who is always there for me and always keeps me focused on the things that matter.

Chapter 1 Introduction: The Lowly Status of the Ed School

On Sunday, February 16, 2003, the *Detroit News* printed a long story in the first section with the title "He Has $300 Million for Detroit: Bob Thompson Challenges the Establishment by Exhausting Fortune to Build Schools." It tells about a man who made a fortune building his own asphalt paving company, sold the business, and retired. "Now Thompson plans to spend almost all of his remaining $300 million on a blunt challenge to educators. Open a Detroit charter high school, graduate 90 percent of the students, send them to college or other training, and he'll give you a new building for $1 a year."[1]

The article explains how Thompson sympathizes with kids who have trouble doing well in school—as so many students in the Detroit school system do these days—because of his own experiences in education:

> A lousy high school student, Thompson figured on a life on the family farm in Hillsdale County until his mother insisted on college. He hitch-hiked to Bowling Green State University south of Toledo. The world opened up. He joined the ROTC, roomed with guys from New York City and met a girl from Cleveland named Ellen who would become his wife.

But the class work was overwhelming. The man who later would devour Michener, *Out of Africa,* and thick biographies failed freshman English three times. He fell back on his farming instincts, rose at four in the morning to study, and took the easiest route to graduation: a major in education.

"It's the only thing I could do," says the man who would one day sell a business for $422 million. "I wasn't smart enough for business school."

He soon learned how tough it is to teach.

Bob and Ellen married after graduation and took classroom jobs in Detroit. Thompson quit after six weeks in a tough junior high. Boys urinated on the radiators. Mounted police shooed kids away after class.

"It was like being on Mars," he remembers. "I was an absolute failure."[2]

Many aspects of this story are familiar to anyone attuned to American culture. It's an inspirational tale of success in the face of adversity: farm boy becomes multimillionaire businessman, overcoming failure in school to achieve great things in business. It's also a heartwarming tale of a good man, grateful for his good fortune, who is trying to give something back in the community.

But nestled in the middle of the story is another familiar piece of Americana: a casual swipe at university schools of education. After initially failing at his studies, and figuring out that he "wasn't smart enough for business school," Thompson decided to take "the easiest route to graduation: a major in education." Note that neither he nor the reporter felt the need to explain this reference, since everyone understands that schools of education are as low as you can go in the hierarchy of academic challenges. But note also that, although education schools are easy, education itself is very difficult: he "was an absolute failure" as a teacher. Apparently, then, there is a serious mismatch between the weak resources of the education school and the powerful needs in the public schools. Which is why Thompson, the businessman outsider, felt it necessary to issue "a blunt challenge to educators" through his offer to build charter schools. Education, it seems, is just too important and too troubled to be left in the hands of educators, who have been ineptly trained by teacher educators in schools of education, and whose efforts to deal with school problems have been inaccurately informed by the ed schools' researchers.

This book is an interpretive essay about the curious nature of the American education school. Institutionally, the ed school is the Rodney Dangerfield of higher education: it don't get no respect. The ed school is the butt of jokes in the university, where professors portray it as an intellectual wasteland; it is the object of scorn in schools, where teachers decry its programs as impractical and its research as irrelevant; and it is a convenient scapegoat in the world of educational policy, where policymakers portray it as a root cause of bad teaching and inadequate learning. Even ed school professors and students express embarrassment about their association with it. For academics and the general public alike, ed school bashing has long been a pleasant pastime. It is so much a part of ordinary conversation that, like talking about the weather, you can bring it up anywhere without fear that you will offend anyone.

Of course, education in general is a source of chronic concern and an object of continuous criticism for most Americans. As the annual Gallup poll of attitudes toward education regularly shows, however, citizens give good grades to their local schools at the same time that they express strong fears about the quality of public education in general.[3] The vision is one of general threats to education that may not have reached the neighborhood school quite yet but may do so in the near future. These threats include everything from multicultural curricula to the decline in the family, the influence of television, and the consequences of chronic poverty.

One such threat is the hapless and baleful education school, whose incompetence and misguided ideas are seen as both producing poorly prepared teachers and promoting wrong-headed curricula. For the public at large, this institution is remote enough to be suspect (unlike the local school) and accessible enough to be scorned (unlike the more arcane realms of the university). For the university faculty, it is the ideal scapegoat, which allows blame for problems with schools to fall upon teacher education in particular rather than higher education in general. And for critics of public education, the ed school's low status and its addiction to progressive educational rhetoric make it a convenient target for blame.

There is a vigorous and expanding literature that fortifies the already robust consensus about the negative influence of education schools. One example is Rita Kramer's 1991 diatribe *Ed School Follies: The Miseducation of America's Teachers,* which draws its spirit and its subtitle from James Koerner's 1963 classic in this genre, *The Miseducation of American Teachers.* Others include Thomas Sowell's 1993 book *Inside American Education: The Decline, the Deception, the Dogmas,* whose chapter on ed schools has the title "Impaired Faculties," and the 1996 book by E. D. Hirsch Jr., *The Schools We Need and Why We Don't Have Them,* whose chapter on the progressive ideology of ed schools is called "Critique of a Thoughtworld." Let's consider some of the images of the ed school that come out of this vast critical literature.

THE LOWLY STATUS OF THE ED SCHOOL

Perhaps the most striking aspect of the critical literature on ed schools is its scornful tone. There is a quality about some of this writing which suggests that teacher education is—almost, but not quite—beneath contempt. In his exposé *The Miseducation of American Teachers,* James Koerner describes his subject in a language that underscores the lowly position of teacher education in the educational hierarchy. Faculty, students, curriculum—all come under his verbal lash. In the middle of a list of grievances, he issues the following indictments:

(5) It is an indecorous thing to say and obviously offensive to most educationists, but it is the truth and it should be said: the inferior quality of the Education faculty is *the* fundamental limitation of the field, and will remain so, in my judgment for some time to come. . . . Until the question of the preparation and the intellectual qualifications of faculty members is faced head-on in Education, the prospects of basic reform are not bright.

(6) Likewise, the academic caliber of students in Education remains a problem, as it always has. . . . Education students still show up poorly on standardized tests and still impress members of the academic faculty as being among their less able students. . . .

(7) Course work in Education deserves its ill-repute. It is most often puerile, repetitious, dull, and ambiguous—incontestably. Two factors make it that way: the limitations of the instructor, and the limitations of the subject-matter that has been remorselessly fragmented, sub-divided, and inflated, and that in may cases was not adequate to its uninflated state. . . . The intellectual impoverishment of the course work remains a major characteristic of the field.[4]

People frequently complain about professional education in a wide range of fields other than teaching, but they don't generally adopt this same tone of scorn when they discuss the preparation of doctors and lawyers. Something about the status of the ed school makes it an easy target, a free-fire zone in the realm of higher education. Sterling McMurrin, a former U.S. commissioner of education, notes this in his introduction to Koerner's book: "As is well known, for the past several years criticism of the professional education schools has been a favorite sport among the faculties of other professional schools and of the sciences and arts."[5] Yet, though he adopts a more judicious approach to the subject than Koerner, McMurrin still agrees with the latter's central judgment:

"While recognizing the outstanding work of both individuals and institutions in pointing new directions in teacher education, I must agree with Mr. Koerner that when one views the national scene as a whole the quality of our teacher education schools and colleges is a weak element in our educational complex, a weakness at the point where the most damage can be done—and where all too often it is done."[6]

Historian Donald Warren lists a whole series of colorful slanders on teacher education issued during the 1980s:

> One report announces that "never before in the nation's history has the caliber of those entering the teaching profession been as low as it is today" (Feistritzer, 1983, p. 112). Colorado Governor Richard Lamm comments, "List the ten most somnolent courses in a university, and nine of them will be teacher courses." That remark pales in quotability next to Gary Sykes' characterization of teacher preparation as "higher education's dirty little secret." H. Ross Perot, the Texas industrialist credited with the recent passage of that state's school reform bill, likens teacher education to a fire drill. . . . The hyperbole borders on silliness, but it gives historians something to chew on.[7]

Even when the tone of the critical voice softens and the gaze turns more sympathetic, many of the same themes continue to emerge. The underlying charge remains that teacher education as an enterprise suffers from a basic condition of *inferiority.* Judith Lanier, who co-wrote an influential review of "Research on Teacher Education," is certainly a sympathetic voice.[8] As the dean of an education school and the president of the Holmes Group, she constructed this review as a platform from which to launch the Holmes Group's effort to reform both teaching and teacher education. Yet her list of ailments requiring a remedy sounds similar in substance if not in tone to the list spelled out by Koerner. Like him, she finds teacher education cursed with an inferior status and finds the roots of this status in part in characteristics of its faculty, students, and curriculum.

On faculty: "There is an inverse relationship," she notes, "between professorial prestige and the intensity of involvement with the formal education of teachers."[9] When one examines the characteristics of the professors themselves, the "research, in general, suggests that education professors differ from their academic counterparts in that they have less scholarly production and lower social class origins."[10] Such faculty members demonstrate "conformist orientations and utilitarian views of knowledge," which helps "explain why teacher educators, as some researchers have observed, 'have difficulty in adjusting to and accepting the norms and expectations of academe.'"[11] On students: "Here the research seems unequivocal. Those who teach teachers encounter a substantial number of learners with average and high scores on standardized measures of academic ability. But the overall group norm for teacher education students falls below the average for all college students due to the larger numbers of learners scoring in the lowest ranks on such measures."[12] And on curriculum: "The research is unequivocal about the general, overall course work provided for teachers. It remains casual at best and affords a poorly conceived collage of courses across the spectrum of initial preparation and an assembly of disparate content fragments throughout continuing education. The formal offerings lack curricular articulation within and between initial and continuing teacher education, and depth of study is noticeably and consistently absent."[13]

This kind of complaining about ed schools is as commonplace as griping about the cold in the middle of winter. But there is something new in the defamatory discourse about these beleaguered institutions, and that is the fact that the attacks are now also coming from their own leaders. The deans of many of the leading education schools in the country issued a report in 1995 that indicted their own colleges for crimes against education, prescribed a radical regime of rehabilitation, and called for the death penalty for any institutions that resisted.

This report was the culmination of a process that began ten years earlier, when the deans from approximately one hundred research-oriented colleges of education in major universities formed themselves into an organization known as the Holmes Group for purposes of promoting educational reform. During its brief existence (in 1996 it reconstituted itself as a network of schools, universities, and other organizations called the Holmes Partnership),[14] the Group issued reports calling for change in three major areas of American education. It argued for the professionalization of teaching in *Tomorrow's Teachers* (1986), for the development of school-university partnerships (known as professional development schools) in *Tomorrow's Schools* (1990), and for the transformation of ed schools in *Tomorrow's Schools of Education* (1995). The last report presented a harsh attack on the Holmes Group's own member institutions, those university-based education schools that produce the bulk of the nation's educational research and educational doctorates.

In the report, the deans donned what they called "the hair shirt of self-criticism" (p. 5), accusing education schools of "dwell[ing] in a bygone era" (p. 7) and being engaged in practices that "cannot be tolerated and will only exacerbate the problems of public education" (p. 6). The faculty—afflicted with a "negative attitude," "lack of will," and "considerable inertia" (p. 88)—were

portrayed as frequently "ill-equipped to help without professional development" or as "diehards who hold the potential to undermine the entire [reform]
effort" (p. 92).

Not a pretty picture, certainly, but it gets worse. For the problem seems to go
beyond issues of competence and will, extending into the very ethos of the institution. According to the report, these education schools are so caught up in
the futile pursuit of academic credibility within the university that they have
chosen to turn their backs on the needs of the students and teachers in America's schools.

> Many [education school] professors go about their teaching and research with hardly
> a nod toward the public schools, seldom if ever deigning to cross the thresholds of
> those "lowly" places. Such attitudes transmit an unmistakable message. The people
> most intimately responsible for children's learning in elementary and secondary
> schools are not sufficiently valued by the education school. Schoolteachers and
> young learners, who should be the focus of the education school's concern, are kept
> at arm's length. They are a sideshow to the performance in the center ring, where
> professors carry out their work insulated from the messiness and hurly-burly of ele-
> mentary and secondary education. (p. 17)

Under these circumstances, it is no wonder that the report called for education
schools to change their ways "or surrender their franchise" (p. 6).

Therefore it seems that education schools are not only characterized by weak
faculty, students, and curriculum—the gist of the standard critique—but they
also don't seem to care about teachers and students, and they have chosen to
turn their backs on the pressing needs of American education. The difference
this time was not only that the critique of these institutions had been enlarged
but also that it was coming from their own deans. With friends like these, who
needs enemies? One reading of this report suggests that education schools have
been the object of ridicule for so long that their own leaders have started joining in—on the theory that it is better to try to lead the opposition to your own
institutions than to attempt a defense of the indefensible. Under these circumstances, it is no surprise that the Holmes Group promptly disbanded after publication of the third report.

So how did things get this bad? What are the conditions that bring a field to
the point at which the victims start joining the victimizers? What *is* the trouble
with ed schools anyway, and what are the major sources of this trouble?

No occupational group or subculture acquires a negative label as widely accepted and deeply rooted as this one—to the point that its own leaders accept

the label and chime in to confirm its validity—unless there is a long history of status deprivation. Chronic status problems have clearly been the historical norm for the American ed school, but the reasons for this situation are rarely given much consideration by either external or internal critics of these institutions, on the apparently sensible grounds that there is little use in belaboring the obvious: Ed schools are weak and irrelevant because everyone and everything associated with them is inferior, so why look further?

These truisms mask a more interesting story, however, one that presents a more sympathetic if not much more flattering portrait of the education school, but one that also portrays the ed school's critics in a manner that is less self-serving than in the standard account. Part of this story is historical, focusing on the way that American policymakers, taxpayers, students, and universities all ended up collectively producing exactly the kind of education school they wanted. Part of it is structural, focusing on the realities the ed school has had to face, given the situation it has been in and the functions it has been asked to serve—especially in preparing teachers, doing educational research, and preparing educational researchers.

Ironies abound in this story of American education schools. In part, these institutions may have acquired—and earned—their universal disrepute by successfully adapting themselves to all of the demands that we have placed on them. And in part, this disregard may have come about because of their all-too-frequently unsuccessful efforts to have a positive impact on an area about which Americans care a great deal, their public schools. By way of comparison, it is interesting to note that most of the other academic units in the university maintain their high social standing by studiously avoiding this kind of commitment to social problem-solving, which would put to the test their claims of educational effectiveness.

The result is that by examining the trouble with ed schools we may be able to gain insight into some of the problems affecting American education at all levels. So let's look at some of the basic elements that define this story and consider the lessons that might emerge from it.

FRAMING THE ARGUMENT

The lowly status of the education school—defined here as a college, school, or department of education within a university—is the issue that defines the starting point of this book. Why, I ask, does the education school get no respect? This leads me first to look at its historical development, in order to figure out how it evolved into its current unenviable position in the academic hierarchy, and then to explore the contemporary factors that continue to reinforce that position, including its continuing role in serving a variety of stigmatized populations. From there, I move on to examine the major functions of the education school—preparing teachers, producing educational knowledge, training researchers—and the peculiar problems these pose for the institution. Finally, I look at the history of its romantic attachment to educational progressivism and the consequences of this attachment for American schools. Throughout I maintain a position of principled ambivalence about the cumulative qualities of the education school—admiring its quixotic persistence in pursuing worthy pedagogical and intellectual aims that have been studiously avoided by the rest of higher education, while at the same time decrying its mediocrity, its romantic rhetoric, and its abject compliance with the demeaning and frequently dysfunctional role assigned to it.

That's what the book is; here's what it is *not*. It is not a comprehensive history of the education school. It is not the report of an empirical study of the way education schools developed or how they currently function. It is not a reform document, proposing the changes that are needed in order to rescue the education school from its present sad state. It is not intended as an attack on this institution, a defense of it, or a prescription for it. Instead, the book is no more and no less than an interpretive analysis of the American education school as an institution. The aim is to explore the roots and the implications of education's problems of status and function and not to cure these problems. During the course of laying out the book's main argument, I draw heavily on the existing literature in the history of education, sociology of education, philosophy of education, educational policy, and teacher education. I do so selectively, however, for the book is not an effort to encompass and summarize this literature but to build a particular interpretation grounded in it. The interpretation is the centerpiece, and the sources are drawn in as needed and as appropriate to provide substantiation and examples for this interpretation. As a result, readers who know education schools and the literature about them will find many of the components of this argument familiar. What is new here, however, is the way I have sought to synthesize these insights around two closely related themes—the causes and consequences of the education school's lowly status, and the peculiar nature of the pedagogical and intellectual work that the education school is called upon to do—and organize them into a coherent and balanced characterization of the institution as a whole.

In this book, I use the approach of historical sociology in developing an understanding of the American education school. The aim is to explain the emergence of some of the most salient characteristics of the education school as a social institution, in the sociological meaning of that term. That is, I am seeking to establish general patterns that characterize education schools as a whole, that define them as a social type whose norms and structures serve as a model for the individual educational organizations that seek to function under the label of the education school. From this perspective, I focus primarily on the regularities that cut across the array of education schools rather than the particular qualities that distinguish individual instances of this type from each other. In addition, within this general framework I concentrate primarily on the structural constraints and incentives embedded within this institutional archetype, which shape the limits and possibilities for any unit within the university that seeks to function as an education school. This means that the story I tell does not delve into the goals and practices of individual actors or into the cultural norms and social patterns of individual education schools. In the same manner, this story does not concern itself very much with the nuts and bolts of how education schools variously carry out their programmatic work of preparing teachers, training researchers, and producing scholarship. These are all important topics that are worthy of close study, but to carry out such a study is not the intent of this book.

This relentless focus on the categorical characteristics of the education school may at first seem hopelessly abstract, especially in light of the current trend in the discourse of educational research toward emphasizing the particular and the personal. But the argument I develop here suggests that the American education school has evolved over time into a distinctive institution with a recognizable set of forms and functions and with a peculiarly unfavorable public persona. And these structural elements have a significant and ongoing impact on the particular programs, practices, and people that operate within individual schools of education—with ramifications for their clients, the educators and students in the public schools . As a sociologist I assert without hesitation or apology that structures matter, categories have consequences, and labels can hurt, and this book explores the ed school as a case in point.

Okay, so the book's methodology is drawn from historical sociology, focusing on the emergence of the structural characteristics of the education school as an institution. But within the general confines of this approach, the interpretation I develop revolves around two main interlocking themes. One is the formative nature of the institution's professional status, and the other is the distinctiveness of the institution's social role.

First, my argument is that the lowly status of the education school has been a critically important fact of life for this institution. The consequences of its status have been enormous—shaping the quality and duration of its programs, the kinds of students and faculty that it can recruit, the way the university and public respond to the knowledge it produces, its impact on schools, and its ability to shape its own destiny. Consider, for example, the latter effect. High status allows some educational institutions to buffer themselves from outside interference, develop their own educational vision, and impose this vision on their social environment. But institutions with low status, such as education schools, do not enjoy these luxuries. Instead, their most prominent organizational and programmatic characteristics are frequently imposed on them by a variety of interested parties in the social environment who feel no need to yield to the authority of an institution that has been drastically enfeebled by its position at the bottom of the academic status order. In light of the salience of status for the education school, it becomes critically important to understand the causes and the consequences of this status, both for the institution and for the main parties whose interests are affected by it.

This status perspective on the education school draws from a long-standing tradition of theoretical work on social stratification. That work seeks to explain a wide range of status-related issues, such as the way systems of social hierarchy develop, the form and function of these hierarchies, the factors that shape social mobility and status preservation, the kinds of groups that succeed and fail in the competition for status, and the social consequences of all this. Within this literature is a body of work that focuses on the process of status attainment and in particular on the role that education plays in this process. The argument in this book finds its inspiration most directly from a segment of this work that derives from Max Weber's analysis of the way the competitive pursuit of status in a stratified society transforms education into a valuable form of cultural commodity. From this perspective, the individual uses of education within the competition over status frequently overwhelm education's broader social functions (socialization, providing human capital) in ways that distort the organization of both school and society. The pursuit of credentials undercuts the pursuit of learning, and the credentials themselves become subject to market forces of supply and demand, much like other commodities. As a result, the accumulation of rational market-based choices by individual educational consumers often leads to collective irrationalities such as overproduction of educational diplomas, credential inflation, and intensified competition.[15]

The second theme that characterizes the argument of this book is that the nature of the work that the education school is assigned gives it a distinctive social role. The defining function of the education school is the preparation of teachers. This poses special instructional problems because teaching is a peculiarly complex and difficult form of professional practice. Teaching is grounded in the necessity of motivating cognitive, moral, and behavioral change in a group of involuntary and frequently resistant clients. It depends heavily on the teacher's ability to construct an effective and authentic teaching persona and use it to manage a complex and demanding emotional relationship with students for curricular purposes. It lacks a valid and reliable technology of instruction, a set of norms defining acceptable professional practice, clear goals for instruction, clear ways of measuring pedagogical effects, or even a clear definition of the clientele to be served. As a result, there is arguably no realm of professional education that faces a challenge more daunting than the challenge presented to teacher educators.

In addition to preparing teachers, the education school is responsible for the production of educational research. Key characteristics of educational knowledge both constrain and enable the work of educational researchers, as producers of this knowledge, in ways that distinguish them from other academic researchers. Educational knowledge is distinctive in being particularly soft (rather than hard) and applied (rather than pure), and in providing considerably more use value than exchange value. As a result, knowledge production in education is organized in a manner that is socially egalitarian and substantively divergent. These conditions of intellectual work put a special strain on the third function of the education school, the preparation of future researchers. And further complicating the task is the fact that the students who enroll in ed school doctoral programs are usually former elementary and secondary teachers. This frequently leads to cultural conflict, as they confront the striking differences in the norms of practice in research compared to the norms of practice in teaching. They often feel that they are being asked to change their whole orientation—from normative to analytical, from personal to intellectual, from particular to universal, and from experiential to theoretical.[16]

Although I am stressing the elements of the status and role of the ed school that make it distinctive, I don't want to suggest that it is somehow unique. Instead, I see the ed school as a case that helps illuminate important issues in the history of the professions and in the history of American higher education. Like other occupation groups who aspired to be recognized as professions, teachers sought to make a claim to a professional role by establishing a proprietary body of professional expertise and sought to make a claim to professional status by establishing control over access to their ranks, with professional schools in universities seen as the key to both projects. Their relative failure to accomplish these goals was hardly unusual. Nurses and social workers in the United States made similar efforts and suffered similar defeats.[17] Thus, as you read this story about the ed school, you would do well to keep in mind the larger problem of professional education and the parallel cases of schools of nursing and social work. Likewise ed schools are by no means unique in being driven by market pressures and by concerns about the useful application of knowledge. These are both central characteristics that define what is distinctive about the direction taken by American higher education in general. From early on, the dependence of U.S. colleges and universities on tuition and their relative autonomy from the state have made them vulnerable to consumer demands for forms of education that would enhance individual status and that would address practical problems.[18] Thus it would be helpful as you read this book if you also keep in mind the way this story of the ed school both emerges from and speaks to the history of American higher education.

One last point: This book focuses primarily on one kind of education school, the kind that you find in research-oriented universities. You may well ask why. After all, most of America's teachers are prepared at education schools in the less elevated portion of U.S. higher education, the regional state universities that for the most part evolved from normal schools. The reason for this focus is that research-oriented education schools are particularly influential in a variety of ways. They prepare most of the faculty members who staff the teacher preparation programs in the country; they produce most of the research about education; and they prepare most of the educational researchers. As a result of playing these roles, research-oriented ed schools exert an enormous impact on how we carry out teacher education and about how we think about teaching, learning, educational reform, and educational policy.

THE ORGANIZATION OF THE BOOK

Teacher education is at the heart of the trouble with ed schools, so our story starts, in chapter 2, with an examination of the historical origins of this field's lowly status. The focus is on how market pressures shaped the development of normal schools and the teacher education programs they offered. Pressures came from two sources—employers (pressuring ed schools to meet social efficiency demands) and consumers (pressuring them to meet student social mobility demands). The result was an institution that was part teacher factory and part people's college. In addition, consumer demand for normal schools to provide broad educational opportunity beyond teacher education led to the evolution of these institutions into teachers colleges and eventually into regional state universities, within which teacher education was increasingly marginalized. All three of these developments—the construction of the ed school as teacher factory, people's college, and component of a full-service university—had significant negative consequences on the form, content, and reputation of teacher ed and the ed school.

Chapter 3 examines the problem of teacher education in the present, focusing on the characteristics of this practice that make it particularly difficult. Teaching is a complex job that looks easy, which poses problems for the public's perception of teachers and teacher educators alike. Key components of this paradox are found in the peculiar characteristics of teaching: It is a very visible and familiar form of professional practice (the "apprenticeship of observation" done by prospective teachers); it appears to require rather ordinary skill (teachers teach what adults already know, so what's the big deal?); its practitioners freely give away their expertise (thus rendering themselves unnecessary), rather than (like most professionals) guarding it closely and renting it as needed; and it calls on general subject-matter knowledge acquired outside of the ed school. As a result of these factors, the practice of teacher education is extraordinarily demanding.

Chapter 4 looks at the problem of producing educational research. Here I show that education occupies a knowledge domain that is both very soft and very applied, which makes it particularly difficult for researchers to produce work that carries much credibility. The soft nature of educational knowledge means they have difficulty building towers of knowledge but end up constantly rebuilding the foundations. The applied nature of education means they have to concentrate their efforts on issues that arise from needs in public education rather than those where their expertise is more effective.

Chapter 5 looks at the problem of preparing educational researchers. Doing educational research demands a particularly sophisticated array of skills, which puts severe pressure on doctoral programs in ed schools. However, students coming into these programs, largely from careers as elementary and secondary teachers, face special challenges in acquiring these skills. Often their educational preparation, from bachelor's and master's programs in education, is not well suited to the academic demands of a doctoral program in research. In addition, the work of research calls for an approach to education (analytical, intellectual, universalistic, and theoretical) that is often at odds with the approach demanded by the students' prior role as teachers (normative, personal, particularistic, and experiential).

Chapter 6 examines the origins and consequences of the status problems facing the education professor. Disdain for education professors is near universal, and studies of this group do not paint a pretty picture. We don't show up well in the criteria that matter within the academic status order: research productivity; focusing on hard and pure knowledge; producing exchange value; and association with elite students and professions. One way we adapt is by internally stratifying the education professoriate, as those who do research and teach doctoral students at major universities try to distance themselves from those who do teacher preparation at former normal schools. But these efforts are largely for naught.

Chapter 7 examines the ed school's long-standing romance with educational progressivism. I trace this connection to two elements: the low status of ed school professors and the history of progressivism. Educational progressivism split early into the administrative progressives, who sought to promote social efficiency and curriculum differentiation, and the pedagogical progressives, who sought student-centered instruction and inquiry-based learning. The first group won in practice, I argue, exerting the greatest impact on the form and function of schooling, while the second group won in the theoretical realm, taking command of educational rhetoric and finding its ideological home in the institutional backwater of the ed school.

Chapter 8 analyzes the impact of the ed school. Critics argue that ed school should bear a major portion of the blame for the problems with American schools. In particular, they charge that the ed school's progressivism has undermined academic learning and stratified social access to knowledge. But my analysis shows that, although the rhetoric of pedagogical progressivism played a supporting role in producing these problems, the primary sources of both educational pathologies are the administrative progressivism (and also educational consumerism) that actually shaped practice in schools. Ed schools do indeed promote the rhetoric of pedagogical progressivism, but they don't have the power to impose these practices on schools and don't even practice it themselves, in the teacher preparation programs they run or the research they do. So ed schools have not been in a position to do much harm to American education, but they also have not been able to do much good. Their potential contributions are discounted in advance, because of their low status and their rhetorical predictability. This is a shame, since they are doing important and demanding work, even if not all are doing it that well, and since they have something to say about the major educational issues of the day, even if no one is listening.

In light of all these troubles with American ed schools, then, it's no wonder why a layman like Bob Thompson feels comfortable about bypassing these institutions, ignoring the so-called expertise of the education professors who inhabit them, and, as a businessman, proposing his own answers to the problems of education.

Chapter 2 Teacher Ed
in the Past: The Roots
of Its Lowly Status

The roots of the American education school are in teacher education.[1]
Preparing teachers was the ed school's original function, and this function has continued to the present day as the primary focus of its institutional effort and its primary identity in the eyes of the public. In this
chapter, I examine the historical roots of teacher education's lowly status. There are already a number of good general accounts of the history of teacher education,[2] so I don't intend to repeat that history
here. Instead, I focus on the way this history brought about many of
the status problems that currently plague the ed school. Teacher education, it turns out, is at the heart of the trouble with ed schools.

Despite what critics often suggest, the lowly status of American
teacher education is not a simple reflection of the purportedly low
quality of professional preparation that it offers. Rather than being a
natural consequence of failure, this status is a primary cause of the
kinds of failure that teacher education has experienced over the years.
The evidence shows that market forces have treated teacher education
quite badly over the past 150 years, assigning it to a position of meager
prestige and influence and forcing it to adopt practices that have fre-

quently proved educationally counterproductive. In short, market pressures have in large part led to the low status of teacher education and have contributed significantly to its inability to carry out its functions effectively.

For the purposes of this book, I am defining a market as a social arena in which individual and organizational actors competitively pursue private gain through the exchange of commodities (the buying and selling of goods and services). The value of these commodities, and thus the degree of benefit enjoyed by producers and consumers, is established by the relationship between supply and demand rather than by any intrinsic qualities in the goods or services themselves. This means treating the market analytically—as a mechanism for shaping the behavior of individuals and organizations and for establishing the economic value of goods and services—in the manner employed by Max Weber in *Economy and Society*, Randall Collins in *The Credential Society*, and Karl Marx in his essay "The Fetishism of Commodities and the Treatment Thereof" in volume one of *Capital*.[3] This analytical usage of the term *market* is quite different from its deployment as an ideological epithet in much of the current literature in critical theory, where the term carries the freight of moral disapproval of the social exploitation attributed to neoliberal economic policies.[4]

By choosing to focus on the status of teacher education rather than its social role, I skip past a wide range of important issues. For example, a status perspective naturally leads me to concentrate more on the position that teacher education occupies in the social and educational hierarchy than on the quality of its performance in carrying out professional education, to focus on matters of form more than content. This means that I say little about the content of the curriculum in teacher preparation programs and a great deal about the prestige of these programs and the way in which they became placed within the stratified array of educational options. To take this approach is not to deny the significance of the curriculum but to assert that curriculum issues have often been shaped significantly by the status concerns of the various parties involved in teacher education.

A status perspective tends to treat teacher education as a marketable commodity, whose function is to meet the status needs of the educational consumers who acquire it, rather than as a process of socialization, whose function is to transmit useful skills to prospective teachers. From this angle, then, the key measure of the worth of teacher education is its exchange value, which is determined by factors of supply and demand in the market for educational credentials. This exchange value may fluctuate according to market conditions and quite independently of the program's use value, which is a measure of the usable practical knowledge acquired there and applicable to the work of teaching. Again, the point here is not that the degree of useful knowledge acquired in a teacher education program is irrelevant to the work of teaching but that it may well be irrelevant to the social position occupied by teachers (or teacher educators). In fact, I suggest that the focus within American teacher education on practical knowledge over high-status liberal learning has had a negative effect on the exchange value of the credentials of its graduates. Further, I argue that concerns about exchange value have had a powerful effect in transforming the formal setting within which teacher education takes place (from the normal school to the university) and also in diluting the professional content of its curriculum.

By examining the market factor more closely, we can gain insight into some of the characteristics that distinguish American teacher education from similar programs in other countries. Of the nations with the highest degree of economic development, the United States is the most market-oriented and has been since the mid-nineteenth century. Nowhere else has the doctrine of laissez-faire attained such earnest and long-lasting acceptance. No other industrial power has so persistently protected private enterprise from public interference, so effectively fragmented the state and limited its power, and so prominently elevated the idea of market competition to a central ideological principle.

In such a market-centered society, it is not surprising that education too finds itself subject to a wide range of persistent market pressures. Consider the example of the high school. As I have argued elsewhere, early in its history the high school emerged as a valued commodity that gave some consumers the means to enhance or reinforce their social position.[5] As a result of this market pressure, high schools became stratified—across programs within individual schools and across different schools within a community—according to the exchange value of the credentials offered by each program or school. Martin Trow and others argue that higher education in the United States has been particularly sensitive to market forces, especially given the glut of colleges and universities, the lack of centralized state control over this sector, and the resulting dependency of these institutions on the consumer preferences of students.[6]

Given the market-saturated environment in which it arose, American teacher education throughout its history has been subjected to a degree of market pressure well beyond that experienced by teacher education in other societies. As a result, focusing on market effects may well inform our understanding of the special character of teacher education in the United States from a comparative perspective. One theme in this history is the problem posed by the insatiable demand for teachers from a burgeoning public school system. Another is the problem of how to meet the social aspirations and credentialing requirements of students who entered normal schools. A third is the impact of these problems on the evolution of teacher education from its original setting in the normal school to the teachers college and eventually the university, and, in turn, the impact that this evolution had on people, programs, and status. With regard to the present, the question becomes how much market conditions have changed and the implications for teacher education today.

A SHORT HISTORY OF MARKET INFLUENCES ON TEACHER EDUCATION

Market pressures have affected teacher education in three ways: by pushing the education school to become a teacher factory, by encouraging it to evolve into a people's college, and by elevating it to the university level. Let us consider each of these in turn.

The Teacher Factory: Filling Empty Classrooms

The biggest single problem facing American school officials in the nineteenth and early twentieth centuries had nothing to do with curriculum or pedagogy. Instead, the persisting challenge was to find a way to build enough classrooms for all the students who required education and to fill these classrooms with teachers. The aim of the common school movement, which swept out of New England and across the country in the years before the Civil War, was to have each community establish a publicly funded system of elementary schooling that would provide a common educational experience for all of the young people in that community. In keeping with the American suspicion of centralized state power, the responsibility for paying for the new schools and hiring the new teachers that were required by this expansion fell primarily on local government.

By 1870, when the federal government began gathering data on schools, there were already 200,000 public school teachers in the United States, and the number doubled by 1900. At this point, when the supply of elementary schooling was finally beginning to catch up with demand, the sudden growth of high schools set off another dizzying spiral of educational expansion, which by 1930 once again doubled the size of the public school teaching force, bringing the total in that year to almost 850,000.[7]

In the mid-nineteenth century, the insatiable demand for teachers—combined with the radical decentralization of control over schools and the absence of consistent standards for certification—meant that the emphasis was on finding warm bodies to fill classrooms rather than on preparing qualified professionals. The following examination of a teacher candidate in a New England town during the 1860s was not unusual:

CHAIRMAN: How old are you?

CANDIDATE: I was eighteen years old the 27th day of last May.

CHAIRMAN: Where did you last attend school?

CANDIDATE: At the Academy of S.

CHAIRMAN: Do you think you can make our big youngsters mind?

CANDIDATE: Yes, I think I can.

CHAIRMAN: Well, I am satisfied. I guess you will do for our school. I will send over the certificate by the children tomorrow.[8]

As Sedlak concludes in his review of teacher hiring in this period, "A general teacher shortage, combined with wildly fluctuating and inconsistent prerequisite qualifications, virtually assured any prospective teacher some sort of job, and secured someone for most communities needing a teacher."[9]

It was in the midst of this difficult period in the history of the market for teachers that the American normal school appeared on the scene. By many accounts, the first public normal school opened in 1839 in Lexington, Massachusetts, under the leadership of Cyrus Peirce.[10] Looking back on this experience a dozen years later, Peirce spelled out the aims of his pathbreaking institution in a letter to Henry Barnard, sounding themes that defined the core concerns of the whole normal school movement.

I answer briefly, that it was my aim, and it would be my aim again, to make better teachers, and especially, better teachers for our common schools; so that those primary seminaries, on which so many depend for their education, might answer, in a higher degree, the end of their institution. Yes, to make better teachers; teachers who would understand, and do their business better; teachers who should know more of the nature of children, of youthful developments, more of the subject to be taught, and more of the true methods of teaching; who would teach more philosophically, more in harmony with the natural development of the young mind, with a truer regard to the order and connection in which the different branches of knowledge should be presented to it, and, of course, more successfully.[11]

This was a tall order indeed. And although "the formal history of American teacher education and professionalization is conventionally a story of one triumphal march,"[12] the reality was a story of rear-guard action by the stalwart normal school advocates while the opposing hoard swept around them on both flanks. By the time of the Civil War, there were only twelve state normal schools in existence in the entire country,[13] so that in spite of the high ideals of these institutions, their actual impact was minimal at best. Throughout most of the nineteenth century, the large majority of teachers entered into the classroom without benefit of a normal school diploma. There was a wide range of ways for a prospective teacher to acquire training and obtain a job. The larger cities often set up their own normal schools to supply teachers to the local elementary schools. High schools frequently offered a short course in pedagogy toward the same end. At an even more rudimentary level, local school districts would provide a brief preparation in the grammar school so that graduates could almost immediately return to their old classrooms as the teacher. A widespread network of teacher institutes offered training during the summer, both for new teachers and, after the fact, for teachers already on the job. But there were also a large number of teachers who were hired and kept on the job with no formal training and no qualifications at all except the ability to make the "big youngsters mind."

Consider the problems that this situation posed for the status of the normal school. In order for a form of professional education to attain a high status in the educational marketplace, it must meet two primary prerequisites: monopoly and selectivity. The current situation of law schools and medical schools serves as a case in point. Each of those types of schools has established itself as the only door through which a person can gain entry to the profession. And each has made it difficult to get through that door, by instituting restrictive admissions and rigorous programs of study. When Cyrus Peirce and Horace Mann and others established the first normal schools, they chose to ignore the market situation and concentrate on developing a sound program of professional preparation for future teachers. However, the problem was that the professional schools they nurtured into life ran the risk of being completely irrelevant to the realities of the job market for teachers. Since no one had to attend a normal school in order to teach and since all the alternative modes of access to teaching were easier and less costly, the normal school leaders found themselves standing on the sidelines while the real work of training and hiring teachers played out before them.

In short, normal school leaders faced a choice between selectivity and monopoly. They could remain as elite institutions providing an idealized form of professional preparation for a small number of aspiring teachers—"teachers who would understand, and do their business better," in Peirce's words—and allow other routes to teaching to remain dominant. Or they could expand the system to meet the demand for teachers, establishing an eventual monopoly over access to the profession while risking the dilution of the normal school ideal in the process. They chose expansion.

Between 1865 and 1890, the number of state normal schools grew from 15 to 103.[14] A key element in this expansion was the growing tendency for state governments to employ certification as a mechanism for restricting the pool of teacher candidates from which local districts could hire their faculty and to employ teacher education as a criterion for certification. "By 1873, according to a leading analyst of this issue, policy deliberations were beginning to recognize credentials from normal schools as 'professional licenses,' and several states were relying on them as the basis for certification. By 1897, twenty-eight states accepted normal-school diplomas, and by 1921 all but one state "recognized graduation from normal schools and universities as evidence of qualification for certification." By the World War I era, therefore, certification policies that bestowed licenses on the basis of credential acquisition had become the rule nationwide."[15] The expansion of normal schools and their growing monopoly over access to teaching was accelerated "as graduates of professional programs assumed leadership roles in state departments of education."[16]

Once normal schools moved toward establishing a monopoly on access to teaching, they also took on the responsibility for meeting the full weight of the market's demand for teachers. The natural result was that teacher education came under intense pressure to produce large numbers of teachers as quickly and cheaply as possible. Two factors served to intensify this pressure. One was the feminization of the teaching force and the kind of career pattern that accompanied this shift. The standard pattern in the late nineteenth and early twentieth centuries was for young women to enter teaching for a half dozen years or so, beginning in their late teens and ending with marriage. The short tenure in the classroom for the average teacher meant that normal schools had to produce large numbers of graduates in order to keep replacing young teachers who were leaving the classroom. The other was a fiscal problem. If teacher training took on aspects of mass production, and if the product was not expected to last very long anyway, then the cost of producing each unit had to be kept down in order to sustain the operation. Under these circumstances, an intensive and prolonged process of professional education was difficult to justify to legislators and taxpayers.

The pressure for warm bodies to fill empty classrooms continued throughout the nineteenth and early twentieth centuries, and the impact on both the content and the status of teacher education was devastating. All three problem areas in teacher education that were identified by James Koerner and Judith Lanier in the passages quoted in the previous chapter—faculty, students, and curriculum—have their origins in considerable degree in this pressure to meet the demand for teachers. The burgeoning normal school system had to mass produce faculty members to staff its own classrooms, without the luxury of being particularly selective about whom to admit into these positions or of being especially thorough in the preparation of these people for the role of teaching teachers. As for students, the rapid expansion of normal schools in the late nineteenth century necessarily meant that these schools had to open their doors wide to admit the flood of candidates that were required to meet demand. The normal school became, as Herbst points out, a true people's college, which offered a chance at advanced education to a wide range of the population that had previously been confined to a grammar school education.[17] And the curriculum felt the effects of this market pressure as well. The need to produce a large number of teachers quickly meant that normal schools could not enforce an extensive and rigorous professional education. These schools operated under the constant threat of being bypassed. If they made access to or completion of teacher education very difficult, the number of graduates would decline and school districts would be forced to find other sources for teachers. One way or the other, the classrooms would be filled, and the normal school leaders chose to fill them with their own graduates, whatever the cost.

The cost, I suggest, was high. A thinly educated faculty, academically weak students, and a foreshortened and unchallenging curriculum—all were consequences of the effort by normal schools to meet the continuing high level of demand for teachers. As a result, the normal school became a kind of teacher factory, mass producing as many practitioners as the market required. But by pressing the normal school to choose quantity over quality, the market exerted an impact on the status of this institution as well as its content. Selectivity is a crucial component of the status of an educational institution. The current status hierarchy of American higher education is closely related to the degree of difficulty students experience in gaining access to credentials of individual colleges, which range from highly selective Ivy League-type schools at the high end of the scale to open-admissions community colleges at the low end. The normal school was the community college of the late nineteenth century, easily accessible and thus lacking in distinction. By choosing to meet the demand for teachers, this institution gave up any claim it might have once had for elite status. By becoming socially useful, it lost social respect. What this suggests is that much of the scorn that has been directed at teacher education over the years can be traced to the simple fact that it has earnestly sought to provide all of the teachers that were asked of it.[18]

The People's College:
Meeting Consumer Demand

We have already seen that one market influence on American teacher education came from *employers,* as school districts demanded a large number of teachers and normal schools chose to supply this demand in spite of the negative impact on both the content and the status of teacher education. But another market influence came from educational *consumers,* as students demanded a particular kind of educational product and normal schools chose to give it to them. The first imposed a *social-efficiency* function on these schools, which required them to subordinate concerns about institutional status and effective professional education to the pressing social need for teachers. However, the second market influence imposed a *social-mobility*[19] function, which required the schools to provide the kind of educational choices that would best serve the needs of students who were competing for desirable social positions.

The reverence for individual freedom of choice—construed both as political choice and consumer choice—has deep roots in American cultural history. Louis Hartz, in his classic *The Liberal Tradition in America,* defined the issue this way: "Here, then, is the master assumption of American political thought, the assumption from which all of the American attitudes discussed in this essay flow: the reality of atomistic social freedom. It is instinctive to the American mind, as in a sense the concept of the polis was instinctive to Platonic Athens or the concept of the church to the mind of the middle ages."[20] This assumption is at the heart of the market as a social institution. In a market system, consumers exercise individual freedom of choice by expressing their personal desires, and entrepreneurs prosper by more efficiently meeting these desires.

As Martin Trow has put it so succinctly, in America "the market preceded society," with the result that the consumer has long been king.[21] This central characteristic of American social life has been a powerful force contributing to the distinctiveness of American educational institutions, which have been shaped by consumerism to a far greater extent than educational institutions elsewhere in the world, as Trow explains: "We in the United States, surely the most populist society in the world, accept a larger role [than do Europeans] for the influence of consumer preference on cultural forms—even in the provision of what and how subjects are taught in colleges and universities. Europeans try to reduce the influence of consumer preference in a number of ways. Most importantly, they try to insulate their financing of institutions of higher education from student fees. By contrast, in the United States, enrollment-driven budgets in all but a few institutions, both public and private, ensure that most institutions are extremely sensitive to student preferences."[22] In a setting where the educational consumer is highly influential, educational leaders are compelled to respond in a thoroughly entrepreneurial fashion if they wish to thrive or even survive. If they fail to meet consumer demand, students will vote with their feet by enrolling elsewhere in a school that is all too eager to give them what they want.

This was the situation facing normal school leaders in the second half of the nineteenth century.[23] More specifically, they had to confront two characteristics of the educational market during this period. First, anyone who wanted to become a teacher could do so without ever attending a normal school. Although gradually, through increasingly restrictive certification requirements, teacher education would attain a monopoly over access to the teacher workforce, this was a long time in coming. Second, there was a glut of post-grammar-school educational institutions that were competing for the student's tuition dollars. In 1880, for example, there were more than sixteen colleges and universities for every million in the population, the highest ratio ever in American educational history.[24] As a result of these market conditions, the potential normal school student had a variety of options for becoming a teacher and for receiving advanced education, options that allowed her to bypass this institution altogether. Therefore the normal schools had to find a way to make their programs attractive to prospective consumers, and this meant listening very closely to the educational preferences being expressed by students.

What students were saying was clear. They didn't want to be trapped in a single-purpose school that provided them with a narrow vocational education and then channeled them into a single occupational slot. Instead they wanted an advanced educational setting that would, in the classic American fashion, provide them with the maximum degree of individual choice of programs and with access to the widest array of attractive occupational possibilities. In short, they wanted to pursue social mobility and wanted educational institutions to facilitate this pursuit. But this was not a vision that fit comfortably with the alternative visions of the normal school that were also in place: The founders of normal schools saw them as places for instilling sound professional skills; school districts saw them as one among several sources for warm bodies to fill empty classrooms; and students saw them as one among several places where they could acquire the credentials that would enhance their future status. The possibilities for conflict over the purposes of these schools were great, leaving them subject to an array of competing pressures.

In spite of efforts to put normal schools into the service of teacher professionalization or social efficiency, social mobility quickly emerged as a central function through the medium of students exercising their consumer choices. And this form of pressure was there from the very beginning. Cyrus Peirce ran into the problem shortly after he opened the first normal school in Lexington. "Peirce's frustrations increased as time went on. He was particularly chagrined to find that some of his students did not even want to become teachers, and others did not have the necessary ability."[25] When Herbst examined the records of Wisconsin's first state normal school in Platteville, he found that, between its founding in 1866 and 1880, "on the average no more than 45 percent of all attending students were enrolled in the normal classes."[26] Bowing to this demand for a broader and less vocationally oriented educational experience, normal schools began to offer increasing numbers of liberal arts courses. The consequences are described by Altenbaugh and Underwood:

> Many students, especially those who lived near the colleges, came for those courses rather than the teacher training curriculum that formed the original mission of such institutions. Other students used the normal school as a "junior college," completing its program as a step toward enrollment at a state university. To ensure that students who entered the normal departments would actually teach, Illinois Normal not only required that they pledge their intent to teach for three years after graduation; students also had to report their employment, whatever it was, to the state superintendent of public instruction. Signing a pledge to teach and signing a contract with a school district were two different matters. Records at Illinois indicate that only 30 percent of the alumni during the 1860s spent any time in teaching.[27]

For many American families, who otherwise would never have considered pursuing advanced education, normal schools provided an opportunity to gain social advantages that previously had been restricted to the more privileged members of society, who could afford to send their children away to college. In the eyes of these families, the normal school became more than a place for training teachers; it became a kind of people's college. Herbst puts it this way: "Normal schools, rather than the land grant universities, were the pioneers of higher education for the people. Almost everywhere the state universities and agricultural and mechanical colleges were developed at a central location or state capital, whereas the normal schools were scattered to the small country towns across the prairies."[28] These schools "took higher education to where the people lived and worked."[29]

While some normal schools tried to remain focused on their original professional mission, most gradually yielded to the pressure to broaden their vocational curriculum in order to meet the persistent demand for general academic education and social opportunity. The lure of expanding enrollments was difficult for them to resist, especially in the tuition-driven educational economy in which they had to operate. In addition, shifting in the direction of servicing the community rather than simply training teachers also gained them the support of legislators, who found that promoting people's colleges was good politics.

What effect did this consumer pressure have on normal schools? Essentially, it served to undermine, marginalize, and diffuse the goal of teacher professionalization that had led to the creation of these schools in the first place as well as the professionally oriented curriculum that had accompanied this goal. Normal schools were evolving away from single-purpose vocational schools toward general-purpose schools of advanced educational opportunity, within which teacher education was just one program, and not necessarily the most popular or prestigious one at that. One result was a growing confusion about the identity of these schools: Were they teacher training schools or people's colleges? Another was a watering-down of the professional curriculum. It was difficult for normal schools to maintain a rigorous and focused program of teacher preparation when many, often most, of the students wanted something different and when even prospective teachers intended to move on to business and professional careers after a short stint in the classroom.[30] This curriculum diffusion problem was exacerbated by social efficiency pressures, which prodded normal schools to turn out graduates in large numbers.

Under these circumstances, normal schools were under considerable market pressure to make teacher education as undemanding as possible. In their twin roles as teacher factories and people's colleges, these schools were compelled to make the teacher preparation program: easy, so students would be encouraged to sign up for it rather than other potentially more attractive but also more difficult alternatives; flexible, so they could fit it into a larger set of studies that would grant them opportunities outside of teaching; and inexpensive, so the state could afford to produce teachers at a unit cost commensurate with their brief shelf life in the classroom, and so students would consider the program a worthwhile investment, given their modest commitment to a career in teaching.[31]

All in all, the impact of the market on American teacher education has hardly been elevating. The pressure from both the job market and the credentials market, from both employers and consumers, has tended to marginalize, minimize, and trivialize the process of educating future teachers. And, as we will explore later, this disabling legacy continues to affect the way in which teacher education carries out its work. But first, we need to examine the impact of these market factors on the status of teacher education.

From Normal School to University:
Effects on Status

Between the 1890s and the 1970s, market factors propelled the normal school through a process of institutional evolution that eventually transformed it into a general-purpose university. The consequences of this change for the status of teacher education were both profound and profoundly mixed. To put it simply, the institutional status of the normal school rose dramatically during this period while the status of teacher education within the institution declined just as dramatically. Let us consider the causes and effects of this transformation.

The outlines of this evolutionary development are clear. Normal schools experienced a remarkably linear process of institutional mobility. In the words of William Johnson, "the history of twentieth-century teacher training can be seen as a series of institutional displacements, with normal schools becoming state teachers colleges, then multipurpose liberal arts colleges, and now, in many instances, regional state universities."[32] But, as Altenbaugh and Underwood note, "Normal schools actually began this transition well before the turn of the century." As they expanded their academic course offerings and broadened their appeal, normal schools "began to raise admission standards, requiring high school diplomas, and to extend the program of study." During most of the nineteenth century, normal schools had been operating at the same level as high schools, taking in grammar school graduates and sending them out with something like a high school diploma. But by 1900 these schools were beginning to look more like junior colleges, and "after 1920, two- and three-year normal schools evolved to four-year teachers colleges." One indicator of the rapid pace of this change is that between 1920 and 1933 the number of state and city normal schools fell from 170 to 66 and the number of state teachers colleges rose from 46 to 146.[33] "By 1940, the term *normal school* had become obsolete. . . . State teachers' colleges likewise experienced a short life, since by the 1960s they had begun to evolve into multipurpose state colleges or state universities, which granted liberal arts and other degrees as well as education degrees."[34] At the same time that normal schools were turning into universities, already-existing universities were incorporating at least an attenuated form of teacher education within their own programs.

Market factors are what propelled this remarkable process of institutional mobility, whose final outcome was to move teacher education from its own niche at the lower fringe of American higher education and lodge it firmly within the confines of the university.[35] Later the fiscal cost and social inefficiency of the transformation became clear (more on this subject later). But this elevation of the status and function of the normal school took place primarily because of the overwhelming demand for it that developed from all sides. It seemed to benefit everyone concerned. Through the mechanism of the expanding and rising normal school, citizens received access to higher education far beyond what was available through state universities and land grant schools. Legislators won a politically popular program on which voters were eager to spend tax dollars. For students, the upward movement meant that they could gain the advantages of both a normal school education (accessibility, low cost, and teacher certification) and a college education (bachelor's degree, institutional prestige, and access to a wide range of white-collar jobs beyond teaching). For teachers, the change meant a symbolic elevation, as a college diploma came to represent the minimum educational requirement for entry into the occupation. Teacher educators found themselves evolving from trade school instructors into college professors, a heady increase in occupational status. And universities found in teacher education a lucrative cash cow, which attracted large numbers of students, and a political blessing, which demonstrated to the state legislature the practical benefits of a university education.[36]

Compare this market perspective on the evolution of the normal school to the traditional view of this transformation that has been espoused by the educational establishment. Merle Borrowman captures the essence of this view: "The formal history of American teacher education and professionalization is conventionally a story of one triumphal march from Samuel R. Hall's Concord, Vt., normal school in 1823 to the modern National Education Association and the great graduate schools of education. This version of history is misleading."[37] What is misleading about it is the assumption that the institutional elevation of teacher education represents progress, that is, a steady and ineluctable improvement in the quality of teacher education and (consequently) of teaching. Instead, I suggest, the elevation of the status of the normal school and the incorporation of teacher education within the university have less to do with the quality of the professional education of teachers than with the quantity of consumer demand for higher education and the market conditions that encouraged educational institutions to meet that demand. Thus the content of teacher education was less important to this process than its institutional form, and preparing people effectively to carry out the role of a teacher was less important than simply providing them with the status of a college graduate.

The transformation of the status and locus of teacher education had wide-ranging effects. It reduced the social efficiency of these programs, undermined their ability to provide professional preparation, stratified the way in which they were delivered, and marginalized them within their home institutions. Let us consider each of these points in turn.

First, the elevation of normal schools and their transformation into general-purpose universities signaled the subordination of the original social efficiency goal of the normal school to the social mobility goal that came to dominate American higher education more generally. While providing enhanced educational and social opportunities for a wide array of Americans, this change introduced a radical degree of social inefficiency into the task of preparing teachers. Providing individuals with open access to higher education through an expanded and broadened system of teachers colleges may be very attractive to the individuals who benefit from it and may be justifiable politically as an effort to democratize the delivery of education, but it is hardly an efficient investment of social resources. This educational expansion was not based on the social need for skills that could be provided only through a college education but on the individual desire for improved personal status. And it did nothing to meet the need for qualified teachers to staff the nation's classrooms. The normal schools that were created to meet the latter need were thus subverted by the market, transformed into institutions of general education in response to pressing consumer demand. In short, teacher education ended up subsidizing individual ambition and social opportunity at the expense of preparing teachers.

Second, this reorientation of the normal school away from social efficiency and toward social mobility also had the effect of undermining professional education. Originally, these schools were seen by their founders and by many of the students attending them as places that focused on providing a practical education in the knowledge and skills required to be an effective teacher. That is, their function was to provide an education with considerable use value. However, this function changed when consumers asserted their strong preference for an institution that would provide them with educational credentials carrying substantial exchange value. This inevitably shifted the focus within the schools from the content to the form of education, since increasingly students attended them less for the kind of usable knowledge they could acquire there than for the kind of social advantage they could gain by attending.

In this manner, the transformation of the normal school was a key step in the commodification of American higher education during the twentieth century, as status attainment shouldered aside learning as the central aim of students and as colleges and universities quickly adapted themselves to this changing consumer demand.[38] In this commodified setting, the kind of practical learning represented by teacher education lost appeal because students were driven by concerns about the marketability of education more than its applicability. From the consumer's perspective, who cared what you learned in college as long as your diploma gave you access to a good job? Under these circumstances, the former normal schools that became state colleges and universities had no market incentive to sustain a rigorous program of professional teacher preparation. As a result, it is not surprising that even sympathetic observers have often found these programs feeble and undemanding.[39] The market-centered environment of American higher education has provided little incentive to make them otherwise.

Third, the evolution of the normal school also tended to reinforce the stratification of the various functions of professional education. In a market setting, where entrepreneurial educators needed to be concerned about maintaining the exchange value of their educational credentials, there was a strong incentive to focus an institution's attentions on those parts of the educational task that would bring the greatest prestige and influence. As Herbst has pointed out in some detail, this meant, as much as possible, turning one's back on the low-status task of preparing elementary teachers and catering to the more prestigious parts of the education market.[40] Even the early normal school leaders in Massachusetts tried to adopt this strategy. "The educators . . . tended to assign the preparation of elementary teachers to short-term city training schools. Most of the educators preferred to use their state normal schools for the training of secondary school teachers and administrators as well as educational specialists."[41]

By the early twentieth century, however, the structure of teacher education had become considerably more complex and more stratified, with the result that the various professional preparation functions were allocated across a wider span of institutions. Normal schools, as the lowest rung in the ladder of teacher education, were responsible for the education of elementary teachers, the group no one else wanted. Colleges and universities dominated the market for preparing secondary teachers. And the new graduate schools of education at leading universities took on increasing responsibility for the preparation of school administrators and nonteaching educational professionals.[42] However, when normal schools evolved into general-purpose colleges and universities, the distinction between the two lower rungs of the ladder became unclear. The preparation of both elementary and secondary teachers became the responsibility of four-year institutions in general, with the primary distinction being that former teachers colleges drew a larger share of teacher candidates of all types.

This led to a fourth effect of the elevation of the normal school. The incorporation of teacher education within the university meant that the tendency to stratify teacher education functions now became an internal matter defining the relationships between university departments. The result was that teacher education came to occupy a marginal status in the academic hierarchy of the university. This is even true to a significant extent, as Goodlad has noted, within the universities that were once teachers colleges.[43] One reason for this marginality is that teacher education programs concentrate on providing students with usable knowledge about teaching. In the commodified setting of American education, usable knowledge is low-status knowledge. The more removed knowledge is from ordinary concerns and the more closely associated it is with high culture, the more prestige it carries with it. Just as the low-track English class in high school focuses on reading job applications while the high-track class focuses on Elizabethan poetry, at the university teacher education is seen as following the low road of practical instruction while the arts and sciences departments pursue the high road of more esoteric knowledge.[44]

Another reason for the marginal status of teacher education in its new home in the university was that it was designed to prepare students for a marginal profession. Medical schools and law schools both provide intensely practical education to their students, but this does not harm the high standing of these schools because of the elevated status of the professions for which they are preparing students. In this sense, then, the high exchange value of a medical or law degree—measured by the high status of the positions to which these degrees provide access—means that no one considers these programs "vocational" in the pejorative sense that is applied to programs in auto repair and hairdressing or, at a more middling status, in nursing or teacher education. In part, then, the status of teacher education in the university has been inseparable from the status of teaching in American society.

Teacher educators therefore have come to be doubly stigmatized within the university, because of their association with low-status practical knowledge and because of their association with an occupation seen as a semiprofession. In combination this has put them at the lowest tier of the academic hierarchy. "It is common knowledge that professors in the arts and sciences risk a loss of academic respect, including promotion and tenure, if they assume clear interest in or responsibility for teacher education. Professors holding academic rank in education units are in even greater jeopardy of losing the respect of their academic counterparts in the university, because their close proximity makes association with teacher education more possible. And, finally, those education professors who actually supervise prospective or practicing teachers in elementary and secondary schools are indeed at the bottom of the stratification ladder."[45]

DEALING WITH THE LEGACY: CHANGING CONDITIONS

Given the market influence in shaping the history of American teacher education, a key issue is to define to what extent this legacy is still exerting a lingering impact on American teacher education. Have things changed substantially, or are many of the same market factors still exerting pressure on these programs?

Social efficiency: Many of the factors that promoted the original social efficiency pressures on teacher education in the nineteenth and early twentieth centuries have indeed changed. There are periodic teacher shortages (including one at the start of the twenty-first century), but these shortages are no longer chronic. The rapid growth in enrollments that drove so much of the demand for teachers has been replaced by a more stable demographic situation. Also, although turnover remains relatively high and commitment to the job remains relatively low, teaching is no longer the temporary pursuit that it once was. Since World War II, teaching has turned into a career that women and men with growing frequency have pursued all the way to retirement. In large part this is because of the gains in pay, job security, and fringe benefits that teacher unions achieved during this period.

However, in spite of these changes, social efficiency pressures on teacher education still exist, albeit in reduced intensity and altered form. In 1993 there were 2.8 million elementary and secondary teachers in the United States, and replacing those who quit or retire requires about 15 percent of the entire crop of new college graduates every year.[46] Teacher education, as always, is under pressure to meet this continuing demand. It holds a stronger monopoly over access to teaching than it ever did during the normal school era, which intensifies the pressure to produce the numbers that are required every year even if the numbers themselves are not expanding at the same rate. And reinforcing this pressure is an old threat that has returned in recent years, the threat of bypassing teacher education in the hiring of teachers. A number of state legislatures have put in place or proposed plans for "alternative certification," that is, certifying teachers based on work experience or academic major but without benefit of traditional teacher education. Market rhetoric has supported these plans as ways of restoring choice and opportunity to a teacher job market too long constrained by the education school monopoly. Reinforcing this trend is the move toward mobilizing market forces in K–12 education through such mechanisms as schools of choice and charter schools, which could free schools to hire teachers without the usual restrictions imposed by certification rules. The message seems to be that if teacher education fails to become more efficient in cranking out teachers, the state or the market will find other ways to fill classroom vacancies.

Fiscal pressure on state universities has also intensified in the last few years as state appropriations have leveled off or even declined, which has left universities more dependent than ever on tuition as a source of revenue. Under these circumstances, universities are unlikely to do anything to undercut the traditional profitability of teacher education programs, with their high enrollments and low costs. The result is a familiar pattern: Teacher education is being asked to produce a large number of teachers as efficiently and inexpensively as possible or else these teachers will be hired elsewhere. There is little in this market situation to encourage teacher education to move away from its historic pattern of maintaining programs that are easy, flexible, and cheap.

Social mobility: Teacher education is no longer asked to serve as the conduit for Americans' social aspirations. There are now a large number of people's colleges—including a thousand community colleges and a wide array of nonselective four-year colleges and universities (the latter drawn largely from the ranks of former normal schools)—through which people can gain a chance at social mobility. But the long-term effect of consumer pressure on the normal school and the teachers college (the pressure to provide students with marketable credentials that can be exchanged for a good job) has been to locate teacher education within an institution, the university, where it is looked upon with disdain. In the stratified world of contemporary American higher education, teacher education occupies an anomalous position. It is the low-status option for students in the high-status institution; it offers a practical education in a decidedly academic setting; and it sells itself as a provider of occupational use value in a market that ranks educational products on the basis of exchange value.

In this commodified educational world that consumer demand helped create, teacher education finds itself thoroughly marginalized. The preparation of teachers is no longer under its control but is spread across the various colleges within the university, where it is shaped by a number of people who view the whole enterprise with suspicion. As a result, its purposes are diffused and teacher educators find themselves marginalized even within the teacher education program. It is not surprising, then, to find that there is little incentive within the university to enhance the quality, tighten the focus, heighten the field-experience component, or raise the standards of teacher education.

SERVING STIGMATIZED POPULATIONS

This historical analysis suggests that market pressures have seriously undercut both the status and the role of teacher education—that is, both teacher ed's location in the hierarchy of higher education and its ability to carry out its educational functions effectively. Aggravating these problems still further is the fact that teacher ed has been asked to serve a wide array of stigmatized populations.

One such population is *women*. At the point in American educational history when the goal of universal enrollment first emerged (in the middle of the nineteenth century), teaching came to be defined as women's work, and it has largely remained so ever since. (Currently, about 70 percent of teachers are women.) One reason for this was ideological, since nurturing the young and providing moral education were seen as naturally within the female sphere. Another was practical, since women would work for half the pay of men, and they thus helped subsidize the rapid expansion of school enrollments. But the end result is that teaching, like nursing and secretarial work, have been indelibly identified with women. And this has made the task of educating teachers less prestigious than the task of preparing practitioners for traditionally male-dominated occupations, such as law, medicine, engineering, and business.

Another stigmatized population served by the education school has been the *working class*. Teaching has been and continues to be in many ways the archetypal middle-class job—respectable knowledge-based white-collar work. But at the same time, it has offered modest pay and no career ladder for future advancement. (The starting teacher and the veteran of thirty years both occupy the same position; the only chance for "promotion" is to leave the classroom and enter administration.) The result is that teaching has often been more attractive to candidates from the working class, for whom it represented an accessible way of attaining middle class standing, than for middle-class women and men (especially men) who had other prospects. This means that the education schools that taught these students have been seen by others in the university as bearing the stigma of the parvenu. Not only are education schools latecomers to the university, but also their own students have often come from a lower class background than the average liberal arts student.

A third stigmatized population served by the education school is *children*. The status hierarchy of education is clear in linking the status of the teacher closely with the age and academic stage of the student—from doctoral study at the high end of the scale all the way down to preschool at the low end. Anyone who doubts the lowly status associated with working with children should only consider the pay and prestige of the child-care worker, who stands at the bottom of this particular age-graded spectrum. Part of the problem with education schools, therefore, is that they are indelibly associated with children, in a society that rewards adult-contact work more than child-contact work and in a university setting that is more concerned with serious adult matters than with kid stuff.

Finally, there is the uncertain position of the *teacher* herself in American life. It is not enough that teachers carry stigmatized associations of gender, class, and age, but they also suffer from an American bias in favor of doing over thinking. Teachers are the largest and most visible single group of intellectual-workers in the United States—that is, people who make their living through the production and transmission of ideas. More accessible than the others in this category, they constitute the street-level intellectuals of our society. In fact, teachers are the only intellectuals with whom most people will ever have close contact. Therefore teachers take the brunt of the national prejudice against mere book-learning and those pursuits that are scornfully labeled as only "academic." Whereas real professions transplant hearts, defend criminals, design skyscrapers, and build businesses, teachers worry about textbooks and tests and homework exercises. Of course the work of the lofty university professor is even more academic in all senses of the word, but it so thoroughly abstruse as to be out of reach and beyond the experience of the ordinary citizen. The education school professor, however, is associated with the practitioner of what are apparently the most mundane of intellectual tasks, which are seen as neither particularly useful nor especially obscure.

Consider some other reasons for the relatively low status of teaching in the United States. First, with 2.8 million teachers on the job at any one time, teaching is a mass occupation and as such cannot credibly claim to be an elite profession. And with more than 150,000 new recruits called for every year, teacher education is never going to be an exclusive form of professional preparation. Second, since teacher salaries are dependent on the public purse, and since voters have the opportunity to express their preferences about school funding through frequent millage elections, there is an effective ceiling on what members in this occupation can make. Under these circumstances, it is unlikely that American teachers will ever be able to earn an income that puts then substantially above the level of the average taxpayer. And third, public school teachers suffer from the negative image of public employment that characterizes this market-oriented society. Market ideology in the United States labels private-sector workers as productive and public employees as drones. The high professions have played into this ideology effectively by identifying themselves as mini-entrepreneurs operating under the fee-for-service model. Teachers cannot make this same claim.

My point here is a simple one: Market pressures have played a significant role in shaping the distinctive history of American teacher education, and they have left it with a disabling legacy. Education schools have been, and continue to be, torn between competing concerns about social efficiency and social mobility. And they continue to occupy a status at the lower end of the educational hierarchy, which has both undermined their ability to carry on sound programs of professional preparation and interfered with efforts to strengthen these programs. In the next chapter, I examine the nature of teacher education as a mode of professional practice and the things about it that make it so difficult for ed schools to carry out effectively.

Chapter 3 Teacher Ed in the Present: The Peculiar Problems of Preparing Teachers

The problems that afflict teacher education are not only the result of a history of being battered by market forces but also the result of the peculiar nature of the task itself.[1] Preparing teachers, it turns out, is extraordinarily demanding, in large part because of the complexities of teaching itself as a form of professional practice. The core problem is this: Teaching is an enormously difficult job that looks easy.

Both parts of this proposition have caused severe difficulties for teacher education. The sheer complexity and irreducible uncertainty surrounding teaching as a practice have made it unusually difficult for education schools to develop effective programs for preparing practitioners in the field. And this difficulty is exacerbated by the common perception, among prospective teachers and the public alike, that learning to teach is no big deal. As a result, although teacher education programs struggle mightily and often in vain to prepare teacher candidates for the challenges they will face in the classroom, they earn only disdain for their efforts. Both teacher candidates and educational observers berate these programs for making a simple induction process unnecessarily complicated. Only a relentlessly wrongheaded institution like an education school, say the critics, could mess up something as easy and natural as learning to teach. Therefore any effort to enhance the professional role and status of teachers through improved teacher education must first overcome the credibility chasm that afflicts education schools.

To understand the roots of this gap between the reality and the perception of learning to teach, let us look at some of the characteristics of teaching that make it such a difficult form of professional practice, and what it is that makes the process of becoming a teacher seem so uncomplicated.

TEACHING IS A DIFFICULT JOB

One reason that teaching is such a difficult profession is that its aim is to change the behavior of the client, and thus its success depends on the willingness of the client to cooperate in that enterprise. This effort is complicated by the fact that the client is brought to the classroom under compulsion. Teachers and students are thereby thrown into an intense emotional relationship, which the successful teacher has to manage with great skill and at substantial cost in order to bring about desired educational outcomes. Because of the conditions of structural isolation under which teachers must carry out their practice, they must work through all these dilemmas on their own, without much help either from the administrative hierarchy or from fellow teachers. Finally, in part for these reasons, teachers must live with an extraordinary degree of chronic uncertainty about the effectiveness of their efforts to teach.

The Problem of Client Cooperation

At the core of the difficulties facing teachers is that, as David Cohen has put it in his lovely essay on the nature of teaching, "Teaching is a practice of human improvement. It promises students intellectual growth, social learning, better jobs, and civilized sensibilities. Teaching is one member of a modest but growing family of similar practices; psychotherapy, organizational consulting, some parts of social work, and sex therapy are a few others. Practice in all of them is quite unique. Practitioners try to produce states of mind and feeling in other people or groups by direct work on and with those they seek to improve."[2] One big problem that arises from being in such a practice is that "practitioners depend on their clients to achieve any results. In most practices, practitioners rely on their own skill and will to produce results. They depend on clients or customers for approbation, applause, purchases, and the like. But in psychotherapy, teaching, and related practices, clients co-produce results. Students' and patients' will and skill are no less important than practitioners'. No matter how hard practitioners try, or how artfully they work, they can produce no results alone. They can succeed only if their clients succeed."[3]

A surgeon can fix the ailment of a patient who sleeps through the operation, and a lawyer can successfully defend a client who remains mute during the trial; but success for a teacher depends heavily on the active cooperation of the student.[4] The student must be willing to learn what the teacher is teaching. Unless this intended learning takes place, the teacher is understood to have failed. It was this reciprocal notion of the teacher-student relationship that Dewey had in mind when he said, "There is the same exact equation between teaching and learning that there is between selling and buying."[5] That is, you can't be a good salesperson unless someone is buying, and you can't be a good teacher unless someone is learning.

Consider how terribly difficult this makes things for teachers and others trying to work as practitioners of human improvement. They must devote enormous amounts of skill and effort to the task of motivating the client to cooperate, and still the outcome is far from certain. The client may choose to spurn the practitioner's offer of improvement—out of apathy, habit, principle, spite, inattention, or whim. In such a field, success rates are likely to be low, and the connection between a practitioner's action and a client's outcome is likely to be at best indirect. Therefore the effectiveness of the practitioner becomes difficult to establish.

Within the field of medicine, we can see some of the consequences of this reciprocity problem for professional preparation. Medical schools can train physicians to treat many somatic ailments (an inflamed appendix, a bacterial infection) with a high degree of success by means of a direct physical or chemical intervention by the practitioner on the body of the patient. But they are less effective at showing physicians how to treat disorders such as obesity or neurosis, in which the treatment requires patients to change behaviors that are damaging to their health. As a result, medicine tends to push such low-yield therapies into the hands of human improvement practitioners, such as counselors, while retaining control over the treatments that are most successful. Ed schools don't have this luxury. They're stuck with the task of preparing practitioners for a profession in which changing people is the whole job.

The Problem of a Compulsory Clientele

The difficulty of gaining the compliance of the student is made even worse for the teacher because the student is only present in the classroom under duress. A central fact of school life is that, given the choice, students would be doing something other than studying algebra or geography or literature or biology. Part of the compulsion is legal. Most states require students to attend school until the age of sixteen, whether they want to or not.

Of course, the heavy hand of the law is probably not the primary factor pushing students to attend school. They are likely to feel the pressure more directly from their parents (who want school to take care of children during the day, to help them get ahead, even to educate them), from the market (which makes school credentials mandatory for access to a good job), and from their own social desires (school is where their friends are). But the looming presence of a legal sanction is not a minor issue for either student or teacher, and it certainly helps distinguish the classroom from other venues of professional practice, both human improving and not. After all, how often does a truant officer come knocking when a patient misses an appointment with the counselor or dentist? In addition, most of the incentives to go to school, legal and otherwise, have to do with encouraging students to attend rather than to learn. Students may have to be in school and may even want to be there, but they are not necessarily there to learn, at least not to learn the official curriculum. If they learn school subjects while attending school, it is because a teacher has actively sought to make that happen.

If successful teaching, as we have noted, requires the willingness of the student to learn, then success is even more difficult to obtain because the student is there involuntarily. Motivating volunteers to engage in human improvement is very difficult, as any psychotherapist can attest, but motivating conscripts is quite another thing altogether. And it is conscripts that teachers face every day in the classroom.

No one writes about the consequences of involuntary learning on both teacher and student in more depth or with greater bile than Willard Waller does in his classic book *The Sociology of Teaching*:

> The teacher-pupil relationship is a form of institutionalized domination and subordination. Teacher and pupil confront each other in the school with an original conflict of desires, and however much that conflict may be reduced in amount, or however much it may be hidden, it still remains. The teacher represents the adult group, ever the enemy of the spontaneous life of groups of children. The teacher represents the formal curriculum, and his interest is in imposing that curriculum upon the children in the form of tasks; pupils are much more interested in life in their own world than in the desiccated bits of adult life which teachers have to offer.[6]

Control is therefore the central problem facing the teacher, according to Waller, and every novice approaching the classroom for the first time would certainly agree with him. Just ask students in teacher preparation programs, and they will tell you that they have learned too much about theories of curriculum and pedagogy and not nearly enough about classroom management, the thing that most worries them about being able to teach. In fact, as Cusick argues in *The Educational System,* this problem does not go away with time and experience: "The argument is not that classrooms are out of control. Instead, the argument is that control is the major issue and always at the center of teacher-student relations. Orderly behavior can never be expected; it is always problematic and always requires attention."[7]

Of course, teachers have a huge advantage in this struggle for control. They have institutional authority, superior knowledge, and parental sanction, and they are usually bigger too. But students are not without weapons of their own. Waller again: "Whatever the rules that the teacher lays down, the tendency of the pupils it to empty them of meaning. By mechanization of conformity, by 'laughing off' the teacher or hating him out of all existence as a person, by taking refuge in self-initiated activities that are always just beyond the teacher's reach, students attempt to neutralize teacher control."[8]

The key here is the ability of students to empty teacher rules of their meaning. If the purpose of control for teachers is to facilitate learning, then the best way for students to exact revenge for compulsory education is to comply with the formal reality of teacher control without giving in to its substance by actually learning anything. The result is a compromise in which students acknowledge the teacher's control and the teacher uses this control lightly, making only modest demands on the students as learners. In *Selling Students Short,* Sedlak and coauthors call this form of accommodation in the classroom "bargaining";[9] in *The Shopping Mall High School,* Powell, Farrar, and Cohen call it constructing "treaties";[10] and in my previous book, I call it a game of *How to Succeed in School without Really Learning.*[11]

Waller goes out of his way to focus on, even caricature, the traditional teacher, who relies on direct control to manage the classroom (in characteristically epigrammatic form, he asserts, "Every teacher is a taskmaster and every taskmaster is a hard man.").[12] But teachers in the progressive tradition also necessarily exert control in the classroom. The difference is that they do so in a manner that is less direct, less visible, and therefore more manipulative than Waller's taskmaster: by engaging interest and finding ways of attaching it to the required curriculum; by indirectly promoting and modeling correct behavior rather than imposing it by fiat; and by creating an emotional bond with students and using this to motivate compliance with the social order and learning process in the classroom. This softer approach to classroom management may be experienced by students as more benign and friendly than the heavy-handed imposition of authority that characterizes the traditional approach. It may even be more effective in general as a way to motivate students to learn what the teacher is teaching. But it is no less a mechanism for controlling student behavior.

In countries other than the United States, the structure of education sometimes strengthens the teacher's hand in managing student learning—for example, by organizing the educational system around high-stakes testing of students at critical transition points in their careers in school. Outside the United States, students often have to pass an intensive and comprehensive examination of what they have learned in order to get into the most desirable high school or university. An interesting side effect of this is that it shifts responsibility for compelling students to learn the curriculum away from teachers and onto an examination over which the teacher has no control. In the American classroom, where the teacher is responsible for both delivering the curriculum and evaluating the success of students in learning it, the teacher is in the disadvantageous position of having to say to students, "Learn this because I said so" (which provokes student opposition) or "Learn this because you're going to need to know it some day" (which provokes student skepticism because that day seems so far away). In a system driven by outside examinations, however, teachers can portray themselves as the allies rather than taskmasters of the students in their classes. Under these conditions, the teacher can say to students, "You need to learn this for the exam, which is coming up shortly and will have a big impact on your lives, and I can help you pass it." This approach helps teachers undercut some of the student resistance and apathy toward learning, but it doesn't eliminate the problem that compulsion poses for teachers. In fact, high-stakes exams may well exacerbate students' sense of learning under duress—and of learning itself as the acquisition of what Waller called "desiccated bits of adult life"—even as it transfers some of the blame for this away from the teacher.[13] To the extent that the standards movement is now driving the United States in this direction, it too may encounter the pedagogical costs and benefits of high-stakes testing.

The Problem of Emotion Management

Another characteristic of teaching that makes it difficult is the way it requires teachers to establish and actively manage an emotional relationship with students. This is in striking contrast to the norms that govern most professions, including those that focus on human improvement. So consider for a moment some of the characteristics of the prototypical professional relationship, and then consider the implications for teaching that arise from the sharp differences between this and the teacher-student relationship.

First, professional practitioners in general are permitted, even required, to maintain a distinct emotional distance between themselves and the client. They construct the role-relationship around a norm of affective neutrality, according to the rationale that the services of the professional will be most effective in meeting the needs of the client if the professional is able to approach matters from a stance of objectivity. From this perspective, emotional involvement with the client is counterproductive, because it distracts the professional from deploying the analytical and technical skills that will be most valuable in serving the client's interests.

Another characteristic of the professional-client relationship that reinforces the norm of emotional distance is the distinctive narrowness of this relationship. That is, the professional focuses on the particular problem that brings the client to seek professional help in the first place rather than construing this interaction as a diffuse relationship between two people. The doctor focuses on the client's fever, the accountant on the client's tax liability, and the therapist on the client's compulsive behavior. To get involved with the client in the more intense and wide-ranging manner of a close friend may be counterproductive in handling the problem that brought the client to the professional in the first place and therefore may well be defined as unprofessional conduct.

A third characteristic that defines the professional-client relationship is its achievement orientation. It exists in order to get the job done, and the client will judge its success by how well the professional performs in resolving the problem that originally propelled the client to seek professional help. A fourth characteristic of this relationship is the self-interestedness of the actors. They approach each others as independent agents pursuing their own ends, not as members of a collectivity with shared ends. A fifth characteristic of professional relationships is that they are supposed to be governed by universalistic rather than particularistic rules. This means following procedures that are the same across all relationships, without favoring or discriminating against any clients.

These five characteristics of professional-client relationships are drawn from the "pattern variables" developed by Talcott Parsons, which are five pairs of alternative orientations that can be used to define distinctive types of role relationships.[14] He called them: affective neutrality vs. affectivity, specificity vs. diffuseness, achievement vs. ascription, self vs. collectivity-orientation, and universalism vs. particularism. As the theory goes, professionals in their interaction with clients are supposed to be governed by the first orientation in each of the five pairs. In this regard, they fit in a large category of roles that sociologists call secondary roles. Secondary role-relationships make up that vast array of limited and utilitarian social connections that people engage in as a means toward particular ends—such as employer-employee, customer-clerk, and pilot-passenger. The purpose of a secondary role-relationship is to accomplish ends that extend outside the relationship itself: the client gets a problem solved, the professional gets paid. The relationship is not its own reward but is a means toward other ends for each of the parties involved. Primary roles, in contrast, are small in number, intensely emotional, and highly particularistic. The relationship—close friend, spouse, parent, gang member—is defined as an end in itself and not as a means to ulterior ends.

In real life, of course, these theoretical distinctions between roles tend to blur. Boss and employee sometimes become friends, professional and client sometimes fall in love. But the difference between primary and secondary roles still carries meaning. Thus much of the distinctive nature of professional relationships is usefully captured by the ideals of emotional neutrality, narrowness of focus, achievement orientation, convergence of self-interest, and due process.

In comparison to the relative clarity of the role defined for the typical professional, teachers find themselves in a much more complicated role environment. For example, adopting a posture of social distance from students is likely to undermine their ability to teach these students effectively. Gary Fenstermacher argues that "teachers may . . . at times wish for social distance from the complex, tangled, and sometimes destructive lives of their students, but they cannot teach well and ignore the many dimensions of the lives of their students. Teaching well requires as broad and deep an understanding of the learner as possible, a concern for how what is taught relates to the life experience of the learner, and a willingness to engage the learner in the context of the learner's own intentions, interests, and desires. Social distance of the variety favored by many physicians inhibits the capacity of teachers to do their job well."[15]

Teachers need a broad understanding of the whole student—emotional life, family situation, social condition, cultural capital, cognitive capacities—which precludes the narrowly defined approach of most professional associations. By narrowing the focus to the particular task at hand—a math problem, spelling list, or science project—the teacher is likely to miss the information about the student that may help determine the most effective approach to make in promoting learning for that student.

But the issue is more than a matter of developing a broad relationship with students for the purpose of understanding their learning needs and learning problems. The teacher also needs to establish an emotional link in order to be able to motivate the student to participate actively in the learning process. As we have already established, motivating students to learn is not easy. Students are conscripts in the classroom, and as a result teachers are more often successful at containing students' overt behavior than at promoting learning within. Dewey, among others, noted that "children acquire great dexterity in exhibiting in conventional and expected ways the form of attention to school work, while reserving the inner play of their own thought, images, and emotions for subjects that are more important to them, but quite irrelevant."[16] What this means is that teachers are never sure whether what they are observing in the classroom is active engagement in an inner-directed pursuit of learning or merely formal compliance with teacher authority. And the most powerful tool teachers have to encourage engaged learning is their emotional connection with their students.

Teachers devote a lot of care and energy to constructing a social and emotional atmosphere in the classroom that is conducive to learning. This means creating a setting that is inviting and comfortable, so that attending class is a pleasurable rather than dreadful experience. In particular, it quite often means establishing a relationship with students that is warm and affectionate and using this relationship as a lever for learning. A basic rule of teaching is "Like me, like my subject." The ultimate aim of a teacher is to get students so engaged in the intrinsic pleasure of learning that they forget she is there and pursue it for its own rewards, but the teacher's most powerful mechanism for launching them into the learning process initially is their affection for her and their eagerness to please her by learning what she asks them to learn. So the conscious or unconscious strategy for most teachers is to establish a close emotional bond with students and then seek to convert emotional engagement with the teacher into cognitive engagement with the curriculum.

I am not arguing here that all effective teachers are cuddly teddy bears to their students, nor that students cannot learn from teachers they dislike. One of the daunting mysteries of teaching is bound up in the dazzling variety of approaches by which teachers establish an emotional relationship with students, approaches that range widely according to the gender and personality of the teacher, the nature of the subject, and the age of the student. Women and men, extroverts and introverts, science teachers and literature teachers, at the elementary level and the university level—all establish different ways of connecting with their students, but the most effective of them do indeed make this connection in some form or another.

At the start of their careers, teachers fumble around for a way to establish an emotional link with students that is effective and sustainable, for the teaching persona that works best for them. This persona is both natural, in that it draws on characteristics and strengths of the teacher as a person, and constructed, in that it is put together in order to serve the ends of promoting learning in the classroom. Samuel Freedman provides a nice window into the process of persona construction through his portrait of a New York high school English teacher named Jessica Siegel:

> She wants to draw in the students, to thrill them a little. The bulletin board is part of the strategy, and so is her penchant for bright, funky attire. Today she wears four earrings and five rings, two silver on her left hand and three gold on her right, and a dress from Pakistan, bone-white cotton printed with blue designs that are as cryptic and angular as cuneiform. . . . A student once asked, "Miss Siegel, do you water that dress?"
>
> Even as Jessica tries to captivate her students, she wants to control them—not to dictate or deaden, but not to abdicate authority either. . . . It took her years to develop a classroom presence that felt organic, for she was naturally a listener, a backbencher, a person who began countless sentences, "I don't know a lot about this, but. . . ."
>
> Gradually, she created from pieces of herself a persona that might best be called The Tough Cookie. She stands this morning with right hand on the hip, head cocked slightly, eyebrows arched in mock disbelief; every so often, she shoots a phrase Jersey City style out of a gully at the corner of her mouth. "Gimme a break," she says to a lying latecomer. Her students will hear her say the same thing a hundred times before the term is over, hear her bite down hard on "Gimme" and stretch "break" into an aria of annoyance.[17]

There are several characteristics of this need to establish an affectionate relationship with students that add profoundly to the difficulty involved in being a good teacher. First, there is no guidebook for how to accomplish this for any particular teacher in a particular classroom. Like other practitioners in the professions of human improvement, teachers have to work things out on their own, without being able to fall back on standards of acceptable professional practice such as those that guide lawyers and doctors and accountants.

Second, the practice of teaching—with its requirement for a broadly diffuse relationship with students grounded in part in emotion—throws the teacher into an extraordinarily complex role that in awkward fashion puts together characteristics of both primary and secondary relationships. In Parsons's terms, the teacher role combines a mandate for emotional closeness and diffuse interaction, both characteristic of primary roles, with mandates for achievement (giving students rewards based on performance, not ascribed traits), independence (encouraging students to develop and rely on their own skills and knowledge), and universalistic application of rules (treating all students the same, rewarding everyone according to the same criteria), all of which are characteristic of secondary roles. Teachers are asked to use the leverage obtained from their primary relations with students to support the teaching of a curriculum that is quite external to these primary ties. In short, this means creating affectionate ties and then using them to promote student learning. To be really good at teaching requires a remarkable capacity for preserving a creative tension between these opposites, never losing sight of either teaching's relational means or its curricular goal.

Balancing these two kinds of roles in the same position is awkward at best. It is not surprising that teachers often resolve the tension between the primary and secondary elements in one direction or the other—by leading a forced march through a curriculum that no one is motivated to learn or by settling for a feel-good classroom where no one is pushed to learn. In the latter case, teachers get so caught up in the need to be liked by their students that they lose track of the pedagogical purpose of establishing an emotional link with their classes and convert the teacher-student relationship into a simple primary connection, where the positive feeling in the group becomes its purpose. In these cases, the pedagogical logic reverses itself, as teachers seek to win the affection of their students by reducing the pressure on students to learn: "If I get you to like my subject, then you'll like me." One of the most difficult parts about teaching is that good teachers have to be willing to risk their relationship with their students in the pursuit of student learning, to use the leverage of being liked to push for a level of student performance that may result in being disliked.[18]

Third, teachers face the strain of trying to manage the emotional relationship with students by maintaining the teaching persona that makes this relationship work. Maintaining the teaching persona is an exhausting task of what

Arlie Hochschild calls "emotion management." In her book *The Managed Heart* she explores a variety of "jobs that call for emotional labor. Jobs of this type have three characteristics in common. First, they require face-to-face or voice-to-voice contact with the public. Second, they require the worker to produce an emotional state in another person—gratitude or fear, for example. Third, they allow the employer, through training and supervision, to exercise a degree of control over the emotional activities of employees."[19]

Hochschild never refers directly to teachers in this study, focusing attention instead on the cases of flight attendants and bill collectors, but her analysis fits teachers all too well. These kinds of jobs, she argues, are particularly difficult and stressful because the only way you can produce the desired emotional state in the other person is by effectively managing your own emotions. The role of the teacher, like the role of other emotion workers, cannot be taken on superficially if one is going to be effective in this role. The aim is have an impact on the emotions of the student, and in emotional matters students, like all of us, have well-developed antennas for detecting a fake. Teachers are playing a role, but they need to play it in a thoroughly convincing manner, to come across to their students as fully authentic. "We all do a certain amount of acting. But we may act in two ways. In the first way, we try to change how we outwardly appear. As it is for the people observed by Erving Goffman, the action is in the body language, the put-on sneer, the posed shrug, the controlled sigh. This is surface acting. The other way is deep acting. Here, display is a natural result of working on feeling; the actor does not try to seem happy or sad but rather expresses spontaneously, as the Russian director Constantin Stanislavski urged, a real feeling that has been self-induced."[20]

Good teaching, then, is deep acting. Effective teachers feel the role deeply and express it naturally, without affectation or artifice. Like the best method actors, they plunge into the role, drawing on their own emotional life for inspiration and example, and then construct a persona that is an authentic expression of real feeling, even though this feeling is brought to bear on a role that is consciously constructed to serve a particular purpose—to promote learning in the classroom. Jessica Siegel's persona is a useful artifact that she developed in order to be more effective as a teacher, but it only works because she has found an authentic emotional ground for it in her own personality. The result is a role that is not worn lightly or discarded with a flick of the wrist but a role that arises from within a person who teaches and that takes over that person while teaching. This is why Waller is quite right in asserting that "teaching makes the teacher. Teaching is a boomerang that never fails to come back to the hand that threw it. Of teaching, too, it is true, perhaps, that it is more blessed to give than to receive, and it also has more effect. Between good teaching and bad there is a great difference where students are concerned, but none in this, that its most pronounced effect is upon the teacher. Teaching does something to those who teach."[21]

In explaining this phenomenon, Waller characteristically places the greatest weight on the problem of control and the way the role of teacher as taskmaster affects the teacher more than the student. "Subordination is possible only because the subordinated one is a subordinate with a mere fragment of his personality, while the dominant one participates completely. The subject is a subject only part of the time and with a part of himself, but the king is all king."[22] With this emphasis on the inhuman consequences of control for schooling, Waller (as Cohen has pointed out)[23] is adopting a thoroughly romantic vision of education as a contest between natural and forced learning. The implication is that a more child-centered and interest-based mode of instruction, such as promoted by educational progressivism, would resolve the control problem and relieve teachers from having to suffer the dire consequences of playing the teacher role.

But Hochschild suggests a more complicated interpretation. By taking on the progressive version of the teacher role—which involves knowing the student in depth and working to draw that student into the learning process through affection and interest—a teacher is adopting a persona that requires an sizeable degree of emotion management. In short, the child-centered instructor no less than the traditional taskmaster is deeply shaped by the role he plays. To paraphrase Waller, the student is a student only part of the time and with part of the self, but the teacher is all teacher.

The Problem of Structural Isolation

Exacerbating the teacher's problem in trying to motivate the captive learner is the condition of structural isolation within which the teacher has to operate. Ever since the invention of age-graded education early in the nineteenth century, teachers have found themselves plying their trade within the four walls of the self-contained classroom. Before this time, a school tended to be little more than a large room where the learning of students with a wide mix of ages and abilities was managed by one teacher or by a cluster of assistant teachers under the supervision of a principal teacher. The shift to age grading allowed for curriculum specialization, whole-class instruction, comparative evaluation, and a staged educational experience for students, but it also left the teachers with the difficult task of trying to work out the problems of professional practice on their own.

Teachers normally teach behind closed doors under conditions in which they are the only professional in the room. They are left to their own devices to figure out a way to manage a group of twenty-five or thirty students and move them through the required curriculum. They traditionally get little help from other teachers, who are trying to work out an accommodation with the students in their own classroom down the hall, or from administrators, who have their own problems to contend with, who are architecturally barred from knowing exactly what is going on inside the classroom, and who are therefore largely unable to help teachers do their job. Except for lunchtime conversation or the occasional visit from the principal, teachers are usually left alone to work out a way to teach effectively.

One consequence of this is to reinforce the teacher's focus on control issues. Vastly outnumbered by students and cut off from professional support, teachers are left to confront what Deborah Britzman sees as the "two rules governing the hidden tension of classroom life: unless the teacher establishes control there will be no learning, and, if the teacher does not control the students, the students will control the teacher."[24] In order to rise to the challenge of establishing and maintaining control, the teacher must turn the classroom into a personal fiefdom, a little duchy, complete with its own laws and its own local customs.

Another consequence of isolation is to create a vision of learning to teach as a private ordeal[25] and a vision of the emergent teacher as self-made.[26] This leaves little room for the construction of a shared professional culture for teachers across classroom domains, and it certainly undercuts the value of teacher preparation programs. Teaching comes to be seen as an individual accomplishment, a natural expression of a teacher's personality. The idea that teachers are self-made "is a highly individualistic explanation which reinforces the image of the 'natural teacher,'" according to Britzman. "More than any other cultural myth, the dominant belief that teachers 'make' themselves functions to devalue teacher education, educational theory, and the social process of making value systems explicit."[27]

The Problem of Chronic Uncertainty about the Effectiveness of Teaching

In 1986, U.S. Secretary of Education William J. Bennett published a booklet that was widely distributed across the United States with the title *What Works: Research on Teaching and Learning*.[28] As Bennett put it in his foreword, the booklet was "intended to provide accurate and reliable information about *what works* in the education of our children."[29] The unintended consequence of publishing this booklet, however, was to show how little clarity and certainty there is in what we know about effective teaching. Findings reported in this document turn out not to be very helpful in defining what it takes to teach well. Some findings are mere tautologies: "How much time students are actively engaged in learning contributes strongly to their achievement"[30]—that is, students learn more if they spend more time learning. Some are misleading: "Parental involvement helps children learn more effectively";[31] but in fact involvement by parents with high cultural capital provides a big educational advantage for their children over the children of involved parents without this cultural capital. And most findings are simply too vague to be implemented: "Successful principals establish policies that create an orderly environment and support effective instruction,"[32] which begs the question about what constitutes an orderly environment and instructional support.

A troubling fact about teaching is that there is no established set of professional practices that have been proven to work independent of the particular actors involved and the particular time and place of the action. The technology of teaching is anything but certain, and teachers must learn to live with chronic uncertainty as an essential component of their professional practice.[33] One reason for this is that teachers have to operate under the kinds of daunting conditions I have been outlining, conditions that introduce unpredictable elements of will and emotion into the heart of the teaching and learning process. Teachers can only succeed if students agree to cooperate; cooperation is problematic because students are thrust into the learning situation involuntarily; a key factor in enlisting cooperation is the teacher's ability to establish an emotional relationship with students and harness it for curricular ends; and all of this has to be worked out under conditions of immersion with students and isolation from professional peers.

Even if we focus on the more predictable factors shaping teaching and learning, however, teaching remains an uncertain enterprise for a second reason: its irreducible complexity. What we know about teaching is always contingent on a vast array of intervening variables that mediate between a teacher's action and a student's response. As a result, there is always a *ceteris paribus* clause hovering over any instructional prescription: This works better than that, if everything else is equal. In other words, it all depends. It depends on the subject, the grade level, and the community; on the class, race, gender, and culture of the students; on the pedagogical skills, academic knowledge, personality, and mood of the teacher; on the time of day, day of week, season, and barometric pressure; on the content of the students' last meal and the state of their parents' marriage; on the culture and structure of the school; on the available curriculum materials, the teacher they had last year, and their prospects for getting a job when they graduate; and so on. There are simply too many people and too many factors involved in shaping the learning process for us to be able to point to a particular pedagogical technique and claim that it produces successful learning independent of other factors.

A third source of uncertainty in the work of teaching is that we are unable to measure adequately the effects that teachers have on students. What we can measure most precisely about teacher effects is most thoroughly trivial. A teacher can measure how many of the spelling words introduced this week a child can spell on a Friday quiz, how well a student can solve word problems of the type just covered in class, or how many facts a student can remember from a recent textbook chapter about the French Revolution. But what does this show about the larger and more meaningful aims the teacher had in mind in teaching these subjects? What does it show about how well the teacher enhanced the students' literacy and love of literature, empowered students with the capacity to use logic and numerical skills to figure out real life problems, and provided students with the resources to understand alternative ways of bringing about social change? How can we measure these outcomes, and how can we trace specific outcomes in the lives of former students to specific teachers and particular lessons? The most important outcomes that we want education to make possible—the preparation of competent, productive, and socially responsible adults—are removed from any particular classroom interaction between teacher and student by many years and many other intervening factors. There is simply no way to attribute a causal link between a person's capacities in adulthood and the pedagogical technique of an individual teacher early in that person's career, because of the cumulative impact on that person of so many other teachers and choices and contingencies over time.

A fourth source of uncertainty in teaching is the complex and often contradictory purposes that societies impose on the whole educational enterprise. In some ways we want education to promote democratic equality, providing all students with the skills and values they need in order to function competently as citizens. At the same time, we also want education to promote social efficiency, providing students with the highly differentiated skills and knowledge they will need in order to function productively as workers in different occupational roles. And we also want education to promote social mobility, giving individuals the kinds of cultural and credential advantages they need in order to get ahead socially in competition with others. Yet the kind of teaching and learning that will be effective varies radically depending on whether the primary aim is to prepare citizens or workers or social climbers, since teaching that is good for accomplishing one of these goals may be bad for accomplishing another. For example, placing students in ability groups may serve the ends of social mobility by creating distinctions between students, but it is likely to work against democratic equality for the same reason, and it may or may not serve the ends of social efficiency, depending on how well students learn useful job skills in the different groups.[34]

A fifth source of uncertainty is that teachers are not even in a position to establish clearly the identity of their client. At one level, the client is the student. After all, the student is the one facing teachers in the classroom, the one toward whom teachers direct all of their people-improvement efforts. But keep in mind that the student has not contracted with the teacher to deliver desired instructional services. In this sense, the involuntary student is more an object of teaching than a client requesting professional help. At another level, the client is the parent of the student. Parents often see themselves as collaborating with the teacher in the larger project of socializing their children and preparing them for adult life. In private schools—and in a variety of school voucher models— the parents more or less openly contract with schools and teachers to provide professional educational services to their children in line with the parents' educational wishes. But at a third level, the teacher's client is the community at large. In public schools, it is the citizenry as a whole that pays for and governs education, not just the parents of schoolchildren. And in the case of private as well as public education, the community as a whole—in addition to the student and the parents of the student—is a major consumer of the teacher's educational services. The quality of life for all members of the community depends on an educational system that is able to produce competent citizens and productive workers, and therefore everyone suffers from bad teaching and benefits from good teaching. Keeping the client happy is not an easy matter in any profession, but consider how much more difficult it is to satisfy the demands of three entirely different clienteles, especially when they are likely to have conflicting ideas about what makes good teaching and good learning.

Consequences for Teacher Education

As we have seen, teaching is an extraordinarily difficult form of professional practice. It is grounded in the necessity of motivating cognitive, moral, and behavioral change in a group of involuntary and frequently resistant clients. It depends heavily on the teacher's ability to construct an effective and authentic teaching persona and use it to manage a complex and demanding emotional relationship with students for curricular purposes. It lacks a valid and reliable technology of instruction, a set of norms defining acceptable professional practice, clear goals for instruction, clear ways of measuring pedagogical effects, or even a clear definition of the clientele to be served.

In light of all this, is there a more difficult task facing practitioners in any other profession? And is there a challenge facing any realm of professional education that is more daunting than the challenge presented to teacher educators? We ask teacher education programs to provide ordinary college students with the imponderable so they can teach the irrepressible in a manner that pleases the irreconcilable, and all without knowing clearly either the purposes or the consequences of their actions. Is it any wonder that these programs are not seen as smashing successes? It seems obvious that a program of professional education in which the goals, techniques, clients, and consequences are well defined is much more likely to win professional respect and public esteem than a program such as teacher education.

TEACHING IS A JOB THAT SEEMS EASY

Teacher educators face more than enough challenge in trying to prepare students for a profession as diabolically difficult as teaching. But that is not the end of the problem confronting them. In addition, they face a situation in which the profession of teaching is generally seen to be relatively easy. And this perception is not simply characteristic of the untutored public; it is also endemic among teacher candidates.

One reason for this perception is that prospective teachers undergo an extensive apprenticeship of observation before assuming the teaching role themselves. Another is that the substantive skills and knowledge that teachers teach seem to be all too ordinary. Also, teacher educators have little claim of special expertise in the subjects they teach, expertise that resides primarily in the disciplinary departments across campus. And finally, the pedagogical skill involved in teaching comes across as anything but obscure or mysterious, because teachers freely give away this capacity to their students in the expectation of making themselves superfluous.

Apprenticeship of Observation

Dan Lortie makes a convincing case that prospective teachers spend a long time as students observing the way teachers ply their trade, and as a result they feel they know how to teach in some depth before they take their first course in a college of education.

> Those who teach have normally had sixteen continuous years of contact with teachers and professors. American young people, in fact, see teachers at work much more than they see any other occupational group; we can estimate that the average student has spent 13,000 hours in direct contact with classroom teachers by the time he graduates from high school. That contact takes place in a small space; students are rarely more than a few yards away from their teacher. The interaction, moreover, is not passive observation—it is usually a relationship which has consequences for the student and thus is invested with affect. . . . The student learns to "take the role" of the classroom teacher, to engage in at least enough empathy to anticipate the teacher's probable reaction to his behavior. This requires that the student project himself into the teacher's position and imagine how he feels about various student actions. . . . It may be that the widespread idea that "anyone can teach" . . . originates from this; what child cannot, after all, do a reasonably accurate portrayal of a classroom teacher's actions?[35]

In comparison with teaching, other occupations—particularly other professions—remain largely a mystery. Students may spend fewer than a dozen hours observing doctors before entering medical school, and they may never see a lawyer or accountant or architect at work before entering into professional preparation for one of these fields. In such fields professional education serves the function of revealing the secrets that lie under that cloak of mystery. By contrast, teaching is thoroughly familiar to prospective teachers, and teacher education programs seem to represent less a window into the mystery than an arbitrary barrier without any useful purpose.

The mistake in this reasoning by prospective teachers, however, is this: Their apprenticeship of observation shows them a lot about what teachers do but almost nothing about why they do it. As Lortie describes it, "It is improbable that many students learn to see teaching in an ends-means form or that they normally take an analytic stance toward it. Students are undoubtedly impressed by some teacher actions and not by others, but one would not expect them to view the differences in a pedagogical, explanatory way. What students learn about teaching, then, is intuitive and imitative rather than explicit and analytical; it is based on individual personalities rather than pedagogical principles."[36] Teaching from this observational and nonanalytical perspective appears to be simple action, guided either by custom (this is the way teaching is done) or by nature (this is the kind of person I am). In neither case would teacher preparation be necessary or even useful. If teaching is bound by custom, students already know these customs as longtime observers of the profession; and if teaching is more an expression of personality, then that will arise naturally within the student and can't be taught in a program of professional preparation.

What students don't see is the thinking that preceded the teacher's action, the alternatives she considered, the strategic plan within which she located the action, or the aims she sought to accomplish by means of that action. These are the things that teacher preparation programs seek to teach, and legitimately so; but in so doing, they run into enormous resistance from teacher candidates who don't think they need this kind of professional education.

Ordinary Skills and Knowledge

Another impediment facing teacher education is the general perception that the substantive skills and knowledge that teachers possess are thoroughly ordinary. The root of this problem is that elementary and secondary education is imposed on the entire populace. It is not elite education; it is mass education. If it does its job well, the kinds of skills and knowledge that it transmits to students become generic in the population at large. That is, it teaches the things that average adults know. On the skills side, this include things such as how to read novels, magazines, and newspapers and how to write letters, applications, and essays; how to calculate change, figure prices per item, and measure the area of a lot. On the knowledge side, it includes such things as the story of Huck Finn, the causes of the First World War, the way gravity works, and the meaning of a numerical average.

Unlike college professors, who are expected to be experts at a level well beyond the understanding of ordinary citizens, schoolteachers are the masters of what most people of voting age already know. What they teach isn't rocket science; it's common knowledge. And teacher educators, though technically college professors, are not involved in an enterprise that is either awe inspiring or even seen as particularly necessary; instead they are seen as simply teaching prospective teachers to teach what everyone already knows.

Subject Matter Expertise That Belongs to Others

Worse yet, teacher educators have no legitimate claim to special expertise even in the substantive fields where they ply their trade. They may be specialists in mathematics education, literacy or English education, social studies or history education, and science education, but they do not have academic credibility as mathematicians, linguists, literature specialists, historians, or scientists. Substantive expertise does not reside within the education school that prepares teachers but in the disciplinary departments across campus—where professors carry out specialized research and run advanced graduate programs that explore the more esoteric realms of these disciplines, far beyond the reach of ordinary adults and far beyond the mandate or the expertise of K–12 teachers.

Because subject matter expertise is lodged outside the education school, teacher educators are only responsible for part of the preparation of prospective teachers, the part that is seen as having the least credibility and prestige. They are in charge of showing students *how* to teach, which they think they already know, while disciplinary departments are in charge of showing them *what* to teach, which is both a more elevated and an apparently less obvious form of knowledge. This situation not only puts teacher educators at a status disadvantage within in the academic hierarchy, but also puts them in an untenable position in relation to the production of teachers. Teacher education does not have control over providing teachers with the substantive knowledge they will need to teach, but it takes full blame for any deficiencies in knowledge that these teachers may demonstrate in the classroom.

Pedagogical Skill That Is Unobscure and Openly Accessible

Of course, the most appropriate response to all this received wisdom about teaching—the perception that it is an easy practice that is easy to learn—is simply to say that it ain't so. This chapter is an effort to demonstrate the enormous complexity of teaching and the extraordinary challenge of trying to teach people to teach well. The idea is to throw into sharp perspective the chasm between the simplistic perception of teaching and teacher education (held by both the public and the prospective teacher) and the reality of these forms of professional practice. There is no benefit in recounting the points already made or in refuting the more obvious fallacies and misperceptions. Suffice it to say that teacher candidates quickly discover the complexities of the task of teaching after they spend a little time in charge of their own classroom. And if they choose to rise to the challenge, if they strive to teach effectively rather than merely to replicate the traditional forms of teaching behavior learned during their lengthy apprenticeship of observation, they find themselves wrestling with the multitude of pedagogical dilemmas outlined here.

In closing, however, I want to focus on one last point about teaching and about learning to teach that may help put in perspective both the difficulty of these enterprises and the reasons so many people misperceive this difficulty. The point is an obvious one, perhaps, but one that is well worth restating in simple terms: The special expertise of teachers is not the subject matter of the curriculum but the capacity to teach others how to learn this subject matter. And by extension, the special expertise of teacher educators is not disciplinary knowledge but the capacity to teach others how to teach this knowledge effectively.

Other professions share this emphasis on skill in the application of knowledge. Doctors, lawyers, accountants, and architects all have to master their disciplines in order to be effective in their professions, but knowing their subject matter is not sufficient. Professionals are not simply holders of knowledge; they are people who act on this knowledge for the benefit of clients. The difference between teachers and other professionals in this regard, however, is striking. As Fenstermacher points out, most professionals use their knowledge to help the client with a problem, but they don't provide the client with the capacity to figure it out for herself the next time around: "One of the ways that physicians have succeeded in garnering the status and income they presently enjoy is to 'lock up' or mystify their knowledge. Until quite recently, it was extremely difficult to receive any diagnostic instruction from a physician. Physicians saw themselves not as giving their knowledge to the patient but rather as being responsible for making the patient well."[37]

Most professionals rent their expertise without disclosing its mysteries, so they can reserve its power to themselves. The next time clients need help with a medical, legal, or accounting problem, they have no choice but to return to the professional for another fix, another intervention, another rental of expertise. But teachers are different. "Teaching, at least what most of us would regard as good teaching, requires that the teacher give his or her knowledge away to the learner—both knowledge of the subject under study and knowledge of how to learn that subject. Eventually, the good teacher must also give most of his or her knowledge of teaching away to learners, in the hopes that they will learn to be teachers of themselves."[38] They don't rent their expertise, they give it away— and this includes not just their substantive knowledge but also their understanding of how to acquire this knowledge. A good teacher is in the business of making him or herself unnecessary, of empowering learners to learn without the teacher's help. The aim is to enable students to get on with life under their own power and to free themselves from dependency on schools and teachers.

By doing things this way, teachers demystify their own expertise and thus willingly abandon the source of power over the client that other professions guard so jealously. The best teachers are the ones who make learning look the easiest, who make the learner feel smart rather than working to impress the learner with how smart the teacher is.

In the same manner, teacher educators are in the business of demystifying teaching, giving away their own expertise in order to empower the prospective teacher to carry on the practice of teaching without need for continuous consultation and chronic professional dependency. In both cases, teacher and teacher educator put themselves in a position that diminishes their own status and power in order to enhance the capacity and independence of their students. This distinctive mode of professional practice helps explain much of the disdain that both professions must endure, but at the same time this quixotic selflessness also endows teachers and teacher educators with just a hint of frayed nobility.

Chapter 4 The Peculiar Problems of Doing Educational Research

If preparing teachers is a difficult role for the ed school to play, so is the work of carrying out educational research.[1] Researchers in the ed school, it turns out, are compelled to work a distinctive vein of knowledge, which exerts a powerful impact on the kind of research they produce, on the way they produce it, and on the credibility and prestige of their work. Note that the focus in this chapter is on the scholarly work generated by educational researchers, as distinct from the knowledge about teaching practice that experienced teachers have and that ed schools may or may not transmit to prospective teachers; here we are looking at research knowledge rather than practitioner knowledge.

THE KINDS OF KNOWLEDGE
PRODUCED BY EDUCATION SCHOOLS

Tony Becher has written a richly suggestive book about the nature of the knowledge produced by the different academic disciplines and departments within British and American universities. In this work— with the wonderfully evocative title *Academic Tribes and Territo-*

ries[2]—he considers the impact of these knowledge differences on both the nature of the intellectual work carried on by academic practitioners and the form of organization employed to sustain this work. He starts with a familiar pair of distinctions—between hard and soft knowledge and between pure and applied knowledge—and builds his analysis from there. Although he mentions education schools and other professional schools only in passing, his argument provides lovely insights into many of the most familiar and significant characteristics of educational research.

Hard vs. Soft Knowledge

Disciplines seen as producing hard knowledge are those that are most successful in establishing the rhetorical claim that their research findings are verifiable, definitive, and cumulative. The natural sciences are the leading examples in this arena. Practitioners in the natural sciences have developed scientific methodologies, procedures, and verification rules that allow them to produce findings that can be reproduced by others, defended against challenges, and thereby gradually validated to the point that the claims come to be accepted as definitive—seen as an accurate depiction of "what we know" about a particular component of the natural world. Once this kind of finding is established as functionally definitive, at least temporarily, within a scientific discourse community, then others can build upon it, pushing the pursuit of knowledge in that field to the next level.

Disciplines that produce soft knowledge, by contrast, find themselves working an intellectual terrain that is considerably less clearly defined. The humanities and most of the social sciences are the leading examples of this kind of intellectual endeavor. Research practitioners in these areas pursue forms of inquiry in which it is much more difficult to establish findings that are reproducible and whose validity can be successfully defended against challenges by others. Supporting causal claims is particularly difficult in these fields, so the producers of soft knowledge necessarily focus the bulk of their attention on the problems of description and interpretation: how to portray and make sense of the texts or events under study, in the absence of clear decision rules and validating methodologies. And practitioners in these fields never have the luxury of being able to build upon a solid foundation of previous findings, because these findings are always subject to challenge by researchers who adopt a different interpretive approach. As a result, producers of soft knowledge find themselves constantly rebuilding the foundations of their disciplines, as they continually reinterpret the most fundamental issues in their fields.

I'm not arguing that hard knowledge is foundational and soft knowledge is not, only that hard knowledge producers are in a stronger position rhetorically to make the claim that their work is definitive and therefore cumulative. After all, interpretation and intent are irreducible components of all inquiry. The claims of hard science are limited by community norms and purposes, and they are subject to revision and rejection by future researchers whose norms and purposes are different.[3] As a result, the validity claims of the hard disciplines are still only claims—difficult to contest but still contestable, durable in the short term but vulnerable over time. The advantage of hard over soft knowledge may be short-lived and largely rhetorical, but that doesn't make it any less substantial for practical purposes in the contest for contemporary credibility.

Two characteristics in particular make it difficult for researchers in soft knowledge fields to establish durable and cumulative causal claims. One is that, unlike workers in hard knowledge fields, they must generally deal with some aspect of human behavior. This means that cause becomes effect only through the medium of willful human action, which introduces a large and unruly error term into any predictive equation. These billiard balls are likely to change direction between the cue ball and the corner pocket. The other is that research projects in behavioral fields have embedded within them the values and the purposes not only of the researchers (like hard fields) but also of the actors under study. The result is a messy interaction of the researcher and the research subject.

From this perspective, education emerges as the softest of the soft fields of inquiry. Problems of teaching and learning, curriculum and governance, educational organization and educational reform—all of these resist efforts by researchers to establish causal claims about them that are verifiable, definitive, and cumulative in anything like the way hard-knowledge disciplines can. For one thing, of course, education is the social product of actors—teachers, students, administrators, parents, and policymakers—whose actions both shape this institution and are shaped by it. In addition, educational processes are fundamentally political, reflecting social purposes—such as democratic equality, social efficiency, and individual opportunity—that embed contradictory pressures within education and provide conflicting criteria for evaluating educational success.[4] As a result, educational researchers are able at best to make tentative and highly contingent claims that are difficult to sustain in the face of alternative claims by other researchers.

In spite of these difficulties, educational researchers have not been willing to abandon the effort to make their soft knowledge harder. Like knowledge producers in other fields that are grounded in human behavior, they have sought to establish ways of conceptualizing educational processes (such as behaviorism) and methodologies for analyzing these processes (such as statistics) that promise to enhance the claims they can make for the validity and reliability of the resulting educational knowledge. Within limits, this effort has been quite successful. An empirical science of education emerged at the start of the twentieth century and grew into a position of dominance in the field within a few decades, and it is still a strong presence in spite of the recent rise to prominence of an explicitly interpretive approach to educational research.[5] However, the science of education has encountered severe limitations for its claim to produce hard knowledge. It has been much more successful at describing the ways education works and identifying loose relationships between educational variables than at explaining educational outcomes in light of educational causes. These limitations have confined educational number crunching to the soft side of the knowledge spectrum, since the hardness of the hard sciences is expressed most distinctively in the ability to predict the effects arising from particular causes. But the only causal claims educational research can make are constricted by a mass of qualifying clauses, which show that these claims are valid only within the artificial restrictions of a particular experimental setting or the complex peculiarities of a particular natural context. Why? Because the impact of curriculum on teaching or of teaching on learning is radically indirect, since it relies on the cooperation of teachers and students whose individual goals, urges, and capacities play a large and indeterminate role in shaping the outcome. And at the same time, education as an area of inquiry is more a public policy field than an intellectual discipline, whose central orientation is irreducibly normative—to improve education—and whose research practitioners are less united by a common technical orientation than they are divided by the different educational goals they espouse.[6]

As a result, despite their best efforts there is little that researchers can do to construct towers of knowledge on the foundations of the work of others. Within a particular research group (defined by shared values and interpretive approaches), it is possible at best to construct Quonset huts of knowledge through a short-term effort of intellectual accumulation; but these huts are seen as structurally unsound by researchers who do not share the values and interpretive approaches of those within that group's intellectual compound.

Pure vs. Applied Knowledge

Disciplines that produce pure knowledge are primarily oriented toward the construction of theory. Practitioners in these fields work a terrain that is abstracted from particular contexts, focusing on establishing claims of a more universal and generalizable sort than one could make if trapped within a local setting. There is an echo here of Robert K. Merton's distinction between cosmopolitans and locals, which is grounded in the scope of the cultural group to which people see themselves belonging.[7] In this sense, pure knowledge researchers are the cosmopolitans of intellectual inquiry, seeking to gain distance from the local scene in order to establish a sense of the larger pattern that is hidden in the clutter of detail within the close-up view. Much of the work in the natural sciences fits in this domain, but the latter also encompasses the most theoretical work that goes on in a wide range of disciplines, from philosophy to sociology and from literary criticism to mathematics.

Disciplines that produce applied knowledge, in contrast, focus primarily on the practical issues that arise from specific contexts. The aim here is not to establish general patterns but to solve particular problems. Success is measured in relatively modest ways, according to whether or not a particular approach works in a particular setting better than alternatives that are available at the time in question. Professional schools in general have an applied orientation to knowledge, and so do a wide array of disciplines—for example, geology, psychology, and English—when they focus their attention on problem solving more than theory building.

Of course, pure knowledge disciplines are not cut off from practical applications and problem solving. Theoretical findings in physics and math, for example, have enormous implications for daily life, helping us figure out how to build better airplanes and safer bridges. It is not their potential for useful applications that distinguishes them from the applied fields but their scope; for, unlike the latter, they are largely freed from context, which enables them to develop theoretical concepts whose applications are broader. The problem facing the applied disciplines is the extent to which their findings are confined by time, place, and circumstance.

From this perspective, educational knowledge production is overwhelmingly applied in character. For one thing, as noted above, education is not a discipline in the sense that cultural anthropology and physics are—defined by a distinctive theoretical perspective for viewing the world (culture and motion) and by a distinctive research methodology (field work and time-lapse observation). Instead, it is a public policy field focusing on a particular institutional sector. As a result, educational researchers are under pressure to focus their intellectual energies on the most vexing problems that arise within their institutional purview, rather than enjoying the intellectual freedom of pure knowledge researchers, who can follow the chain of thought embedded within their own intellectual constructs. And for educational researchers, confinement to the educational arena is combined with the necessity of following a normative mandate in exploring this arena. It's not enough to study what is interesting about education; the researcher is under pressure to improve it. Fields like education are sites of public policy, which means they are shaped by public goals for their sectors of society and are responsible in part for the powerful consequences—for good or ill—in the lives of children and the health of society.[8] Students are not learning what they need to know, race and gender skew educational outcomes, teachers are not being adequately prepared and school resources are not equally distributed: these kinds of context-based and time-sensitive problems of practice dictate the direction taken by researchers in the relentlessly applied field of education.

Of course, education is not alone in having to work a terrain that is soft or applied. The social sciences in general have to construct knowledge on a soft and shifting foundation, because of the complex problems posed by trying to understand social interactions embedded in institutional structures. And fields like medicine and engineering are thoroughly applied in character, with researchers forced to explore problems thrown at them from the needs of practice rather than driven by the capacities of theory. But social scientists such as sociologists, psychologists, political scientists, and economists can and do let theory drive their construction of knowledge in the soft arena of social life (doing work that is soft but pure), which enhances the intellectual clarity and public respectability of their work. And researchers in professional domains such as medicine and engineering can employ the quantitative precision and causal clarity of hard science in their work on the applied problems thrown their way (doing work that is applied but hard), which enhances the authority and prestige of their research findings. In contrast, education—along with a few other people-changing professional fields such as social work and counseling—is unusually hampered by being both highly soft and highly applied, thus having strong control over neither its methods nor its subject and producing findings that are neither very clear nor very convincing.

The difficult circumstances under which educational researchers have to function help explain why qualitative research, after a long period of subordination to quantitative research, has grown to become such a widely used methodology for scholars in the field. After a quarter century of debate in the pages of *Educational Researcher,* the consensus seems to be that both methodologies are useful and valid approaches,[9] and that both operate within the same post-

positivist paradigm and are subject to the same basic standards.[10] As its proponents have shown, qualitative research is well suited to the task of making sense
of the socially complex, variable-rich, and context-specific character of education.[11] Quantitative work has a harder feel to it, which helps it produce results
that come across as clearer, more definitive, and more conducive to causal in-
ference. But in the effort to represent what's really going on in education, the
quantitative researcher's press for clarity can come at the expense of accuracy.
To exploit the analytical advantages enjoyed by quantitative methods, researchers often need to make simplifying assumptions about educational processes,
assign educational actions and actors and artifacts to categories in which they
can be counted, collapse and eliminate variables, discount multiple interaction
effects, and generalize across differences of time and place and person. This can
lead to an elegant model and to results that are supported by a clear statistical
decision rule, but both model and results can appear so abstracted from the
messy reality of schools as to call into question their validity and utility.

Thus quantitative researchers in education ultimately are no more able to
construct scholarly high-rises than their qualitative colleagues, since both have
to work the same marshy epistemological terrain. The contrast is that qualitative researchers seek to embrace education in all its complexity and specificity,
attempting to incorporate and elaborate just those elements that quantitative
researchers need to set aside and simplify. As Peshkin defines it, qualitative research in education can produce results that are somewhat different from but
equally useful as those produced by quantitative research.[12] It can describe
(defining processes, relationships, settings, systems, and people in all their con-
textualized complexity); interpret (explaining, developing, and elaborating
concepts; providing insights, clarifying complexity, and developing theory);
verify (assessing the utility of assumptions, theories, and generalizations); and
evaluate (examining the effects of policies, practices, and innovations).

But the central point is this: Regardless of whether researchers use quantitative or qualitative methods, carrying out credible research in education is particularly difficult. Citing such daunting characteristics of educational research
as "the power of contexts," "the ubiquity of interactions," and "the short half-
life of our findings," Berliner calls it "the hardest science of all."[13] "Educational
research is considered too soft, squishy, unreliable, and imprecise to rely on as a
basis for practice. . . . But the important distinction is really not between the
hard and the soft sciences. Rather, it is between the hard and the easy sciences.
Easy-to-do science is what those in physics, chemistry, geology, and some other
fields do. Hard-to-do science is what the social scientists do and, in particular,

it is what we educational researchers do. In my estimation, we have the hardest-to-do science of them all!"[14]

Exchange Value versus Use Value

In addition to the hard-soft and pure-applied distinctions, there is another difference, not mentioned by Becher, which divides university researchers from each other based on the way in which knowledge production within the various fields affects the value of the education that a particular department or program provides for its students. On the one hand, a university education can provide students with exchange value, by giving them a credential that can then be exchanged for something that is intrinsically valuable to the students, such as a good job and a nice standard of living. From this perspective, the content of the curriculum they pursue and the actual learning that they accomplish at the university is less important than the reputation of the university (or the program within it) and the perception of its worth among employers and others in the community. On the other hand, a university education can provide students with use value, by giving them a set of skills and an accumulation of knowledge that will prove useful to them in carrying out their varied roles in later life. From this perspective, the content of the knowledge acquired is the most important element of the educational process, quite independent of the university's (or program's) reputation. Consider how this plays out in a high school setting, where the upper curriculum tracks provide abstract academic knowledge that can be exchanged for college admission and eventually a well-paid job (low use value, high exchange value), whereas the lower tracks provide vocational knowledge that can be exchanged for a lower-level job (high use value, low exchange value).[15]

A distinctive characteristic of the knowledge produced by educational researchers and the education offered by education schools is that they have low exchange value and high use value. As we have already seen, education is marked by a variety of stigmas that undermine its ability to provide credentials with high exchange value—for example, an association with women, the lower classes, public employment, and a "semiprofession," along with its weak academic standards and modest institutional origins. In addition, the broadly confirmed general perception of both the research and the instructional programs of education schools is that they are weak, which further undercuts their exchange value. In part this is because of the hierarchy within academic knowledge pursuits, which dictates that hard knowledge production outranks soft, and pure knowledge production outranks applied. Education is located firmly at the bottom of both of these rank orders.

Of course, the high use value of the knowledge in a field is not necessarily a threat to the prestige of that field. Medicine is an applied field whose knowledge provides high use value for its graduates, while at the same time occupying an extraordinarily high status within the university. Likewise, a number of hard/pure fields with high social standing, such as mathematics or biochemistry, gain in status when their efforts lead to useful social applications, such as computers and genetic testing. The key seems to be that high exchange value and hard knowledge together immunize a field from the potentially demeaning perception of being "merely useful." Medical schools are inextricably linked with the highest paid and most prestigious profession in the American occupational status order, and the demonstrable effectiveness of the hard knowledge they produce reinforces this elevated status. As a result, the exchange value they offer is unassailable. But education schools are bonded to one of the more lowly paid and more ordinary professions (closer to nurses than doctors in the professional hierarchy), and the visible weakness of their soft knowledge base to produce predictable and desirable educational outcomes only reinforces this subordinate position. Cursed with weak exchange value, education schools are doubly cursed by having to justify themselves only on the basis of the use value of the knowledge they produce, even though that knowledge is not very useful.

ORGANIZATIONAL CONSEQUENCES

Becher argues that the kind of knowledge that provides the central intellectual focus for a discipline or an area within a discipline brings with it its own distinctive form of organization.[16] Hard/pure knowledge production calls for a social organization of intellectual practice that he calls *urban* and *convergent.* The nature of hard knowledge is that, for practical purposes in a particular intellectual context, it can be treated as cumulative. This means that at a given stage in the development of a discipline, everyone is focused on solving the same intellectual problems. The intellectual structure has been raised to a particular level, and all of the thought-workers are clustered at that level. The result is that the work takes on a distinctly urban feel. At the same time, this intellectual convergence makes for a social structure that is quite hierarchical. It takes novices a long time to learn the full body of knowledge in the field from the bottom all the way up to the point where the definitive knowledge ends and the real work of intellectual inquiry begins. This means that senior people occupy a highly authoritative position, since only they can direct the work at the very edge of understanding. It also means that the field needs to develop its own shorthand way of communicating within itself, one that necessarily assumes the reader or listener is informed about all the issues that are already resolved. As a result, writers and speakers in such a field can focus on the interesting material at the top of the structure of knowledge without having to bring the non-expert up to speed.

By contrast, soft/applied knowledge production calls for a social organization of intellectual practice that Becher calls *rural* and *divergent*. Researchers cannot build towers on the foundations laid by others because these foundations are always being reconstructed. As a result, research work is spread thinly over a wide area, as individuals and groups continually work at rethinking the most basic issues in the field and as they each pursue their own interpretive approaches. The resulting terrain is laid out in a series of rural dwellings and hamlets rather than in the kind of urban high-rises erected by researchers in a field like physics. Novices in this setting find themselves inducted quickly, since the field is wide open and no issues are considered closed off from reconsideration. Senior people have less control over the work of intellectual production, because their own work is so easily subject to challenge. And the field is less turned in on itself, since its boundaries are permeable, its body of knowledge nonesoteric, and its discourse diffused among a variety of divergent research communities.

The organization of knowledge production within education schools fits the pattern of other soft/applied fields by being thoroughly rural and divergent. Intellectual work within this field is spread all over the terrain. Researchers feel free to charge off in all directions without a great deal of concern about what stage the development of the field has attained at the moment or what directions senior scholars want to set for the field. They constantly reexamine old questions and reconstruct existing theories. What clusters develop—for example, around teacher preparation in one place and subject matter standards in another—are the result of practical needs generated from within the institution of education or from society's concerns about the state of this institution rather than from the internal logic of the research effort itself. And these needs and concerns are so numerous at any given time and so likely to change with changing conditions that they provide only temporary and limited incentives to concentrate resources in the classic urban manner that characterizes the hard/pure realm.

Gary Rhoades provides an insightful and influential analysis of the organizational peculiarities of American colleges of education, one that makes particular sense in light of the preceding discussion about the kind of knowledge that is produced in these institutions.[17] One assertion he makes about ed schools is the following: "Colleges of education are marked by greater technological ambiguity and more resource dependency on well-organized, vocal constituencies in an environment in flux than are colleges of letters and science. As a result, colleges of education have more diversified organizational structures across colleges and are more unstable both within and across colleges than is the case with letters and sciences colleges."[18] Another assertion is this: "Colleges of education faculty are more likely than letters and science faculty to expect and accede to managerial control and are also more divided and thus less likely than letters and science faculty to assert faculty influence, forming coalitions to defend and advance the collective interests of the college faculty. Thus, education deans have potentially more impact than letters and science deans."[19]

This argument by Rhoades follows naturally from the argument that I have been developing about the role of knowledge in shaping the organization of knowledge production in education. As a soft/applied field, education is characterized by high "technological ambiguity" (a diffused intellectual focus) and high "resource dependency" on "an environment in flux" (that is, a need to respond to practical issues arising from school and society rather than from the theoretical logic of the research effort itself). This means that faculty members in ed schools do not have natural intellectual communities to draw on for political strength, at least not in the way that psychologists or astronomers, for example, can draw on their national and international disciplinary communities for support. The intellectual labor of ed school faculty members is in service to diffuse demands from the environment rather than to their own colleagues within the field of educational research. The result is that they do not fall into intellectually distinctive social groupings within or across colleges (ed schools do not have a standard departmental structure), and therefore they have few social resources for asserting faculty power or for countering the managerial authority of the dean.

NEGATIVE CONSEQUENCES FOR EDUCATION SCHOOLS

This analysis of the nature and social organization of knowledge production in education schools has significant implications for the way in which these institutions function and the way they are seen. Consider first some of the negative consequences for education schools and then some of the positive consequences.

Low Status within the University

There is no doubt that ed schools are located at the bottom of the academic hierarchy within the American university. An important source of this low status is the nature of the knowledge produced by faculty members in education, especially its relentlessly soft and applied character. The pinnacles of the academic status order are reserved for the hardest and purest of intellectual pursuits. It is not difficult to see why this would be so. Hard-knowledge disciplines are able to maintain general respect because their claims to validity are so difficult to refute, while the softer disciplines suffer from having to qualify, temporize, and particularize their claims. Whereas the former seem to be standing on a firm empirical platform and speaking with a clear loud voice, the latter wallow around in a swamp of uncertainty and speak in a whisper. There is little doubt which of these will win greater attention and higher esteem. Likewise pure-knowledge fields, by addressing questions of broad theoretical scope, gain a decided status advantage over applied fields, whose scope of address is sharply restricted by time and place.

In addition, educational knowledge suffers from its low exchange value. After all, exchange value is the coin of the realm in the market-based environment of the American university. These universities are unique in their extreme sensitivity to market considerations in comparison to their counterparts elsewhere in the world.[20] Dependent heavily on tuition and forced to compete for customers in a buyer's market for higher-education services, American universities have to give education consumers what they are looking for—credentials that can be exchanged for good jobs and attractive social positions.[21] In this kind of environment, exchange value counts more than use value. And the root of exchange value is the employers' and public's general perception of the reputation of an institution and of the programs within that institution. This leaves education holding, as usual, the short end of the stick. What education offers is soft use value—usable knowledge of marginal validity—which is not a commodity that can compete effectively with the credentials from the more prestigious realms of the university, which offer hard and pure exchange value.

Weak Authority within Education and Educational Policymaking

It follows from the preceding analysis that the nature of the knowledge produced within education schools also makes the authority of these institutions relatively weak, even within their own world of schools and educational policy.

As Cohen, Garet, and Lindblom have pointed out, the impact of social science research on social policy is indirect at best, because of the difficulty it has in representing complex social policy consequences.[22] The more widely researchers throw their net around a complex array of variables, the less valid and reliable their conclusions become; but the more narrowly and rigorously they construct their studies methodologically, the more likely it is that they are leaving out important variables and the more incomprehensible their findings are going to be to policymakers. Educational researchers suffer from this syndrome at least as much as other social scientists. These problems are particularly acute for the empiricists within the field, who are trying to create hard knowledge through educational research. The findings of educational studies that have the greatest claim to validity and reliability—e.g., those that zero in on the effects of a particular experimental treatment by tightly controlling for other variables—are also likely to be the most trivial, since real education takes places in extraordinarily complex settings where variables are inextricably intermingled.

Educational researchers have an additional burden, however, which derives from their low academic status, their weak platform, and their whispery voice. The knowledge base of educational researchers leaves them in a position of marginal credibility with the educators and educational policymakers for whom their research findings should be of the greatest utility. As low-status purveyors of educational knowledge that is soft, highly contingent, and largely ungeneralizable, they are not able to speak in tones that are likely to command respect and to shape educational policy. In short, they can easily be ignored. And with the credibility of the institutional experts on education called into question like this, it leaves the field of educational reform and educational policy wide open to the influence of a wide range of others whose voices are granted at least equal standing.

Pressure to Transform Education into a Hard Science

One natural consequence of all this is that educational researchers would seek to transform the nature of their knowledge production from soft to hard and applied to pure. This has been the mission of the American Educational Research Association over the past forty years. All one has to do is examine the burgeoning production of scientific research on education that has arisen from this organization—as evidenced by the explosion in papers presented at its annual meetings and by the compilations of scientific research about teaching and teacher education that have emerged from its membership.[23]

This movement to make educational research harder and purer came to a head with the issuance of the first Holmes Group report in 1986 (*Tomorrow's Teachers*). In this report, the deans of the leading research-oriented education schools in the United States proclaimed that the research efforts in their institutions over the preceding decades had produced a true science of teaching—with rock-solid validity and sweeping theoretical scope—which could now serve as the knowledge base for the professionalization of teaching. In a recent article in *Educational Researcher,* former AERA president N. L. Gage restated this faith: "In the last 20 years . . . meta-analysis has yielded knowledge concerning the impressive magnitude, consistency, and validity across contexts of many generalizations in the behavioral sciences and promising methods for quantifying and analyzing the generalizability of research results. These arguments, findings, and methods justify . . . continuing the effort to build sciences of behavior."[24]

There is a value in the effort to make educational knowledge more quantifiable and generalizable, since it pushes researchers not to settle for the softest and most equivocal of findings. It is not very helpful if researchers answer every important question in the field by saying, "It all depends." Thus striving to establish and support harder claims is a valuable goal, but there is only so far that we can realistically move in that direction, and that is well short of the condition Gage calls a science of educational behavior. In order to create a solid ground for making hard claims about education, you can try to drain the swamp of human action and political purpose that makes this institution what it is, but the result is a science of something other than education as it is experienced by teachers and students. As I have argued elsewhere, such an effort may have more positive impact on the status of researchers (for whom hard science is the holy grail) than the quality of learning in schools, and it may lead us to reshape education in the image of our own hyper-rationalized and disembodied constructs rather than our visions of the good school.[25]

Another sign of the effort to move education into something like a hard science is the construction in recent years of large federally funded centers for educational research. These centers mimic the urban-style organization of knowledge production in the hard knowledge fields, which is particularly striking in a field as traditionally rural in research practice as education has been. But these centers arise more from the government's desire to increase the efficiency of its research funding and oversight (and the university's desire for large infusions of soft money) than from any discovery that educational knowledge has suddenly begun to accumulate into a rising epistemological structure. If anything, the centers are an effort to compensate for the lack of an accumulation of educational knowledge across studies—by organizing large, loosely integrated research projects as a proxy for this kind of accumulation. The production coming out of a research center gives the impression of systematic construction, but on close analysis this structure quickly disaggregates into an eclectic array of disparate studies operating under the center's umbrella. In this way, an educational research center is no more urban than the shantytown on the outskirts of a third-world city. Each is a collection of villages rather than a true urban community.

Pressure to Transform Education Schools into Pure Research Institutions

The distinctive nature of educational knowledge has produced another related form of negative impact on education schools by putting pressure on them to change their focus from teacher preparation to a more prestigious mission. Trying to mimic those disciplinary departments on the university campus with the highest academic standing, education schools—especially in the most elite universities—have frequently sought to change themselves into graduate schools of educational studies.[26]

Geraldine Clifford and James Guthrie tell the story of this misguided effort in withering detail in their book *Ed School.*[27] The idea has been to back away from too close an identification with teaching and with the production of useful knowledge for schools and to focus instead on developing a body of research that is purer than the education school norm, focusing on general theoretical exploration rather than responding to particular educational problems of practice. In addition, this new research direction would yield a higher exchange value, because of its affinities with the decontextualized and theory-driven (rather than environment-driven) explorations of the more prestigious fields in the academy. As Clifford and Guthrie point out, however, these efforts have not been successful. For one thing, the rest of the university has not accorded the desired higher academic standing to the faculty of these graduate schools of educational studies. For another, these efforts have served to wrench researchers away from real educational knowledge production without changing the soft, applied, political, behavioral, and environment-driven character of the field itself.

A Sense That the Field Is Never Getting Anywhere

One last problem that the form of educational knowledge poses for those who seek to produce it is that it often leaves them feeling as though they are perpetually struggling to move ahead but getting nowhere. If Sisyphus were a scholar, his field would be education. At the end of long and distinguished careers, senior educational researchers are likely to find that they are still working on the same questions that confronted them at the beginning. And the new generation of researchers they have trained will be taking up these questions as well, reconstructing the very foundations of the field over which their mentors labored during their entire careers.

This not only poses a problem for the researcher's sense of professional accomplishment and self esteem. It also leaves the entire field open to ridicule and kibitzing from those who stand outside. If these people can't get to first base in their own field of expertise, then they must not be very good. So maybe they ought to step aside and let a talented outsider stand in and swing for the fences. Could these outsiders do worse than the so-called professionals? (Recall this book's opening vignette, about the Michigan businessman who jumped in with a proposed solution to the problems of Detroit schools.) Since educational researchers are unable to be definitive and to demonstrate that they are making progress, they leave the field wide open to amateur educationists who feel little reason to be reticent about making their own contributions to educational discourse.

POSITIVE CONSEQUENCES FOR EDUCATION SCHOOLS

Having laid out a variety of negative consequences for education schools that arise from the peculiar characteristics of educational knowledge, I now turn to some of the positive outcomes that arise from the same source.

Seeking to Produce Useful Knowledge Is Not a Bad Thing

The close identification of education with use value and its alienation from exchange value has the potential to work to its long-term advantage socially and politically. After all, the university's practice of selling credentials that are based on appearance and reputation more than substance and real learning is one that is quite vulnerable to public challenge. This practice has all the characteristics of a confidence game, since it rests on an interlocking set of beliefs that are quite shaky. The chain goes something like this: it makes sense for consumers to invest in the credentials of a respected university because the prestigious research carried out there produces capable graduates who then deserve preferential access to jobs. Yet each part of this chain of reasoning depends more on faith than fact, and the whole system can collapse if challenged to prove itself. After all, the value of the credentials has more to do with the prestige of the institution than with the knowledge that students acquire there. In addition, the rising fiscal pressure at all levels of American government puts higher education increasingly in the position of justifying the enormous public investment in terms of verifiable outcomes rather than tradition or belief. This problem is exacerbated by a related issue: the gross social inefficiency of providing a public subsidy for an education system that is grounded more in individual social mobility (helping me get the job I want) than in substantial public benefit (providing us with the capacities we need).[28]

In this setting, the strong connection between education and usable knowledge can be a valuable asset. For the most part, educational research arises in response to clear current problems within a preeminently important institutional arena. This timeliness, responsiveness, and potential usefulness makes it much easier to justify—in the emerging era of outcomes measurement and cost-effective public investment—than much of the university's more prestigious but less relevant research efforts. Of course, there are several limitations to this pursuit of applied knowledge. One, discussed earlier, is that the findings of educational research are so soft that this applied knowledge is of limited usefulness. Unlike fields that are comfortably buffered by high exchange value, educational research is eager to help improve the practice of education, but its toolkit does not contain the kind of powerful cures that can be found in the medical doctor's black bag. Another is the relentlessly—even proudly—atheoretical quality of much of this research. Theoretical significance (like empirical validation) is something that educational research should aspire to, in spite of the enormous difficulties that this work poses for such efforts. In the absence of theoretical aspiration, educational research often seems rather pinched and pedestrian. But this failing arises more from intellectual laziness than from the characteristics of educational knowledge. The kind of practical knowledge that educational researchers produce can be theoretically provocative even if it is somewhat restricted in theoretical scope, and in this context its potential social usefulness can be both politically advantageous and vocationally gratifying for the producers in ways that are not available to researchers in less applied fields.

Freedom from Consumer Pressures

A related benefit for education that derives from the kind of knowledge it produces is that it is relatively free from the consumer pressures that have shaped the rest of the university. In general, the American university has been compelled to bend to the demand from consumers for programs and credentials that will serve individual ambition in the pursuit of social position. But the close identification of education schools with the vocational preparation of teachers and with the production of research to meet practical educational needs means that these schools are constructed around the accomplishment of social rather than individual ends. Their primary concern is social efficiency rather than individual mobility. This certainly puts constraints on both research and programs, since both must be responsive to the most urgent and current societal concerns. As a result, educational researchers do not enjoy the luxury of pursuing pure inquiry in whatever direction theory might lead them—or pursuing idiosyncratic inquiry in whatever direction personal preference might propel them. But at the same time they are liberated from involvement in a market-dominated instructional process that requires them to provide fickle educational consumers with whatever courses and programs the latter demand. And they have the satisfaction of knowing that they are working on issues that matter, both for the individual actors within education (like teachers and students) and for the larger society.

Freedom from Disciplinary Boundaries

Another advantage that accrues to educational researchers from the nature of the knowledge they produce is that they are free to deal with educational questions from whatever disciplinary perspective or methodological approach they find appropriate. This, as in the previous example, involves several tradeoffs. One is that they give up freedom of institutional focus—since educational researchers are compelled to focus on education—in return for considerable freedom in the way they choose to explore this subject. Researchers in other disciplines are often subject to a test of disciplinary correctness that can be quite confining. "Is this really political science?" they are asked (or history or philosophy or biology). If not, it doesn't count in the internal status order as measured by merit pay, promotion in rank, and professional recognition. But educational researchers are free to be as eclectic as they wish in the way they choose to intermingle disciplinary perspectives or methodological orthodoxies. There is an attractive pragmatism within educational research, which prefers to reward approaches that work rather than those that are canonical within a particular theoretical subculture. The downside here is that, at the same time that educational researchers cut loose from unnecessary disciplinary constraints, they also frequently lose some of the methodological rigor that comes from working within a clearly defined disciplinary research tradition. The result is a tolerance for poor research design and sloppy thinking. However, there is nothing in the nature of educational knowledge to prevent researchers in education from creating their own standards of rigor and from policing their own ranks in light of these standards.

Freedom from Hierarchical Constraints

The thoroughly rural and divergent character of educational research makes for a social organization of research effort that is relatively egalitarian. Senior researchers are not in a strong position to control the research process because their authority rests on shaky foundations. The noncumulative character of educational knowledge makes entry into the field easy and leaves newcomers in a position to make contributions that are arguably as valuable as those by the old hands. The same characteristics of educational research that allow policymakers to ignore it and other academics to ridicule it—namely its structural underdevelopment and its vulnerability to challenge—make it a field that is remarkably open and endlessly fascinating in the variety of its voices. There is nothing like confusion to create opportunity. The rural landscape of educational research produces endless possibilities for intellectual homesteaders to stake a claim and start developing their own little piece of the terrain. Of course, large federally funded centers for educational research represent an important countertrend to this pattern, since they resemble urban enclaves in a largely rural field and inevitably establish a kind of status order within them. But what is different about these centers in education compared with large projects in hard knowledge fields is that they are best understood as collaborations among loosely related independent research projects, pulled together for the effort to obtain funding but not integrated into a strong social or epistemological hierarchy.

Producing Soft Knowledge Is Now
the In Thing

In the past decade or two, there has been a strong and highly effective series of attacks on positivism and on the validity of quantitative research.[29] This process has affected a wide range of fields, beginning with the philosophy of science and moving eventually into education. All of this is thoroughly familiar to the members of the American Educational Research Association, who have seen the argument played out at great length in the pages of *Educational Researcher* over the past twenty years. As a result of this epistemological effort, the consensus has shifted toward a position that asserts the essential softness of hard knowledge and the essential uncertainty at the core of the validity claims made by the hard sciences. This means that soft-knowledge fields such as education can now breathe a sigh of relief, since softness is now a generalized condition and not an affliction only affecting educational researchers.

Unfortunately, the newly relaxed philosophical position toward the softness of educational knowledge—combined with its freedom from disciplinary constraints and its openness to newcomers—can (and frequently does) lead to rather cavalier attitudes by educational researchers toward methodological rigor. As confirmation, all one has to do is read a cross section of dissertations in the field or of papers presented at educational conferences. For many educational researchers, apparently, the successful attack on the validity of the hard sciences in recent years has led to the position that softness is not a problem to be dealt with but a virtue to be celebrated. Frequently the result is that qualitative methods are treated less as a cluster of alternative methodologies than as a license to say what one wants without regard to rules of evidence or forms of validation.

I bring up this point about the dangers of soft knowledge (paralleling the earlier point about the dangers of applied knowledge and of non-discipline-based research) as a caution to educational researchers against embracing too warmly the necessity imposed on them by the kind of knowledge they produce. For in looking for the silver lining in the cloud of problems surrounding the production of educational knowledge, we should not ignore the significance of the cloud itself. The characteristics of educational knowledge present researchers with both advantages and disadvantages. These elements do not cancel each other out, but instead in combination they define a universe of working possibilities and enduring dilemmas within which educational researchers have to forge their way.

An Ability to Speak to a General Audience

From the perspective of someone in the harder and purer disciplines, educational researchers speak with a voice that is laughably amateurish. Their lack of professionalism is apparent in a discourse that does not have the esoteric language and verbal shorthand of a truly advanced field of study. A paper that is truly interesting in a field such as math or biochemistry—that is, at the leading edge of theoretical development—is one that should be completely incomprehensible to an apprentice in the field, much less a layperson. By comparison, the discourse within education is transparent in language and widely accessible in meaning. All the complaints about "educatorese" only serve to prove the point, since they tend to come from those completely outside the educational research community. They are not saying they cannot understand what the researchers are saying, only that they themselves could say it better. But none of these critics would think of trying to read the cutting-edge research in math or biochemistry or to complain about math- or biochemist-speak, because these fields are supposed to be esoteric and beyond the reach of the layperson. Education, however, is largely accessible to outsiders and therefore vulnerable to discursive critique from nonexperts.

This situation puts educational researchers in a position to become public intellectuals in a way that is not possible for scholars in fields whose knowledge development makes them incomprehensible to the ordinary citizen. It is easy for outsiders to look into education—to contribute, criticize, and kibitz. But at the same time, this makes it easy for educational insiders to reach out directly to members of the public and make a case to them about the problems facing education and the ways we can deal with these problems. In this sense, educational researchers may not have the kind of authority that comes with hard/pure science, but they have a ready rhetorical access to the public that is lacking in more authoritative fields. As a result, the lesser form of knowledge produced by educational researchers may in fact offer them a political and social opportunity that is largely closed to the more prestigious realms of the university.

Chapter 5 The Peculiar Problems of Preparing Educational Researchers

Ed schools are not only responsible for preparing teachers and producing educational research; they also have to prepare future researchers.[1] Like the other two roles they are required to play, preparing researchers is fraught with special difficulties. In this chapter, I explore these difficulties, with particular attention to the work of doctoral programs in ed schools that aim to turn experienced educational practitioners into accomplished educational scholars.

FRAMING ISSUES: INSTITUTIONAL SETTING AND KNOWLEDGE SPACE

Two issues that are peculiar to the ed school frame this discussion of the problems it faces in preparing researchers. Both were examined in earlier chapters. One issue is the lowly status of the ed school, and the other is the special problems posed by the kind of knowledge it has to pursue. Let's consider each of these in turn.

Training in a Low-status Institution

Most researchers who focus on education are trained in education schools. In light of this, what are the effects of preparing educational researchers within the tainted confines of this institution? First, in education schools, as in other schools for the lesser professions, the prestige of the faculty comes less from their standing as members of the profession—as teachers—than from their standing as university professors with specialized academic skills.[2] Frequently the result is a sizeable cultural gap between the teaching profession and the education school faculty, which means that teachers who enter doctoral programs in education often feel they are being asked to abandon teacher culture in favor of a new academic culture in order to become educational researchers. This jarring discontinuity can undermine the education school's ability to effect a smooth induction of their students into the community of educational scholars. Second, the low status of the education school further weakens the position of the faculty to socialize doctoral students as future teacher educators and educational researchers. Professors in law and medical schools are generally seen as more learned and respected than those in education, which means that the latter may have more difficulty establishing their authority over students and spurring emulation.

Pursuing a Peculiar Form of Knowledge

As we saw in the previous chapter, educational researchers work a domain of knowledge that is particularly difficult because it is very soft and very applied. What, then, are the effects for education schools of having to prepare educational researchers to function within this soft/applied knowledge space? A key result is that, to be effective in studying this space, educational researchers need to develop an extraordinary degree of methodological sophistication and flexibility. It is not enough to be good at a particular mode of research and to be satisfied with a career of applying this approach in a series of studies. Where the terrain that needs mapping is this complex, researchers need to bring an equally complex variety of research methods to the task if they want to be able to view the subject in its many forms. Education starts to become understandable only when it is approached from multiple perspectives. This means that educational researchers need to have a broad comprehension of the foundational questions about the nature of their inquiry, instead of relegating this skill to those in the philosophy of science.[3] It also means that a program for preparing educational researchers needs to provide students with exposure to and competence in multiple research paradigms, unless it wants to relegate them to a parochial corner of the discourse in this multidimensional field.

A recent special issue of *Educational Researcher* reported on efforts at several universities to provide such training,[4] and a special issue of *Journal of Teacher Education,* devoted to a review of the literature in teacher education, turned into a similar discussion about the need for multiple research perspectives.[5] This does not necessarily require that every researcher be equally expert in multiple research methods. They should, however, be aware of the limitations of their own approach and the value of alternative approaches, and they should be capable of working in conjunction with researchers doing work quite different from their own. In 2002 a committee of the National Research Council published a report on *Scientific Research in Education,* which argued that, since "there are many legitimate research frameworks and methods" in education, "contradictory conclusions may be offered, adding fuel to the debates about both the specific topic and the value of educational research. The challenge for the diverse field of education is to integrate theories and empirical findings across domains and methods. Researchers from a range of disciplines working together, therefore, can be particularly valuable."[6] The report goes on to spell out the severe challenge that this situation poses for programs that seek to prepare effective researchers in education:

> Finally, this proliferation of frameworks, coupled with the sheer scope of the myriad fields that contribute to understanding in education, make the development of professional training for education researchers particularly vexing. The breadth and depth of topical areas as well as multiple epistemological and methodological frameworks are nearly impossible to cover adequately in a single degree program. Conceptualizing how to structure the continuum of professional development for education researchers is similarly challenging, especially since there is little agreement about what scholars in education need to know and be able to do. These unresolved questions have contributed to the uneven preparation of education researchers.[7]

In sum, education schools face a multidimensional dilemma in their effort to prepare researchers. First, their lowly status within higher education puts these schools in a relatively weak position to provide students in their research preparation programs with the expertise they need and to induct them into the community of educational researchers. Second, the soft and applied nature of the knowledge that educational researchers need to produce, combined with the dispersed and rural organization of the educational research effort, make it particularly difficult to design programs that would adequately prepare graduates to work effectively and credibly in this field. And third, the epistemological and social complexity of the field makes it essential for educational researchers to have a firm grasp of the foundations of inquiry, a solid understanding of and appreciation for multiple methods for pursuing inquiry, and a willingness and ability to work with researchers of different types to synthesize theories and findings in the field—all of which puts an even greater pressure on research preparation programs. As a result of all this, we should not be surprised to find that these programs often fail to produce all that we ask of them.

THE FOCUS AND ROOTS OF THE ARGUMENT

Below I explore some key implications of the special institutional and epistemological situation that faces American education schools in their efforts to prepare teachers as educational researchers. Why focus on this particular combination of people and places? Education schools are not the only institutions in which someone can be trained in educational research, and teachers are not the only source of prospective researchers; but former teachers trained in education schools dominate the world of educational research, so understanding the problems that arise from their training process is undeniably important. In particular, I focus on the cultural clash that frequently occurs when representatives of two distinct realms of professional practice—the K–12 teacher and the university researcher—collide in a research-oriented doctoral program in education. This clash plays out in part as a problem of how to accommodate potentially conflicting professional worldviews between teacher and researcher to the satisfaction of both, and in part as a problem of how to agree on the kind of educational experience that is needed for teachers to become effective researchers without abandoning their teacherly values and skills.

The argument in this chapter emerges from two interrelated sources. One is an analysis of the structural situation within which doctoral programs function at education schools. That is, continuing the analysis developed above, I examine the various conditions and constraints that affect the way these doctoral programs operate, based on the institutional differences between schools and universities and the differences between the work roles of teachers and researchers. The other primary source for the arguments in this essay is my own experience with the preparation of researchers in one college of education. For eighteen years I was intensively involved in the doctoral program in Curriculum, Teaching, and Educational Policy within the College of Education at Michigan State University.

THE TRANSITION FROM TEACHER TO RESEARCHER: WHAT MAKES IT EASY

In many important ways, the transition from teacher to educational researcher is a natural and easy one. As prospective researchers, teachers bring many traits that are ideal for this new role, including maturity, professional experience, dedication, and good academic skills.

Maturity

One striking characteristic that distinguishes doctoral students in education from their peers in disciplinary departments is that they are grownups. In arts and sciences departments, students frequently enter doctoral study right after completing their bachelor's degree, but in education they typically arrive at this stage only after first serving at least a few years as an elementary or secondary teacher. Nationally, 49 percent of all graduate students in education (master's and doctoral level) are over thirty-five, compared to 29 percent of those in other fields.[8] The median age for a person receiving a doctorate in education is forty-four—compared to thirty-six in business, thirty-five in humanities, thirty-four in social sciences, and thirty-two in life sciences.[9]

Doctoral students in education have already lived a life. They have spent at least some time, generally a lot of time, doing something other than being a good student. They have usually pursued careers as teachers, and along the way they have accumulated the experiences and obligations of adult life. They pay taxes. They often have a pension plan, car payments, and a mortgage. Frequently they are married and have children, or start having them while in graduate school. All of this puts a distinctive spin on the experience of doctoral study. Unlike many of their peers in the arts and sciences, who drift into graduate study out of inertia or avoidance, doctoral students in education choose to enter doctoral study as a deliberate step in the early or middle stages of a viable career as a classroom teacher. As adults, frequently the same age as their professors, they are not willing to be treated as kids just because they are students. One result is that they are likely to take charge of their doctoral program and make it serve their own needs instead of waiting for the program to shape them.

Professional Experience

As experienced classroom teachers and school administrators, these students bring a wealth of professional expertise to their doctoral studies in education. Unlike their counterparts in disciplinary departments across campus, they have more than an abstract conception of the subject they will be studying in their doctoral program. Their work in the program builds on an intensive and extensive involvement in elementary and secondary education, which gives them a sense of the subject that is much richer than what could be obtained by pursuing an undergraduate major in it, the usual preparation for doctoral study in the disciplines.

Teachers have a feel for the breadth, depth, and complexity of education as an institution that cannot be picked up by reading about it or observing it.[10] This means they bring a storehouse of data to doctoral study, which they can and do draw upon in evaluating the utility and validity of the theories they encounter there. Though neophytes in the business of theorizing about education, they are old hands at the practices that are the subject of this theorizing. Even Cronbach and Suppes, who in their 1969 report on educational research for the National Academy of Education favored recruiting nonteachers as educational researchers, recognized that such recruits will need to pick up some of the teacher's knowledge of schools through such means as school-based internships and extensive classroom observation.[11]

Teachers and administrators also bring to doctoral study a set of plausible and professionally tested understandings about what makes education work and not work. They come in with a sense of what is happening in the institution they will be studying. This means they don't want the doctoral program to explain to them what they already know but instead want it to allow them as scholars to continue exploring issues they already started examining as practitioners.[12]

Dedication to Education

A major task in a doctoral program in the disciplines is to convince students that their studies have value. Sure, they already have an interest in the subject, since they selected themselves into a doctoral program in that area. But they may not necessarily think of this area of intellectual pursuit as being more than an object of curiosity or a mode of personal expression. As a result, doctoral programs need to provide a process of induction into a career, and a key part of the process is to emphasize the importance of this career. That is a harder sell for a program in history or English than in education, because students coming into education are already thoroughly invested in the field.

The most visible characteristic of new doctoral students in education schools is their passionate commitment to education. These students express a calm certainty that the future of their country and its children depends on the quality of teaching and learning in schools. As a result, their goal in pursuing doctoral study is not to explore an abstract question or follow a whim. Instead, in their view their mission as doctoral students—and later as teacher educators and scholars of education—is, overwhelmingly, to improve schools. This powerful sense of mission is a rich resource from which the faculty members in an education school can build a program of doctoral study, where they already have the rapt attention and fervent commitment of their students to the object of study. As we will see later, it is also a serious problem for a program seeking to make these dedicated practitioners into scholars of practice.[13]

Good Cognitive Skills

Doctoral students in education tend to have good cognitive skills, although probably not quite as high as those in the social sciences. Consider the evidence from the Graduate Record Examination (GRE). Between 1995 and 1998, the average scores for everyone taking the GRE were 472 (verbal), 563 (quantitative), and 547 (analytical), for a total of 1582.[14] The average for prospective education students was 445/507/533 for a total of 1485, which was lower than all the other major academic groupings (natural sciences, physical sciences, engineering, humanities, and business), including the most comparable group, social sciences, which scored 481/531/555 for a total of 1567. However, this may not be an appropriate comparison. ETS data only show scores by field for students who took the test within two years of graduating from college,[15] but doctoral students in education most often take the test well after this point, since they are about ten years older than other doctoral students when they enter their program. Fortunately, thanks to *U.S. News and World Report*, we do know the average GRE scores for doctoral students at the leading colleges of education. Every year the magazine ranks the top fifty education schools in the United States, using average GRE scores as one criterion. In the rankings for the year 2000, they listed fifty-three institutions (there was a four-way tie for fiftieth place). The average GRE scores for students entering these education schools in 1999 were 522 (verbal), 577 (quantitative), and 583 (analytical), for a total of 1682[16]—200 points above the average of education students who took the exam within two years of receiving a bachelor's degree and 100 points above the average of the whole population that took the exam at that point.

   This comparison, however, is not very fair, since it pits doctoral students admitted into the best education schools against students applying to a wide range of graduate programs of varying quality. The problem is that *U.S. News* ranks social science programs by reputation only and therefore does not record

GRE scores for these programs, so there are not comparable data for social science students. My point, however, is not that doctoral students in education are smarter than those in sociology or psychology but simply that they are—despite the generally bad reputation of educationists—no dummies. And the population of education students represented by the data from *U.S. News* is in fact the group that is of most interest for my purposes. The top 53 education schools (out of a total of about 750 such institutions) produce almost half of the U.S. doctorates in education every year (about 3,100 out of 6,600).[17] Even more important than the disproportionate number of doctorates these top-ranked schools produce is the fact that they train the large majority of the country's educational researchers and teacher educators. They gain a position in the top rank largely because of their research productivity and their focus on the academic preparation of education researchers and professors.

Overall, then, if students in doctoral programs in education face significant problems, it is not because they lack academic ability; nor is it because they lack commitment, experience, or maturity. Such problems arise instead from a potential clash between two distinct professional cultures.

THE TRANSITION FROM TEACHER TO RESEARCHER: WHAT MAKES IT HARD

Professors and students in doctoral programs in education may confront two kinds of cultural conflicts. One derives from potential differences in worldview arising from the nature of teaching as a practice and the nature of educational research as a practice. The other derives from possible struggles over the kind of education one needs in order to become an effective educational researcher. Let's consider each of these areas of potential conflict in turn.

The Problem of Conflicting Worldviews of Teachers and Researchers

As we saw in chapter 3, teaching is a difficult and distinctive form of professional practice, which poses serious problems for programs that seek to prepare students to carry out this practice effectively. At the same time, and for some of the same reasons, the nature of teaching can make things hard for programs that seek to turn teachers into effective researchers, and this problem of transition is exacerbated by the institutional and epistemological problems (as we saw in chapter 4) that make educational research so difficult. Teachers and researchers not only find themselves in two very different institutional contexts—the public school and the university—but they also tend to carry with them sharply contrasting worldviews that arise from the distinctive problems of practice they encounter in their respective roles. Making the transition from teacher to researcher, therefore, calls for a potentially drastic change in the way students look at education and at their work as educationists.

Anna Neumann, Aaron Pallas, and Penelope Peterson provide a rich analysis of this "epistemological confrontation" between teachers and the doctoral programs that are trying to make them into researchers.[18] Drawing on their own experience as teachers in doctoral programs and on the cases of two teachers who made the transition and recorded their reactions, the authors identify three tensions that characterize this confrontation: "One is the tension of agenda, which bears on whose questions get asked: researchers' or practitioners'. Another is the tension of perspective, which considers the ways in which the understanding of educational phenomena flows from the academic disciplines and from educators. The third is the tension of response (and responsibility) to primary stakeholders in the education enterprise, which examines the interplay of researchers' public and intellectual stakes in the study of educational phenomena."[19]

What follows is my effort to tease out the core elements that define the basis of these tensions in research training programs in education, elements that emerge from the conflicting cultures of practice in teaching and research. I argue that the shift from K–12 teaching to educational research asks students to transform their cultural orientation from normative to analytical, from personal to intellectual, from particularistic to universalistic, and from experiential to theoretical. Embedded in these pressures to change is a struggle over the relationship between teaching and research in education and an emergent struggle over the moral responsibility of both kinds of practitioners for education's social outcomes. As a result of this culture clash, students often feel that the programs are challenging the legitimacy of their own teacher-based perspective on education, and they often respond by challenging the legitimacy of the proffered research-based perspective and by resisting key elements of the research training process.

Presenting the issue in this way—as a conflict between two worldviews that are polar opposites of each other—is something of an exaggeration. These dichotomies start to break down when you look at them more closely. As actually practiced, educational research is also, in part and in its own way, normative, practical, particularistic, and experiential. Encouraging doctoral students in education to see this—and encouraging faculty members to make this aspect of their work explicit—is one step toward dealing with the cultural conflicts in education doctoral programs. In recent years major movements have emerged that work to narrow the gap between teacher and researcher. On one side is the movement to encourage teachers to carry out research into issues of practice in their own classrooms and to enhance the legitimacy of this work as parallel to the research generated by university professors. On the other side is the movement to focus university research on issues of teacher practice in the classroom (teacher thinking, teacher decision making, the social construction of teaching and learning within the classroom community) and on parallel issues of practice in school administration, especially through the growing reliance on qualitative research that seeks to capture the full richness and contextual specificity of these practices.[20]

However, the differences in worldviews held by teachers and researchers are not the kinds of academic dualisms that simply disappear under close analysis, nor can they be brought together just by trying to make teachers more research oriented and researchers more teaching oriented. Instead, these cultural differences arise from irreducible differences in the work roles occupied by teachers and researchers. Occupants of both of these roles have to learn how to function effectively in occupational positions that pose for them sharply divergent sets of constraints and incentives. As a result, their jobs present them with different professional purposes, definitions of success, daily routines, time pressures, intrinsic and extrinsic rewards, social status, social expectations, work relationships, administrative regimes, architectural settings, and so on. These different positions set certain limits and enable certain possibilities for the ranges of action and modes of practice that actors are likely to pursue. The durability of each set of positional differences over time leads to a durable occupational culture, which spells out norms of purpose and practice that are integrated into a distinctive worldview. In short, position matters, which is why teachers who enter programs for preparing researchers find themselves straddling two conflicting work cultures. The discussion below is a positional analysis (reinforced by my own experience as a doctoral educator) of this conflict's roots in the work situations of the two sets of participants.

FROM THE NORMATIVE TO THE ANALYTICAL

Classroom teachers bring to doctoral study a perspective on education that is strongly normative. This perspective is deeply rooted in the practice of teaching, which necessarily puts a premium on doing what is best for the student. As a result, there is an element of teaching that is irreducibly moral, which compels us to think of teaching, in the words of Alan Tom, as a "moral craft."[21] This is not to say that technique is unimportant. Teachers spend a lot of time examining their experience to find out what works and what doesn't, and many can deploy their tested instructional technique in a dazzling display of expertise. But the moral factor is still at the heart of the enterprise.

The main reason for this is that, unlike most professionals, teachers do not apply their expertise toward ends that are set by the client. A lawyer, doctor, or accountant is a hired mind who helps clients pursue goals that they themselves establish, such as to gain a divorce, halt an infection, or minimize taxes. But teachers are in the business of instilling behaviors and skills and knowledge in students who did not ask for this intervention in their lives and who are considered too young to make that kind of choice anyway. By setting out to change people rather than to serve their wishes, teachers take on an enormous moral responsibility to make sure that the changes they introduce are truly in the best interest of the student and not merely a matter of individual whim or personal convenience. And this responsibility is exacerbated by the fact that the student's presence in the teacher's classroom is compulsory. Not only are teachers imposing a particular curriculum on students, then, but they are also denying them the liberty to do something else. The moral implications are clear: If you are going to restrict student liberty, it has to be for very good reasons; you had better be able to show that the student ultimately benefits and that these benefits are large enough to justify the coercive means used to produce them.[22]

However, if teaching is a highly normative practice, which focuses on the effort to produce valued outcomes, then educational research is a distinctly more analytical practice, which focuses on the effort to produce valid explanations. The mission of the educational researcher is to make sense of the way schools work and the way they don't. The object of a particular foray into research, as a piece of scholarship, is not to fix a problem of educational practice but to understand more fully the nature of this problem. It is not that scholars are unconcerned about the moral issues that surround the problems they explore or that they ignore the implications for practice that arise from their work. Frequently a moral problem (for example, high rates of educational failure among minority students) provides the initial impetus for a scholar to pursue a particular research project, and frequently the scholar seeks to encourage practitioners and policymakers to act on research findings in a way that might improve some aspect of education. Their primary responsibility as scholars, however, is to work through the intellectual component of educational problems: they seek to clarify and validate arguments about the functions and dysfunctions, causes and consequences of educational practices. Their distinctive contribution as scholars to the discourse on education is to make good arguments, and they pursue this goal on the moral grounds that you can't fix problems of practice unless you have a deep and sophisticated understanding of the nature of these problems and of the contexts within which they arise.[23]

But the scholar's analytical mission is not an easy one to appreciate for practitioners who have been deeply immersed in the arena of moral action. Teachers entering doctoral study in education find themselves being asked to adopt a mode of professional practice that appears to be not only sharply different from their own but also morally suspect. From the teacher's perspective, the scholarly approach to education may seem coldly distant and unconscionably unconcerned about student outcomes. The elementary and secondary classroom is a setting in which it is neither practically possible (given immediate demands to act) nor morally defensible (given the need to do the right thing by one's students) for a teacher to adopt the analytical distance required for scholarship. But scholars of education are freed from direct responsibility for the students in the K–12 classroom, so that, unlike teachers, they have the time and space to focus their attention on what is going on and why, instead of having to focus on what to do and how to do it. At the same time, they are constrained by the scholar's professional mandate to make valid explanations about teaching and learning in the classroom, in contrast to the teacher's professional mandate to make good things happen for students.

As a result, students who enter doctoral programs in education tend to bring a normative view of education that gives them encouragement to resist the pressure they get from their professors to start looking at education as an object of analysis. The faculty pushes them to think and act in ways that are essential for the emerging scholar but highly suspect from the perspective of the teacher: to read extensively and intensively in the literature on education, critique and synthesize the ideas in this literature, develop cogent arguments about educational issues, and use data and logic to validate these arguments. All of this may seem to these students like so much intellectual fiddling while the classroom burns. Posed with a situation in which two children are fighting in the back of the classroom, the scholar wants to ponder the social, psychological, economic, and pedagogical reasons for this conflict, while the teacher wants to separate the combatants. Under the circumstances, it is not surprising that teachers are often reluctant to embrace the analytical practices of educational scholarship. They may well put a lower priority on getting things straight in their heads than on getting things right in the classroom.

In my experience, this reluctance often leads students in education doctoral programs to shift the discourse about educational issues from what is to what should be, looking for practical solutions before explaining the problem.[24] The initial impulse is still to intervene and fix the problem, or critique the actions of the teacher who made the mistake. It also often leads students to frame their own research around educational success stories. The idea is to pick an intervention that promises to improve education—a new teaching technique, curriculum approach, instructional technology, reform effort, or administrative structure—and study it in practice. The desired outcome is that the intervention works rather well, and the function of the study is to document this and suggest how the approach could be improved in the future. This often leads to an approach to scholarship (and eventually to a kind of scholarly literature) that is relentlessly, unrealistically, sometimes comically optimistic—one that suggests that there is an implementable answer to every educational problem and that help is always on the way.

In arguing that teachers see things normatively and researchers see things analytically, however, I am not arguing that teachers don't think and researchers don't care. Teachers are constantly evaluating the effectiveness of their instructional practices and adjusting these practices appropriately. And there are moves afoot to formalize and extend this analytical component. Teacher research[25] and action research[26] together constitute an emerging genre in the field of educational scholarship, which seeks to promote a more analytical approach to education among teachers and other practitioners by encouraging them to carry out systematic research projects within their own context of practice, while at the same time seeking to inject a more normative approach (grounded in the purposes and problems of the practitioner) into a research literature dominated by the analytical perspective of university researchers. In a complementary fashion, researchers are motivated to pursue scholarship in large part by a moral commitment to improve schools. They frequently combine research with development efforts, in which they design forms of curriculum and pedagogy that they hope will enhance the prospects of schoolchildren and then analyze the effectiveness of these efforts. This, after all, is much of what it means to do scholarship in an applied field such as education.

However, differences in the nature of the work done by teachers and researchers set a limit on how far each can and should move toward adopting the perspective of the other, and how much doctoral programs in education can and should incorporate both perspectives in preparing researchers. In a recent exchange in *Educational Researcher,* Anderson argues for using teacher research as a central component in education doctoral studies in order to bridge the gap between teacher and researcher,[27] whereas Metz and Page caution against embracing this approach by pointing to fundamental differences in the two work roles.[28] The problem is that research is defined as a central part of the professor's job but not the teacher's. A university faculty position gives professors the time and space to do research, sets expectations for the frequency and quality of research output, and enforces these expectations with pay and promotion incentives. None of these conditions is present in the position of the classroom teacher. The teacher's job is to teach the required curriculum to the assigned students at an appropriate level of effectiveness, and this leaves no time for carrying out research. Under these circumstances, teachers can do research only if they add it on top of their existing work, which would place an unfair burden on them because of the heavy load they already bear, or if they do research at the expense of their teaching duties, which would unfairly deprive their students educationally. Realistically, then, moral and occupational constraints limit the time and intellectual effort that teachers can devote to research. As a result, Metz and Page argue, "It would be disrespectful both to the effort and professional qualities of teaching and administration in K–12 schools and to the effort and distinctive skills required for research to argue that these students [full-time teachers who are doctoral students in education] can fully accomplish both tasks without loss of quality while most others find it challenging to do either well."[29] To move from being a teacher to being a researcher through the medium of a doctoral program in education, therefore, constitutes a major change in occupational role and requires an accompanying change in professional priorities, which is reflected in part by the shift in emphasis from the normative to the analytical (and, as discussed below, from personal to intellectual, particular to universal, and experiential to theoretical).

FROM THE PERSONAL TO THE INTELLECTUAL

Not only is teaching a normative practice; it is also by nature highly personal. At its core, teaching and learning is about a teacher, a student, and a subject matter; the key to getting students to pursue intellectual engagement with subject matter often lies in the quality of their personal relationship with the teacher. As a result, as we saw in chapter 3, the ability to connect with students is an essential skill for teachers, and teaching takes on the characteristics of what Arlie Hochschild calls "emotional labor."[30] If the teacher succeeds in getting you to like her, maybe you will like the subject she is trying to teach you; or at least you are more prone to go along with the kind of learning she is working to foster in the class, out of a desire to please her if not out of a simple love for learning.

The value of this expertise in fostering a relationship with students is a key component of the worldview that teachers bring to doctoral study, and it can create a degree of cognitive dissonance with the worldview of scholarship that they encounter there. Educational researchers necessarily focus to a considerable degree on relationships as a key object of study; in light of the importance that relationships have in the learning process, they could hardly do otherwise. But the primary currency of scholarship, the thing that distinguishes it from other practices in education and gives it value, is not relationships; it is ideas. The measure of quality in a scholarly work—a book, article, paper, or research report—is in the quality of the ideas it expresses. The criteria we use to evaluate scholarly texts arise from this fact. For example, here are the questions I ask my doctoral students to use in critically examining the texts they read, the same ones I use in evaluating the texts they produce:

- What's the point? (This is the analysis/interpretation issue: what is the author's angle?)
- What's new? (This is the value-added issue: what does the author contribute that we don't already know?)
- Who says? (This is the validity issue: on what (data, literature) are the claims based?)
- Who cares? (This is the significance issue: is this work worth doing, does it contribute something important?)

Teachers encounter these kinds of analytical performance criteria when they enter doctoral study. The way they read, write, and talk about education is evaluated according to their ability to consume ideas and produce ideas in accord with these standards. This single-minded focus on managing ideas about education is often in striking contrast to their own intense experience as teachers, which placed heavy weight on managing personal relationships. For doctoral study not only asks them to change their approach to education from the normative to the analytical, but also asks them to change their approach from the personal to the intellectual. All of those person-centered skills that are so essential to teaching seem to be discounted in doctoral study: establishing rapport with students, mediating conflicts between students, negotiating the tension between making students happy and encouraging them to learn, channeling the teacher's own emotions into an effective and natural teacher persona. All of the professional capacities that enable a good teacher to establish a viable and comfortable learning community seem to matter little in the unnaturally idea-centered world of a doctoral program.

Under these circumstances of clashing worldviews, it is not surprising that many former teachers resist what they see as the oddly intellectualized perspective encountered in doctoral study. Finding the scholarly approach to education cold and impersonal, with little connection to the flesh-and-blood world of emotional interaction they recall in the K–12 classroom, they frequently (in my experience) hang back from embracing the intellectual skills that they need in order to become educational scholars. To adopt the intellectual perspective seems to do a disservice to the teacher's view of teaching, to turn teachers and students into actors who are imprisoned in a world governed not by people but by abstract ideas.

FROM THE PARTICULAR TO THE UNIVERSAL

Closely related to the normative and personal quality of teaching as a practice is its emphasis on the particular. As every good teacher knows, you can't teach effectively unless you take into account the special learning needs of individual students. The general rule of teaching is that general rules don't help very much. The exception is the norm, because every case is different. Some of the differences come from the special traits that students bring to the learning task: their psychological makeup, social background, economic condition, ethnicity, gender, cultural capital, social capital, role in the family, and so on. Some come from the special traits that teachers bring to the task: general education, professional education, subject matter knowledge, pedagogical knowledge, pedagogical content knowledge, plus all of the just-mentioned personal traits, which affect teachers as much as students. And some come from the learning context: the community around the school, the culture of the school, the principal, the grade level, the subject area, the curriculum, the community in the classroom, the time of day, the day of year, the weather, and plenty more.

For teachers, then, education always comes down to cases. But for educational scholars, the emphasis is on the development of generalities that hold across cases. They usually aim to theorize. This means developing ideas about the way education works that apply to more than one student or classroom or school. Of course not all educational research fits this depiction. A number of studies—especially those using qualitative methods—focus on describing and interpreting educational processes, relationships, and systems within a particular context. This work is not conducive to generalization, but, as Peshkin notes, we nonetheless "appreciate the foundational character of good description for all research."[31] The reason is that descriptive research is able to capture precisely those particularities of time, place, and person that teachers know are so integral to understanding how education works. In fact, one of the main factors that has fueled the rapid expansion of qualitative research in education in the last twenty or thirty years is that teachers and researchers alike—growing disillusioned with studies that misrepresented education by ignoring the importance of context—found that qualitative methods are well adapted overall to representing the context sensitivity of education. But most qualitative research, while still sensitive to the particular, aims to go beyond description to pursue forms of analysis that Peshkin calls interpretation, verification, and evaluation. In these modalities, qualitative researchers in education are reaching beyond a single context with the aim, among other things, of explaining and creating generalizations, developing new concepts, developing theory, and testing theory.[32]

Given the particularistic nature of teaching as a practice, this reach for theory and generalization is not necessarily what teachers in doctoral programs want, but it may be exactly the kind of additional perspective on the situation that education needs. The understandings that teachers develop about the particularities of education are critical to their success in helping students learn, but the uniqueness of their sites of practice also leaves them potentially trapped. Unless they work in an unusually collegial school culture, they can be confined to one classroom with one group of students without ready access to what is going on in other classrooms with other teachers and students, which means they are often not able to base their practice on a collective sense of what works in settings other than their own. They are also often trapped in another way, by their own experienced-based sense of teaching as a radically particularistic practice, which means they may harbor a deep suspicion that there are no generalities about teaching—no ideas or theories or modes of practice—that will be of any use to them in dealing with their own unique pedagogical problems.

As Britzman and Lortie and others have noted, this sense of teacher as Lone Ranger is part of the distinctive self-image of the teaching profession.[33] But this image can be both debilitating and wrong. Debilitating because it can force the teacher to work in professional isolation and to reinvent the pedagogical wheel. Wrong because it ignores the ways that problems of practice in one classroom often resemble those in other classrooms, which may be different in some details (as any two social settings will always be) but similar in others. Where similarity exists, there is the possibility of finding practices that teachers can adopt or adapt in order to meet their own pedagogical needs.

This is the professional function that educational scholarship can serve: to develop research findings—concepts, generalizations, theories—that make sense of educational processes across contexts and offer them to teachers and other practitioners. The idea is not to pretend to make claims about teaching and learning that are universal in a literal sense, but instead to provide a theoretical mirror, which teachers can hold up to their own problems of practice in order to see the ways that their problems are both similar to and different from those facing teachers in other settings. In this sense, then, theory allows teachers access to a community of practice that is otherwise often denied them by the tyranny of the self-contained classroom.

FROM THE EXPERIENTIAL TO THE THEORETICAL

One final characteristic of the teacher worldview, implied in the preceding analysis, is the privileged position it assigns to professional experience. This follows naturally from what we know about teaching as a practice. If we think about teaching the way teachers do—as, in large part, a particularistic moral practice involving the management of intense personal relations toward curricular ends—then teachers' own experience as practitioners naturally emerges as their primary bank of professional knowledge. Only their experience fits the particulars of their own practice, while also being grounded in their own conception of moral purpose and their own style of personal engagement with students.

This position encourages doctoral students in education to stay at arm's length from the arguments they encounter in the theoretical and empirical literature. Why? Because at any point in the discussion of an academic paper, the student can (and, in my experience, frequently does) introduce an example from his or her practitioner experience that automatically trumps any claim made by the authors. No matter how much data authors bring to the table or how effectively they make their arguments, personal experience still can carry the day. Just as the teacher reigns supreme in her classroom, the teacher's experience dominates other kinds of knowledge as the basis for interpreting what happens in that domain. From the teacher's perspective, researchers can say what they like about the nature of teaching and learning in general, but only teachers have the expertise to speak with authority about the teaching and learning of their own students.

This perspective causes obvious problems in the effort to socialize teachers into the researcher role. For educational researchers, teacher experience is an important source of knowledge about education, but that does not make it canonical. As the view of an insider and prime actor in the classroom, this form of knowledge has its strengths and weaknesses. It is uniquely insightful because of its rich knowledge about the particular context, the characteristics of the individual learners, and the intent of the teacher. But it is also narrow in scope by being confined to these same contexts, learners, and intentions. Although outsiders, such as researchers, are less knowledgeable than the teacher about the characteristics of the classroom, they are in a better position to put these characteristics in perspective, by comparing them with other actors and settings and by viewing them through the normalizing lens of theory. The problem facing doctoral programs in education, therefore, is not to convince students that education is worth examining (which they already believe) but to convince them that there is something valuable they can learn about education by examining it as an outsider, as a researcher (about which they are skeptical).

Dealing with the Cultural Divide

One way to deal with the cultural divide between teachers and researchers is to acknowledge it explicitly and to sell teacher-students vigorously on the value of adopting the researcher perspective—as an addition to rather than replacement for the teacher perspective. Another approach is to show that the gap is not as wide as it seems, that the differences are more a matter of emphasis in professional practice than of total opposition. Like teachers, researchers take moral responsibility for the consequences of education, and their work in trying to understand this institution is in large part motivated by their desire to rectify the harm done by dysfunctional education. Like teachers, researchers develop close personal relationships with their students and often their subjects as well. The advisor-student relationship in doctoral education is especially close, and managing the complexity of this connection is an important skill of the researcher as research mentor. Like teachers, researchers have to deal with education in all its context-bound particularism, which means that a central problem for them, in both designing research studies and explaining research findings, is to balance the urge to generalize against the need to validate those generalizations about a social phenomenon that is specific to time, place, and person. Finally, like teachers, researchers build on their own experience in important ways that gradually accumulate into individual professional biographies, and these biographies exert a powerful personal impact on the kinds of work they pursue.

A third approach is to narrow the cultural gap between teachers and researchers by designing research training programs that deliberately demonstrate respect for the skills and orientations teachers bring with them and that self-consciously invite these apprentices to develop roles for themselves as researchers who incorporate their teacher identities. This means constructing a hybrid program that marries theory and practice, as is only appropriate for research preparation in a professional school; instead of pushing teachers to drop practice for a new career in theory, it would seek to induct them into a practice of research that draws heavily upon knowledge from the practice of teaching while simultaneously informing that practice. This is the model for the preparation of educational researchers that is proposed by Neumann, Pallas, and Peterson.[34]

But let me come back to an earlier point: Although it may be possible and even useful to reduce the cultural gap between teachers and researchers, that does not by any means imply that this gap can be made to disappear. Teaching and research overlap in values, skills, and orientations, but the difference in emphasis between them is real and substantial because it is grounded in the positional constraints, incentives, and practices of these two forms of work.

The Problem of Mismatched Educational Expectations

Another source of tension in the preparation of teachers as educational researchers arises from conflicting educational expectations. Teachers typically arrive in education doctoral programs with an undergraduate degree in education, or in a disciplinary major combined with teacher certification, and also equipped with a master's degree in education. They did well in their higher education experience, earning good grades and confirming them with strong GRE scores. With a successful educational career behind them, an advanced degree in the field, and rich professional experience in the same field, they feel ready and able to launch directly into doctoral study.

But the faculty members of their doctoral program in the education school tend to disagree. From the point of view of the faculty, the incoming students are seen as generally deficient in the educational preparation they need in order to pursue doctoral work effectively. The students are recognized as smart, capable, and professionally accomplished, but they are seen as having a weak exposure to and understanding of the liberal arts and almost no grounding in the theory and literature of education as a field of scholarship. The students are stunned and offended to hear the faculty telling them that they can't write analytically, can't construct arguments logically, or read critically; that they don't know anything about American history and culture and social theory; and that they don't even know the fundamental issues and basic literature in their own field. All of these forms of academic knowledge and skill, they are told, are essential for an effective researcher in education. Negative comments, bad grades, and ill feelings pile up quickly, and students start doubting their own competence, dropping out of the program, or complaining that they are being treated unfairly.

What's going on here? One way of looking at this problem is as a conflict between the professional and the academic. The faculty complain that the students' preparation has taken place largely within narrowly construed professional programs that are severely starved of basic academic content, which is critically necessary to succeed in an academic doctoral program for future educational researchers. And the students complain that the faculty's vision of a doctoral program in a professional school of education is bizarrely academic in all the most pejorative meanings of that term: abstrusely theoretical, impractical, book-bound, and cut off from the real world of educational practice. Another way to look at the situation is not as a conflict between the professional and the academic but as a conflict between two forms of professional education that are simply not very compatible—the preparation of teachers and the preparation of educational researchers. These two kinds of programs may (or may not) be good in preparing students for their respective professional roles, but—as both are currently constituted—the former does not provide a good foundation for pursuing the latter.

Either way you look at it, there is a mismatch between the education that teachers receive and the education that these teachers are later expected to have and to enhance in order to become educational researchers. So let's look in a little more detail at what is problematic about the education of teachers for programs that prepare educational researchers, adopting the perspective of the faculty in these programs. This is a deficit model for understanding the instructional problem in research-oriented doctoral programs in education. After reviewing the issue from this angle, we will return to the question of whether this problem is a result of the inadequate education of teachers or of the inappropriate framing of the education of educational researchers.

From the perspective of the faculty who prepare teachers to become educational researchers, the education of teachers in the United States is seen as generally lacking in intellectual rigor and academic richness. This is true of their education at every stage along the way, including the general liberal education they received in high school and college, the professional education they received in a program for teacher certification, and the advanced professional preparation they received in an education master's program. Consider the potential problems for researcher education that are presented by the education of teachers in each of these three stages.

GENERAL LIBERAL EDUCATION

Most teachers do not receive a rich education in the liberal arts, but that is true as well for most American college graduates. As I suggested earlier, future teachers are neither the highest nor the lowest achievers within the universe of all U.S. undergraduates. The huge continuing demand for teachers draws such a large proportion of the undergraduate population that, for better and for worse, the average teacher looks a lot like the average college graduate. This is true not only for level of academic ability but also for quality of learning.

The U.S. system of education in general does not put primary emphasis on student learning. In a classic essay Ralph Turner argues that American education is structured around the principle that he calls "contest mobility," which stresses giving students wide access to schooling in order to support the open competition for social position. One result is that "under contest mobility in the United States, education is valued as a means of getting ahead, but the contents of education are not highly valued in their own right."[35] Another is that "schooling tends to be evaluated in terms of its practical benefits and to become, beyond the elementary level, chiefly vocational."[36] A third is that the system leans toward formalism. Through the metric of the credit hour, which uses seat time as a proxy for educational accomplishment, the system guarantees not that students know something about a particular subject but only that he or she might have had the opportunity to learn it. This encourages students to focus on the tokens of learning (grades, credits, and degrees) rather than the substance.[37] As a result, possession of a college diploma does little to assure that a teacher or any other American college graduate has received a liberal education.

INITIAL PROFESSIONAL EDUCATION

If teachers, like most students, fail to gain a solid core of general academic knowledge in high school and college, they are usually not able to make up for this deficiency during the course of a teacher preparation program. As we saw in chapter 3, providing prospective teachers with professional preparation is extraordinarily difficult, given the complexity of skills and knowledge that are required to carry out this mode of practice effectively. Teacher educators have neither the time nor the academic expertise to give students a deep understanding of individual subjects, much less a broad understanding of culture, language, history, and theory. Instead, teacher education, at best, provides a rich introduction to the practice of teaching and leaves responsibility for liberal learning in the hands of disciplinary departments across campus. At worst, it provides a mode of training that is so narrowly practical that it can actually displace and discount the liberal learning that the student may have acquired elsewhere.

Critics have long had fun ridiculing teacher education in books whose titles say it all—such as James Koerner's *The Miseducation of American Teachers* [38] and Rita Kramer's *Ed School Follies* [39]—and they have paid special attention to the intellectual failings of its curriculum. Recall what Koerner has to say on the subject: "Course work in Education deserves its ill-repute. It is most often puerile, repetitious, dull, and ambiguous—incontestably."[40] But even sober and sympathetic observers have been hard pressed to characterize teacher education programs as intellectually rich and rewarding. In his comprehensive scholarly study of twenty-nine teacher education programs across the country, John Goodlad (a former education school dean) concludes that "curriculum development in teacher education is largely absent, inadequate, primitive, or all of these. In the absence of accessible relevant knowledge and potent curricula, both the teacher educator and the teacher are left to their intuitive and practical interpretations. Because intuition is capricious and in short supply among humans, it is not surprising that both teacher educators and teachers are unduly influenced by what appears to work for them or others, has been part of their own experience as students, is well packaged and marketed, or is required by an empowered regulatory agency."[41]

Students entering a doctoral program in the disciplines also may not have received a solid liberal education as undergraduates; in that sense, they enjoy no automatic educational advantage over schoolteachers beginning graduate study in education. But these students do have the good fortune to have avoided the intellectually dispiriting experience offered by many teacher preparation programs. The contrast is particularly striking in the case of elementary teachers, who are likely to have majored in education, which means they took a smaller number of liberal arts courses and pursued these subjects in less depth than their peers in the disciplines. Prospective secondary teachers occupy an intermediate position in this regard. These students normally major in a subject area as undergraduates, and that greater disciplinary depth may be a key reason why they are more likely to pursue doctoral study than are elementary teachers.

ADVANCED PROFESSIONAL EDUCATION

The final and perhaps most telling difference in the educational preparation of doctoral students in education compared to doctoral students in the disciplines, however, is found in their master's programs. Entry into a doctoral program in a disciplinary field is normally predicated on successful completion of an academic master's program in that field. Graduate work in these domains frequently incorporates master's and doctoral study into a single sequence of courses, in which the transition from master's student to doctoral candidate is marked by successful completion of a thesis or preliminary examination or both.

In education, however, master's programs have a very different form and function. Most teachers pursue master's programs in curriculum and instruction or in educational administration, which are not designed as preparatory programs for scholars seeking advanced academic study in the field but as terminal programs for educational practitioners who plan to stay in schools. Unlike disciplinary programs, their aim is not to immerse students in the theoretical and empirical literature of the field but to provide professional development that will enhance the practice of K–12 teachers and administrators. From the best education master's programs, students gain significant help in enhancing their professional practice but little help in developing their academic understanding of the field. From the worst, they gain nothing but bad intellectual habits derived from low academic expectations. And, as Gresham's law would dictate, the debased currency of the worst master's programs threatens to drive other currencies out of the market. For many, perhaps most, practitioners in K–12 education, the primary reason to pursue a master's is simple careerism. The degree helps them meet state requirements for continuing certification, and it grants them a pay increase (because of union contracts that, in part, base pay on number of graduate credits). Under these conditions, education schools have a strong incentive to offer master's programs that make few intellectual demands, for fear that the customer will be able to buy credits more cheaply at the institution next door. And online technology for taking courses now means that a program can be academically low-balled by an institution across country as easily as by one across town.[42]

What a difference this difference makes. Once students have achieved doctoral candidacy in the disciplines, the program faculty can assume that they have mastered the academic foundations of the field—acquired in an undergraduate major and academic master's program and confirmed by a thesis and/

or comprehensive exam. As a result, doctoral study can dispense with courses that survey the field and that transmit fundamental knowledge in order to focus on advanced courses in a particular area of expertise, on research methods training, and on the dissertation.

Not so in education, where the faculty finds that it has to construct doctoral programs that make few assumptions about the prior knowledge of the students. Those who teach in such programs can't assume that their students have a solid foundation in the liberal arts. Instead, they have to find ways to inject that kind of broad and foundational learning into what is supposed to be a specialized and advanced program of study. They also can't assume that their students have a strong background in the academic literature of education, picked up in their programs of initial and advanced professional preparation. Instead, we have to find ways to provide that kind of academic preparation as part of doctoral study. Both forms of instruction coexist within the confines of the same program that gives them advanced expertise in a specialized field, trains them in the craft of scholarly research, and supports them in the production of an original piece of scholarship that will make a contribution to the field. And all of this has to be accomplished during a reasonably short period—say five years in total—in order to make doctoral study seem at all feasible for a mid-career teacher considering a career change. In light of these factors that make doctoral preparation so difficult in education, it should be no surprise to find that so many dissertations in education are academically weak, so many junior faculty members in education are struggling to establish a research agenda, and so much educational research is simplistic and uninteresting.

THE LIMITS IN BRIDGING THE GAP BETWEEN TEACHING AND RESEARCH

This depiction of the education of teachers is relentlessly negative, arguing that teachers are lacking in many of the main forms of academic knowledge and skill that are required by programs for preparing educational researchers. Since the diagnosis of the problem from this perspective is educational deficit, the logical treatment, at least in the short run, is educational remediation: Have doctoral programs try to inject as much of the missing skills and knowledge as possible in the short time that is available. This, as I have suggested, is not easy, especially since these programs are not able to extend the time that students spend in them.

Another response to the deficit diagnosis would be to improve the liberal education of American college students more generally, provide academic enrichment for programs of teacher education, and enhance the academic rigor and depth of education master's programs. However, improving the quality of undergraduate education is a daunting task, well beyond the capacities for influence of the beleaguered and disrespected education school faculty. And efforts to infuse more academic content into teacher preparation and education master's programs could threaten the professional aims of these programs.

A third approach would be to reject the deficit diagnosis of the problem and take seriously the complaints that students make about the academic demands of research preparation programs. This approach would ask programs to move closer to the students instead of the reverse—redesigning curriculum and faculty expectations around a core of knowledge from practice, channeling research toward issues arising from practice, and de-emphasizing academic skills and content.

But programs can move only so far in this direction before they begin to undermine their ability to function effectively as programs of practice in a profession that is related to but distinct from teaching. To a considerable extent, the core knowledge and skills that are required to succeed in the profession of educational research are academic. In order to carry out valid and reliable studies of the workings of teaching, learning, and schooling, researchers need to have command of a rich array of conceptual frameworks; they need a broad and deep knowledge of the history and processes and purposes and functions of the social institutions in their society; and they need to be able to read, write, and argue with rigor and precision.

As a result, doctoral programs cannot avoid responsibility for providing their teacher-students with a strongly academic course of study. But, as we have seen, they encounter a lot of resistance from their students in their efforts to pursue this course. In addition, as we will see in the following chapter, the education professors who staff these programs are often ill-equipped for the job.

Chapter 6 Status Dilemmas
of Education Professors

The analysis thus far has provided an outline of the structural situation that the ed school occupies, including both the social demands placed on it and the social scorn it wins both for meeting and failing to meet these demands.[1] This is helpful in giving a sense of the possibilities and limitations that confront this institution, the responsibilities it bears, and the incentives and disincentives that shape its behavior. But all of these structural elements do not constitute the ed school; they only define the framework within which it functions. To understand what this institution does and why, we need to know something about the people who populate it and the purposes that guide them in their professional work. So in this chapter I look at characteristics of the ed school's professors, the status dilemmas that arise from our situation and intrude on our work, and the largely ineffective ways in which we try to deal with these dilemmas. In the following chapter, I explore the belief system that guides the actions of ed professors, seeing it in large part as a natural expression of and response to our position.

In 1998, there were about 40,000 full-time faculty members spread across the 1,300 or so colleges, schools, and departments of education in the United States. Of these, 58 percent were women and 16 percent minorities. In comparison, among all 560,000 full-time faculty members in higher education, the proportions were respectively 31 percent and 15 percent. About 35 percent of the faculty in education were engaged in the preparation of teachers, and in this group the proportion of women was 64 percent and of minorities 14 percent.[2] Salaries were rather low, an average of $48,000 in education compared to $57,000 for faculty overall. Out of ten academic fields, only two ranked at the same level or below education in pay: humanities ($48,000) and fine arts ($46,000).[3]

SOURCES OF LOW STATUS

A low salary and a high proportion of women are two sociological signals of low status for an occupation group—in this case suggesting that education professors have low status in comparison to our colleagues across campus. Contributing to this situation are several factors, including social origins, education, professional experience, and research productivity. Professors in education are much more likely than those in other fields to come from working-class and lower-middle-class families.[4] According to studies summarized by Ducharme & Agne, the fathers of only 13 percent of education professors had a college degree, and half of these were teachers.[5] Ed professors were most likely to attend a nonselective state college near home and then start teaching school. Of the surveyed group, 71 percent had had appointments in elementary and secondary schools, mostly as teachers, and 87 percent of these had held the position for three or more years. They typically went on to earn a master's in education while continuing to work, and then completed a doctorate in education also on a part-time basis.

Since studies show that the connection of education professors to higher education is primarily with low-status institutions, that our degree programs are almost entirely in education, and our graduate studies involve a peripheral connection to academic life, it is not surprising that we become "uneasy residents of academe."[6] The academic culture of higher education, with its emphasis on research, is neither familiar nor comfortable for us, and as a result we usually end up not doing research or doing it badly. One thorough study from the 1970s recorded that only 19 percent of the 1,367 education schools or departments in the United States were doing any research at all (with research defined as publishing more than one refereed article in any of twenty-six core journals in a two-year period); that is the total for the *institution,* not an average per faculty member. Only 7 percent of ed schools were considered even moderately active in research, defined as producing at least fifteen journal articles in two years. Nearly all of these were in the small subset of education schools that offered doctoral degrees (11 percent of the total); but even in this elite group, 44 percent did not meet the modest criteria for being considered research active.[7] Of course, the pressure to produce research has increased at all levels of higher education in the last thirty years, and education schools are no exception. Faculty members in all of the institutions in John Goodlad's more recent survey of education schools reported steadily increasing demands for research,[8] but education professors still lag behind their colleagues across campus. An analysis of the 1993 National Survey of Postsecondary Faculty (NSOPF) shows that the average education professor had 2.8 refereed publications (of all types) in the previous two years, compared to 3.9 for all faculty members at four-year institutions and 4.1 for those in social science; the only program areas that had comparable or lower levels of productivity were business (2.8) and fine arts (1.5).[9] NSOPF data from 1988 show education professors with an average of 17.5 publications over a career, compared to 25.1 for all professors and 24.7 for those in social science; again, only business and fine arts were lower.[10]

SPEAKING ILL OF THE EDUCATION PROFESSOR

On one thing, it seems, both friends and foes of the education school agree: the education professor occupies a lowly position in the firmament of higher education. One friend, in an editorial in the *Journal of Teacher Education,*[11] put it this way: "Education professors are among the most maligned of academics. Their research is often viewed as lacking scholarship, their classes as devoid of substance, and their intellectual focus as too-school-based. Those who hold the title 'education professor' putatively are held to a lesser standard than faculty colleagues from the liberal arts departments and professional schools across the campus. These and other (mis)conceptions are often difficult to combat, given the realities of academic life."[12] Another pair of the ed school's friends, Theodore Sizer and Arthur Powell, writing as the dean and associate dean of the Harvard Graduate School of Education, captured the same images in much the same way:

> Few academic stereotypes are as pathetic as that of the professor of education. He (or she) is gentle, unintellectual, saccharine, and well-meaning, the bumbling doctor of undiagnosable ills, harmless if morosely defensive. He is either a mechanic (or cook,

as the picture usually paints him purveying "cook-book recipes" of pedagogy), or he is the flatulent promoter of irrelevant trivia. From Abraham Flexner to Hyman Rickover, the silly jargon and grotesque excesses of the "educationist professoriate" have been proclaimed. A good many contemporary critics find the breed so inept as to suggest the cruelest form of genocide: ignoring the professors altogether. The professor's image, to say the least, is at low ebb.[13]

As you may recall from chapter 1, James Koerner, a fierce critic, was even more blunt and less kind in this judgment at the start of *The Miseducation of American Teachers:*

> It is an indecorous thing to say and obviously offensive to most educationists, but it is the truth and it should be said: the inferior quality of the Education faculty is *the* fundamental limitation of the field, and will remain so, in my judgment, for some time to come. Although a number of able men are to be found, as I have said, in Education, particularly among the younger people, their number is minute in relation to the whole. Moreover, there is still a strong strain of anti-intellectualism that runs through the typical Education staff, despite their increasingly frequent apostrophes to academic quality. Until the question of the preparation and the intellectual qualifications of faculty members is faced head-on in Education, the prospects of basic reform are not bright.[14]

STUDIES OF THE EDUCATION PROFESSOR

Whereas negative opinions about education professors are abundant, reliable data are more scarce. This should not be a surprise, since studies of higher education tend to focus on the top of the educational status order. There are many more studies of the Ivy League than the community college, and the medical school is a much more popular topic for research than the nursing school. Scholarly examinations of education professors are few, and they usually come from within the ed school community. Large-scale efforts include, in chronological order: a collection of essays (*To Be a Phoenix: The Education Professoriate*) published by Phi Delta Kappa, the education honor society;[15] another volume of collected papers (*The Professors of Education: An Assessment of Conditions*) published by the Society of Professors of Education;[16] the Research About Teacher Education (RATE) survey (*Teaching Teachers: Facts and Figures*) published by the American Association of Colleges for Teacher Education;[17] a volume of papers (*The Professors of Teaching: An Inquiry*) edited by Wisniewski and Ducharme;[18] *The Lives of Teacher Educators,* a study by Ducharme, published by Teachers College Press;[19] and Shen's *The School of Education: Its Mis-*

sion, Faculty, and Reward Structure.[20] The only major literature review on the subject is by Howey and Zimpher, who manage to add little of analytical value to the sketchy information that was available.[21]

In light of the modest amount of data on the subject, I thought it useful to examine more closely the findings in Ducharme's 1993 book, which is the most recent major study in the field, written by the scholar who has done the most work on the subject. This study, both by its empirical evidence and by its unwitting example, reveals a lot about the nature of education professors. Ducharme interviewed a sample of thirty-four teacher educators from eleven education schools and departments that were housed in a wide array of institutional settings: "four private liberal arts colleges, three former state teachers colleges . . . , two private universities, and two 'flagship' state universities."[22] All of his subjects had been K–12 teachers earlier in their careers. They told him they entered teaching for a variety of reasons: chance (men), lack of alternatives (women), and ease of entry (both). None of them mentioned a passion for children or for teaching a subject. They enjoyed being teachers, but they left it to become education professors because of the isolation, lack of autonomy, and lack of opportunity that the teacher role offered them. They liked their new positions because of the teaching, the intrinsic rewards that came from their relationship with students, and the freedom it granted them, but not because they saw it as a mechanism for reforming education. Ducharme found that "no faculty members . . . indicated any sustained effort on their parts to change the schools in which they were placing their students, but rather addressed the matter of how they might prepare their students well to work and survive in the schools."[23]

All of the subjects said they felt pressure to do research, but they had difficulty explaining the rationale for and substantive value of their research efforts. One said, "Oh, I did a little bit of writing. Put together some presentations, always did something at ATE and that sort. It seemed to do the trick. But as far as substantive work, I didn't do any."[24] Another said, "Well, I'm a compulsive researcher, writer. . . . I've got about 250 things in print; the vitae's about 25 pages long."[25] As Ducharme notes at one point, the respondents' comments about research came all too close to "some of the broader academy's views of some educational research and writing. Done in haste and without real conviction, how valuable can it be?"[26] Ducharme tried to get a sense of the intellectual interests of his subjects by asking them to name three books they would "want their students to have read so as to 'make them better teachers and better people.'"[27] Their responses revealed a depressing lack of intellectual orientation in their work as education professors. One person mentioned *Macbeth*, but most of the titles were on the order of *Up the Down Staircase, Future Shock,* and *Blackboard Jungle.* One professor said, "I read *about* books more than I read books."[28] "There were also several very vague answers containing references to an unnamed book; included in these answers were 'something by Eric Erickson,' 'the Bloom book,' 'a fantastic history book,' and the 'handbook,' which, upon questioning, turned out to be Wittrock's *Handbook of Research on Teaching.* Five interviewees, after thinking for several minutes and talking about the question, named no books or authors."[29]

When you get to the end of this study, it is hard to avoid being depressed about the state of the education professoriate. The book reinforces this impression at two analytical levels. At one level, the data depict a group of faculty members who, as Harry Judge put it in an icily accurate summary in the book's foreword, "went into teaching in a somewhat casual if not absent-minded way, assisted by the absence of high entrance standards or vigorous competition," who left to become education professors because the university "gave them more leisure and less supervision," and who did research as a "small price to pay" for this privilege, without "any vision, intellectual or moral, of what the research in such institutions might or should be about."[30]

At another level, the book makes the point about the weakness of the education faculty through its own example. Poorly designed and laxly analyzed, the study is a model for the kind of superficial research that people commonly accuse education professors of producing. Ducharme's thirty-four subjects, it turns out, were an idiosyncratic convenience sample, who were recommended by informants as representing "a range from 'star' quality to adequate" in order "to reflect something of the range of the professoriate without overly structuring the process."[31] The author asked each of these subjects eleven open-ended questions—such as "Tell me about your introduction to teaching at the lower levels, how you made the decision to teach?"—during an interview that lasted between forty and sixty-five minutes, and he "generally allowed full reign to the respondents."[32] That's his whole methodology. And his approach to analyzing his data is equally simplistic and unsystematic; he just tells us what some of them said. Yet even with an enterprise as uncomplicated as this, Ducharme manages to miss the point of his own study. As nonrandom and unrepresentative as his sample is, the data are nonetheless devastating because of the relentlessly negative evidence they provide of the lack of professionalism, purpose, and intellectual commitment of the subjects. But Ducharme is still able to see the up-side, drawing conclusions that contradict his own evidence: "I remain struck with the decency, integrity, and the values of these faculty. Oh, they

might have disappointed me in their 'failure' to fulfill my hopes for a rich collection of titles of imaginative literature that future teachers should read. But
their interest in their work, their concern for quality, their high hopes for their
students, their thoughtfulness, and their zest for life more than fulfill hopes one
might have for standards about those who work with the young to help them
prepare to be teachers."[33]

In his wry foreword, Harry Judge notes the "optimistic" quality of the author's interpretation and then offers an alternative reading by a hypothetical
"successful French woman academic" whose "comparative perspective would, I
suspect, moderate the optimism."[34] I presented excerpts from this devastating
overview of the evidence earlier. He concludes: "The real satisfactions [for these
professors] lie in working in gentle and hassle-free environments where colleagues are uncritical of one another, and in experiencing a warm good sense of
doing some good."[35] Judge closes by noting that a major value of the book is
"in provoking the reader to make private interpretations of the rich evidence
offered."[36] So true.

IS ALL THIS CRITICISM OF
ED PROFESSORS FAIR?

By this point, readers may be developing a concern that all this disparagement
of education professors is a bit unfair. To which I respond: of course it is. The
purpose of this chapter is to examine the status problem of education professors, and there is nothing fair about status. Status hierarchies are an expression
of social power, as groups with the power to do so establish the particular characteristics that will bring people higher or lower degrees of social respect. Not
surprisingly, the characteristics that garner the most respect are those associated
with the groups who have the most power. And this kind of power often comes
from being there first.

As we saw in chapter 2, education was a latecomer to American higher education. First came the private institutions founded in the eighteenth century
and then the flagship state universities in the early and mid-nineteenth century.
Education didn't begin to emerge as a university subject until the late nineteenth century, and the normal schools didn't complete their evolution from
separate vocational schools to full-service regional state universities until the
mid-twentieth century. By the time education professors arrived in the university, the status order in the professoriate had already been firmly established by
their predecessors. As I showed earlier, this hierarchy granted the highest status

for factors that played to the strength of the institutions and academic specialties that got there earliest, while punishing the latecomers in ed schools. Professors won status rewards for teaching students who were themselves high in status, which favored institutions like the Ivies, which from the beginning drew
upper-class male students, and which favored programs that trained people for
the high professions. But education professors found themselves in universities
and schools of education that were parvenus in the university status order, and
they trained working-class women to take roles in what was considered the
semiprofession of teaching. In addition, the status order of higher education rewarded professors less for teaching than for doing research, especially research
that produced knowledge that could be presented as hard and pure and that
carried more exchange value than use value.

In the evolution of the university status order, therefore, education professors have ended up holding the short end of the stick. There is nothing necessarily fair about this; it's just the way things turned out. Simply because other
professors teach students with higher status and produce research in greater
quantity and with more academic cachet, they outrank education professors—
even though the teaching of prospective teachers that education professors do
is arguably more consequential, and even though the research they do is arguably more relevant to the needs of society. In chapter 3 we saw how extraordinarily difficult it is to operate an effective teacher preparation program, in
comparison to instructional challenges facing the faculty in more prestigious
programs across campus. And in light of the enormous number of students that
teachers influence, the multiplier effect of the ed school's teacher education role
gives its instructional programs a degree of social impact that higher-status academic departments can only dream about. In chapter 4, we saw how complex
and demanding it is to produce credible research in education, in comparison
to the research carried out in other departments where the knowledge domain
is harder and purer. And the applied character of this research gives it a real-
world relevance that is largely missing in the research products of the professors
in the disciplines. If this chapter were focused on the latter instead of the lowly
ed professor, we could have a field day ridiculing their work for its sheer obscu-
rity, tendentiousness, and uselessness, as others have done.[37]

Although, as I have shown, in some ways education professors may have
richly earned disrespect—witness the low levels of performance and aspiration
of Ducharme's interview subjects and the low quality of his own study—the
fact of our lowly location in the status order of higher education is a matter of
historical contingency as much as a matter of just desserts. Whatever the origin,

the results are devastating. As low dog in the pack of higher education, the ed professor is the target of whatever snarls and snaps the others choose to inflict.

STATUS DIFFERENCES WITHIN
THE EDUCATION PROFESSORIATE

As it turns out, there is also a status hierarchy among and within education schools. Consider four related criteria by which education professors are stratified, two of which they have in common with professors in other program areas and two of which are particular to education. Like other faculty members in higher education, professors of education are ranked by the *degree level* of their program and of the university in which it is located, and also by their association with *research*. But within education schools, there are two other distinctions, between faculty involved in *teacher education* and those who are not, and between working in a former *normal school* and working in another institutional location.

Programs and universities that offer doctoral degrees provide higher standing to their faculty than programs and universities that offer master's degrees or those that offer only bachelor's degrees. A simple measure of this difference is in faculty pay: in 2001–2, full-time faculty at doctoral institutions in the United States earned an average salary of $72,000, whereas those at comprehensive institutions earned $58,000 and those at baccalaureate institutions earned $52,000.[38] Closely related to this distinction is another, the relative research orientation of the program and institution. The higher the research orientation, the higher the status of the professors. Again, salary provides a crude measure of this distinction. In 1998–99, average salaries for full-time education faculty in public research institutions was $53,000, compared to $46,000 in public doctoral institutions.[39] Within programs, research productivity also provides a means of ranking faculty, and this too can be seen in salaries. A study using 1988 NSOPF data shows that in public research universities, faculty members with thirty or more career publications had a salary that was 27 percent higher than those whose publications were fewer than two; the salary advantage was 70 percent at private research universities.[40]

Think about what this means for the education professors. In 1999–2000, there were only 245 education schools in the United States that granted doctoral degrees, compared to 1,146 that granted bachelor's degrees, a ratio of one to five.[41] And the Guba and Clark study showed that only a little more than half of these doctoral level education schools are really active in producing research.[42] As a result, only a small proportion of all education professors are working in research-productive and doctoral-degree-granting education schools, and these professors have a markedly higher status than their counterparts in the other ed schools. Accompanying this status difference is a sizeable difference in pay, working conditions, and time allocation.

Closely connected to these distinctions surrounding program level and research orientation is the status assigned to teacher education within the education professoriate. Lanier and Little explain it with commendable clarity:

> There is an inverse relationship between professorial prestige and the intensity of involvement with the formal education of teachers. . . .
>
> It is common knowledge that professors in the arts and sciences risk a loss of academic respect, including promotion and tenure, if they assume clear interest in or responsibility for teacher education. Professors holding academic rank in education units are in even greater jeopardy of losing the respect of their academic counterparts in the university, because their close proximity makes association with teacher education more possible. And, finally, those education professors who actually supervise prospective or practicing teachers in elementary and secondary schools are indeed at the bottom of the stratification ladder.[43]

The loss of status for education professors arising from association with teacher education is a commonplace in the literature on education schools.[44] As noted earlier, 35 percent of education professors work in the preparation of teachers, but this proportion varies considerably according to the level of the institution. The higher one goes up the status order of education schools toward institutions that emphasize doctoral study and research, the lower the proportion of professorial effort expended on teacher education.

Among the faculty members in the education school who are not involved in teacher education, two further status distinctions come into play. For historical reasons, the dominant power position in the education school has been held by the administration department, and the dominant intellectual position by the educational psychology department. During the progressive education reform period, which extended over the first half of the twentieth century, a group known as the administrative progressives became the dominant force in the movement. Their brand of progressivism had the biggest impact on schools, in part because its leaders were powerfully positioned, moving easily between administrative roles in schools and faculty roles in education schools. During this time, administration departments in education schools became filled with experienced and often high-visibility school administrators. (I discuss this movement in more detail in the following chapter.) The combination of leadership experience, association with power in the world of schools, and prominence as progressive reformers put them in a good position to control the governance of the education school as well. Until recently, when teacher education became a major policy issue, deans of education have usually come from the administration department.

At the same time, however, educational psychology departments have usually taken the intellectual lead within ed schools. Education as an area of academic research emerged from the discipline of psychology, and the most influential early researchers in the field, such as Edward L. Thorndike and G. Stanley Hall, were educational psychologists; even Dewey's earliest work on education was done in psychology. Education journals today continue to employ the style manual of the American Psychological Association. Psychology—with its focus on individual characteristics, child development, and learning theory—remains as the basic disciplinary paradigm in the field. As the earliest researchers in the field and as the area in education that is closest to the disciplines, educational psychology retains the most academic and least professional-school orientation of all areas in education, and its scholarship continues to draw more respect than other educational fields from colleagues in the university community. Professors of teacher education, therefore, have traditionally found themselves cut off from both institutional power and academic respect within the education school.

The low status of education professors is not just correlated with teacher education; it is also connected to the institution's historical link to the normal school. As we saw in chapter 2, formal teacher preparation in the United States began in normal schools in the second half of the nineteenth century. These institutions came under strong market pressure from consumers, who wanted them to offer a wider array of educational opportunities and degrees with higher exchange value than a teaching certificate. As a result, normal schools gradually evolved into state teachers colleges granting full bachelor's degrees, then state colleges with a large array of program options, and finally full-service regional universities. At each stage, teacher education retreated a little further from its central role in the institution to a more marginal status, as other programs gradually pushed their way into the curriculum, but the emergent universities still retained the imprint of their origins in the normal school. Not only were they latecomers in the procession of new institutions in the history of American higher education, but they continued to carry the primary burden of preparing teachers, while the more prestigious universities sought to minimize their involvement with this domain.

So there you have the basic hierarchy of education professors. The largest number of education professors with the lowest status focus their efforts on teacher education in former normal schools, where there is little or no emphasis on advanced graduate programs or educational research. At the same time, a small number of high-status professors work in education schools located in institutions (private, flagship public, or land grant) that evolved earlier than and separately from the normal schools, where they are less involved in teacher education and more heavily focused on doctoral students and the conduct of research.

The second group of education professors is the primary focus of this chapter, just as the research-oriented education school is the primary focus of this book. In light of the substantial differences separating these professors from their counterparts at the lower end of the education status order, does it make sense to tar them with the same brush used to blacken the name of the lowly teacher educator in the former normal school? Is it fair to apply to them the epithets hurled at their less fortunate colleagues? In a word, yes. After all, everyone else does. As I noted earlier, status is not a matter of fairness, it's a function of social facts on the ground. And the simple fact is that in the view of policymakers, university faculty, educators, and the public, one ed school is a lot like another. The status differences among education professors matter a great deal to those of us on the inside of this beleaguered community, but to outsiders our association with teacher ed washes away much of the distinction that comes from having a long list of publications and employing the letterhead of a top-ranked university. Low status, after all, is a great social homogenizer. One function that social status serves is to allow members of a society to focus their attention on things that are socially salient and ignore things that aren't. So they spend a lot of time sorting out the distinctions at their own level and above, but they tend to look on people below them as pretty much alike, since the low-status groups are unlikely to have much impact on them. Distinctions among the servants downstairs just don't matter very much to their employers upstairs.

Professors at high-status education schools are not able to use their clout within the ed school community to gain them much respect on the outside. In fact, ed schools in elite universities are often more vulnerable to condescension and discrimination by colleagues across campus than those in less exalted environments, simply because the baseness of education as an academic domain is particularly apparent in a setting where elevated standing is the norm. A strong education school in a weak university can make the university look good, but a strong education school in an elite university can at best avoid being an embarrassment. In such settings the question chronically arises, "Why do we have one of those schools anyway?" And the response, not infrequently, is, "Maybe we shouldn't." Yale eliminated its education school in the early 1950s, Johns Hopkins in the late 1950s, Duke in the 1980s, and the University of Chicago in the 1990s. The University of California at Berkeley came close to doing so in the early 1980s, while at the same time the ed school at the University of Michigan was threatened with severe cutbacks. Harvard's education school is tolerated but it is not allowed to offer the Ph.D., and Teachers College at Columbia can offer the Ph.D. only in conjunction with the graduate school of arts and sciences.

STRATEGIES FOR WRESTLING WITH THE STATUS PROBLEM

The strategies that professors at research-oriented education schools can adopt to deal with their status problem are limited in number and effectiveness. Two strategies in particular have been proposed: embrace the role of university professor and turn your back on teaching and teacher education, or embrace the link with the teaching profession and turn your back on the university. Let's consider each of these in turn.

One proposal was developed by the Holmes Group—a reform organization made up of the deans of leading education schools, which existed from the mid-1980s to the mid-1990s—in its first report, *Tomorrow's Teachers*,[45] and the other was developed by Geraldine Joncich Clifford and James W. Guthrie in *Ed School: A Brief for Professional Education*.[46] Both documents identify the low status of teacher education as a critical problem that affects its ability to carry out its functions effectively and that therefore needs to be resolved. Both of them see professionalization as a key component of any solution to this problem. But each of them takes a very different approach to the task of accomplishing this professionalization, with the Holmes Group advocating a strategy that would tie teacher education more closely to the university and Clifford and Guthrie advocating a strategy that would ally the programs more closely with the teaching profession.[47] In light of the similar goals put forward in these proposals and the different strategies suggested for achieving these goals, the two proposals lend themselves to evaluation in tandem.[48]

Tomorrow's Teachers

Early in its report, the Holmes Group zeroes in on the status problem that has plagued teacher education over the years and connects it to the status problem that has also affected teaching. "Unhappily, teaching and teacher education have a long history of mutual impairment. Teacher education long has been intellectually weak; this further eroded the prestige of an already poorly esteemed profession, and it encouraged many inadequately prepared people to enter teaching. But teaching long has been an underpaid and overworked occupation, making it difficult for universities to recruit good students to teacher education or to take it as seriously as they have taken education for more prestigious professions."[49] Acknowledging that "the legendary problems of teacher education in America have been lamented since the turn of the century," the report charges that the solutions commonly proposed for these problems have not worked in large part because of "a failure to appreciate the extent to which teacher education has evolved as a creature of teaching."[50] If mutual impairment is the ailment, then mutual improvement is the remedy. As a result, as Judith Lanier puts it in the preface to the report, the Holmes Group "is organized around the twin goals of the reform of teacher education and the reform of the teaching profession," where the latter refers to "nothing less than the transformation of teaching from an occupation into a genuine profession."[51]

To professionalize teaching calls for significant changes in the structure of teacher roles and teacher rewards within schools. But institutions like the members of the Holmes Group at the time of the report—approximately one hundred education schools at top research-oriented universities—have little control over these areas, which lie within the province of local school boards. As a result, the report's authors concentrate their attention on the ways that these institutions can draw on their strengths as research-oriented, university-based education schools to promote the professionalization agenda. "The work that we propose is therefore distinctively the province of the university: study, research, and teaching. What is new in our proposals is the idea that these distinctive academic resources be focused on the problems of teacher education, and that the universities make the solution of these problems a top priority."[52]

What education schools can do is create a program of professional education modeled after programs used as preparation for such professions as medicine and law: "The established professions have, over time, developed a body of specialized knowledge, codified and transmitted through professional education and clinical practice. Their claim to professional status rests on this. For the occupation of teaching, a defensible claim for such special knowledge has emerged only recently. Efforts to reform the preparation of teachers and the profession of teaching must begin, therefore, with the serious work of articulating the knowledge base of the profession and developing the means by which it can be imparted."[53] Fortunately, as noted earlier in the report, "Within the last twenty years . . . the science of education promised by Dewey, Thorndike, and others at the turn of the century, has become more tangible."[54]

In sum, the logic of the argument in *Tomorrow's Teachers* is this: Teacher education has a poor reputation in part because it is intellectually weak and in part because teaching itself has a low status. The elevation of teacher education requires the professionalization of teaching. From the vantage point of the university, where education schools reside, the most potent and accessible way to promote the latter goal is to restructure teacher education around a research-based core of professional knowledge. This is a strategy that capitalizes on the historical contingencies that brought teacher education up from the lowly normal school and into the university. Teacher educators are university professors who (can or do) carry out scientific research on teaching in the classic university manner. So why not shore up the intellectual weakness of teacher education (its low-brow practicality, its atheoretical character) with some of this high-status, academically validated knowledge? In effect this means calling on teacher educators to outdo the university at its own game, carrying out academically credible research on teaching and then passing this knowledge on to prospective teachers. The high exchange value of this form of knowledge will then be transferred to both teacher educators and teachers, elevating both to a higher status. This is a pure market-based strategy, which draws on the aura of the university to advance the cause of both groups.

There are two major problems with this strategy, which cast doubt on its effectiveness as a mechanism for enhancing the status of either teachers or teacher educators. First, there is little reason to think that the kind of enhanced professional education proposed by the Holmes Group would bring about a significant improvement in the status of teachers. This would be the case only if use value were the key to occupational status; then, indeed, one's prestige would depend on what one knows. However, in the market for occupational status, it is exchange value that matters most. Medicine and law are high-status professions, I would argue, not because they have rigorous programs of professional education but the other way around. They have highly selective professional education programs because the professions are enormously rewarding and therefore draw many more candidates than can be accommodated.

Raising the credential requirements for a subordinate occupation group raises the cost of entry but it does nothing to raise the power, prestige, or salary of the occupation itself. Nursing has been trying this strategy in recent years, moving toward the point where every registered nurse will be required to hold a bachelor's degree. But this will do nothing to change the way in which nurses remain subordinate to doctors; at best, it will serve to draw a firmer boundary between registered nurses and licensed practical nurses, protecting the former against downward mobility rather than promoting professional advancement.[55] If professional education were the critical factor, then pharmacists would be members of an elevated profession. They pursue advanced study of pharmacology in order to carry out a job that often requires them to do little more than transfer pills from one bottle to another. By pursuing a strategy of increased educational requirements, teaching and nursing likewise may run the risk of overcredentialing people for a job that is not changing to meet the new levels of professional preparation.

In fact, the Holmes Group strategy in *Tomorrow's Teachers* is perhaps better designed to enhance the professional status of the teacher educator than that of the teacher.[56] The effort to install academic research at the center of the professional curriculum serves to displace the clinical knowledge of the practitioner and establish the teacher educator rather than the teacher as the prime authority on correct professional practice. This strategy may actually increase the position of the teacher educator at the expense of the teacher. In addition, it is designed to shore up the status of teacher educators within the university, by highlighting their credentials as academic researchers and knowledge producers. But that leads to a second problem with this strategy: There is little reason to think that this effort to model themselves after the other professors in the university will in fact yield teacher educators the kind of respect we desire. This point is at the heart of Clifford and Guthrie's analysis in *Ed School,* and it forms the basis for their own recommendation for reforming teacher education.

Ed School

Clifford and Guthrie begin their book with a quotation from a president of Harvard, who, as far back as 1865, had the same idea as the authors of *Tomorrow's Teachers.* He felt, as they do, that by investing teacher education with the full prestige of the university, teaching could be elevated to a true profession. In his words, "the establishment of a Normal School in a University, and of a special course for Bachelor of Arts in a Normal School, would be steps calculated to raise the standard of excellence required of teachers, and would lift towards its proper dignity the high profession of teaching."[57] But the authors sharply disagree with this conclusion and announce that the main point of their book is to argue that the approach suggested by this university president 130 years ago has been tried and has been proven a failure:

This book is about those "normal schools in the university" in the United States: about their origins, historical evolution, continuing problems, and future prospects. Our thesis is that schools of education, particularly those located on the campuses of prestigious research universities, have become ensnared improvidently in the academic and political cultures of their institutions and have neglected their professional allegiances. They are like marginal men, aliens in their own worlds. They have seldom succeeded in satisfying the scholarly norms of their campus letters and science colleagues, and they are simultaneously estranged from their practicing professional peers. The more forcefully they have rowed toward the shores of scholarly research, the more distant they have become from the public schools they are duty bound to serve. Conversely, systematic efforts at addressing the applied problems of public schools have placed schools of education at risk on their own campuses.[58]

As we have seen, it was not the benevolent feelings of university presidents toward the profession of teaching that brought the normal school into the university but rather the intense pressure from educational consumers seeking advanced degrees. But once teacher education became lodged in this elevated setting, teacher educators, according to Clifford and Guthrie, began to suffer from "the American disease of 'status anxiety,'" compelling them to cast about for ways to establish their own professional credentials within this new academic setting. Unfortunately, these methods did not succeed: "One presumed route to higher regard was to encourage abandonment of the classroom. . . . Another well-worn path that brought them far short of their destination was to be as academic as possible. The usual and unexpected reward was repudiation by other academics on the grounds that such work could only rarely be as worthy as the same work done in disciplinary departments."[59]

Two key points emerge from Clifford and Guthrie's analysis that are relevant to my discussion of *Tomorrow's Teachers* and of the status of education professors. First, it was concerns about their own professional status rather than the professionalization of teaching that pushed teacher educators to launch full force into the task of constructing a body of academic research about education. Therefore the "science of teaching," which the first Holmes Group report sees as the basis for teacher professionalization, actually emerged as a side effect of the effort by education professors to professionalize ourselves in ways that were more in tune with academic norms than teacher practice.[60]

Second, these efforts failed miserably. "Being as academic as possible"— by engaging in funded research, employing scientific methodology, writing strictly for an academic audience, producing mountains of refereed journal articles—could not erase the stigma of the normal school from the brow of the education professor. The status of teacher educators was fixed by factors outside of our control. As latecomers to the major university faculties, we were fated to play a continuing game of status catch-up. With most of our numbers concentrated in the new regional universities that recently evolved from teachers colleges, we were tied to the low standing of these institutions in the established academic hierarchy. We were unavoidably linked to the practical knowledge and vocational orientation of a teacher preparation program in a setting that looked down on these things. And we were also inextricably tied to the low status of teaching.

For these reasons, Clifford and Guthrie argue, the best strategy for improving teacher education is for education schools to abandon their futile pursuit of academic status and focus attention on serving the profession of teaching. This calls for an abrupt about-face (in direct contradiction to the central thrust of *Tomorrow's Teachers*), with education schools being asked to turn their backs on the university and embrace the schools:

> Schools of education must take the profession of education, not academia, as their main point of reference. It is not sufficient to say that the greatest strength of schools of education is that they are the only places available to look at fundamental issues from a variety of disciplinary perspectives. They have been doing so for more than a half a century without appreciable effect on professional practice. It is time for many institutions to shift gears.
>
> . . . Their prime orientation should be to educate practitioners, and education faculty must be made more cognizant of the technical or experiential culture of schooling for that to happen. To require less is to continue to frustrate both research and training activities. We think it sound policy that faculty appointments in education redress the imbalance that exists on many graduate school faculties by including substantial professional criteria in the guidelines and processes of faculty appraisal. This appraisal should cover both appointment and promotion decisions.[61]

Although Clifford and Guthrie provide a cogent critique of the university-based strategy for reforming teacher education proposed by the Holmes Group, their profession-based strategy poses its own problems. The key problem relates again to the issue of status. It seems wholly unrealistic and even counterproductive to ask education professors to turn our backs on the high status setting in the university that we currently occupy, however uncomfortably, and throw ourselves into the arms of an occupation whose status is markedly lower. Even though education faculty members are not well received within the university, holding the position of university professor carries with it a wide range of external status benefits. Whereas education professors do not add much to the aura of the university, we enjoy being illuminated by its glow. By contrast, as *Tomorrow's Teachers* so accurately points out, the status of teaching tends to exert a downward pull on the public standing of teacher education. This downward pull is the factor that *Ed School* ignores, in the process undercutting the potential effectiveness of its effort to reform teacher education.

Within the category of education schools that produce research and offer doctoral programs, individual schools tend to adopt one or the other of these strategies for dealing with their status problem, with the choice depending primarily on their position in the institutional hierarchy. Education schools in elite universities tend to identify with the university and not the profession, defining themselves as graduate schools of educational studies. They keep their distance from teacher education and/or confine it within a small and marginal program, and they concentrate on carrying out educational research and training educational researchers, functioning more like a disciplinary department than a professional school. Education schools pursuing this course are small in number, including Harvard, Stanford, Northwestern, Berkeley, UCLA, Michigan, Wisconsin, Pennsylvania, and Teachers College. Below this level is a group of institutions that try to balance the scholarly and the professional roles by focusing on both research production and teacher education. These includes places such as Michigan State, Ohio State, and Louisiana State. The largest group of the 250 or so education schools that offer doctoral degrees are in the third tier, where the professional-school ethos is primary and teacher education is the central programmatic effort, with research and doctoral study playing a peripheral part. At all levels you find the same distinctions among faculty members within individual institutions. Some professors focus on research and doctoral programs and others focus on the preparation of teachers, administrators, and other educational professionals, with the proportions in each group varying according to the rank of the institution.

The problem is that there is no easy way out of the status dilemma facing those of us who are professors at research-oriented education schools. Neither of the strategies proposed by the Holmes Group and by Clifford and Guthrie works very well. A professional school cut off from the profession, offering only a pale reflection of disciplinary scholarship, provides no rationale for its continued existence, which is one reason that high-end education schools are the most frequent to bite the dust. And an education school that pursues the professional role, while taking on a bit of research and doctoral study, ends up coming off as lowbrow to the university and as pretentious to the profession. Those few institutions that seriously try to maintain credibility with both of the ed school's main constituencies find themselves in a particularly difficult situation. For them, it is a hard sell to convince either constituency of the ed schools' allegiance, since the relationship with one undercuts that claim in the eyes of the other, which means they need to be twice as academic and twice as professional to overcome this doubt. Under these circumstances, the middle position is a difficult one to sustain, as the two poles draw ed schools to cast their lot with either the university or the schools but not both. As a result, the default position leaves professors at education schools distant from one of these two constituencies and treated with suspicion by the other.

Chapter 7 The Ed School's
Romance with Progressivism

Education professors are in a bad spot, but we are not without resources.[1] True, we have a tough job (as teacher educators, researchers, and educators of researchers), we don't have a lot of professional or academic credibility, and we don't get much respect. But we do have a vision. Most of us are convinced that we know what is wrong with education and how to fix it, and we are eager to make our case to all of the parties who shape the schools: teachers, administrators, parents, policymakers, lawmakers, curriculum developers, textbook writers, test designers, and the media. The vision of education we propose has been around for the last hundred years; it's usually called "progressive education."

The relationship between education professors and our beliefs is particularly important in the current politics of education, because a number of critics blame education professors and our progressive ideology for many of the ills that afflict American schooling. The lowly status of education professors makes us an easy target for critics looking for someone to blame, and key elements of the progressive credo that we espouse so unreflectively enhance the credibility of the charges against us. As I will show in the final chapter, the ed school's vision of progressivism could indeed cause damage in schools if it were in the hands of an institution that was powerful enough to implement this vision, but the ed school is too weak to do so. In this chapter, however, my aim is to develop an understanding of how and why progressivism became the dominant view in schools of education, by analyzing the nature of this vision and its structural roots in the intertwined histories of the progressive education movement and the education school.

TWO VISIONS OF TEACHING AND LEARNING

From the late nineteenth century to the present, two strikingly different visions of teaching and learning have been competing for primacy in American schools. They have gone by a variety of names, some familiar and some more obscure, including: old education vs. new education,[2] curriculum-based vs. child-based,[3] formal vs. informal,[4] mimetic vs. transformative,[5] intellectualist vs. anti-intellectualist,[6] acquisition metaphor vs. participation metaphor,[7] direct vs. indirect instruction, extrinsic vs. intrinsic motivation, and text-oriented vs. project-oriented. The most common labels, however, which capture most of the sense of these various category systems, are teacher-centered vs. child-centered (or student-centered), traditional vs. progressive, and, in what is currently the most popular terminology in education schools, traditional vs. constructivist teaching. For reasons of simplicity, common usage, and historical resonance, I refer to these visions by the names traditional and progressive.

Let's consider the basic differences between the two approaches. A classic comparison can be found in Dewey's *The Child and the Curriculum:*

> One school fixes its attention upon the importance of the subject-matter of the curriculum as compared with the contents of the child's own experience. . . .
>
> . . . Subject matter furnishes the end, and it determines method. The child is simply the immature being who is to be matured; he is the superficial being who is to be deepened; his is narrow experience which is to be widened. It is his to receive, to accept. His part is fulfilled when he is ductile and docile.
>
> Not so, says the other sect. The child is the starting-point, the center, and the end. His development, his growth, is the ideal. It alone furnishes the standard. To the growth of the child all studies are subservient; they are the instruments valued as they serve the needs of growth. Personality, character, is more than subject-matter. Not knowledge or information, but self-realization, is the goal. . . . Moreover, subject-matter never can be got into the child from without. Learning is active. It involves reaching into the mind. It involves organic assimilation starting from within.[8]

Dewey goes on to deconstruct the differences between these two visions, in keeping with his philosophical opposition to dualisms (reflected in the booklet's title: *The Child and the Curriculum,* not *The Child or the Curriculum*). This blurring of the differences is also a useful rhetorical move, one that is quite common in the ongoing debate over the two positions, because it depicts the writer as a reasonable person, a moderate, who does not espouse a black-and-white view of the educational world. Once this nod toward compromise is made, however, the participants in the debate customarily revert with haste to an argument that pushes for one side over the other. Here, as elsewhere, Dewey follows this pattern, concluding the essay with an attack on the "three typical evils" that result from pursuing the traditional method of teaching the curriculum—the lack of organic connection with the child, the lack of motivation to learn, and the reduction of knowledge to meaningless facts[9]—which in turn compel "recourse to adventitious leverage to push it in, to factitious drill to drive it in, to artificial bribe to lure it in."[10]

In order to elaborate on the implications of the two visions for classroom teaching, I draw on Jeanne Chall's *The Academic Achievement Challenge,* a sharp critique of progressive methods that provides a useful comparison of the differences between traditional and progressive instruction for each major component of the teaching process.[11] Table 7.1 below is a slightly revised and abridged version of a chart from her book,[12] which in turn draws on a more elaborate comparison in the appendix.[13] This catalogue of pedagogical differences serves as a useful ground for later discussions of the two positions in this chapter and the next.

THE ED SCHOOL'S COMMITMENT TO
PROGRESSIVISM

For American education schools during the twentieth century and continuing into the present, the progressive vision has become canonical, serving as the definition of good teaching. In these institutions, the purpose of teacher education programs (for prospective practitioners) and teacher professional-development programs (for existing practitioners) is framed as an effort to dissuade teachers from adopting the traditional approach and to enlist them firmly within the progressive cause. There are people in ed schools, like Chall, who choose not to employ the rhetoric of progressivism and even speak against it, but they are a small minority and they know their position is heterodox.

This is not a point about which there is any serious disagreement; both edu-

Table 7.1. Traditional vs. Progressive Instruction

Characteristic	Traditional Instruction	Progressive Instruction
Curriculum	Standards are established for each grade level; specific subject areas are taught differently	Follows student interests; integrates materials across subject areas
Role of teacher	Teacher as leader of the class: responsible for content, leading lessons, recitation, skills, seatwork, and assigning homework	Teacher as facilitator of learning: provides resources, helps students plan, and keeps records of learners' activities
Materials	Teachers work with commercial textbooks	Teachers use a rich variety of learning materials, including manipulatives
Range of activities	A small range, largely prescribed by teacher	A wide range, based on individual interests
Grouping of students	The whole class is moved through the same curriculum at roughly the same pace, with occasional small groups, and individual work	Students work in small groups, individually and/or with teacher guidance based on their own initiative
Teaching target	The whole class	The individual child
Movement	Child-child interactions are restricted	Students are permitted to move around freely and cooperate with others
Time	The day is divided into distinct periods for teaching different subjects	The use of time is flexible, permitting uninterrupted work sessions largely determined by learners
Evaluation	Norm-referenced tests and grade standards; informal and formal testing	Based on individual progress rather than classmates or grade standards; preference for diagnostic evaluation; deemphasis on formal testing
Progression	Students are assigned to grades by age	Students proceed at different rates

Source: Revised and abridged version of Chall (2000, table 1, p. 29).

cation professors and their critics would agree with it. However, the ed school's romance with progressivism, like a high school crush, is at best superficial. As I will show in this and the following chapter, the main thrust of educational research and of teacher education in the United States is not progressive but instrumentalist, aimed at serving the administrative needs of the existing school system, whose teaching and curriculum are largely traditional. But, although the practice of educational researchers and the practice of teacher educators is shaped by the traditional structure of education, the language of both is almost uniformly progressive, so the conceptual framing and linguistic patina of research papers and TE programs carry a persistent progressive gloss. As Lawrence Cremin put it at the end of his history of educational progressivism in the United States, by the 1950s progressivism had become the "cant," "the peculiar jargon of the pedagogues."[14]

A good place to find a clear statement of the ed school's progressive credo is in an institutional mission statement, where the focus is on principles rather than practice. Perhaps the most widely visible such statement of recent years is found in the *Model Standards for Beginning Teacher Licensing and Development,* formulated in 1992 by the Interstate New Teacher Assessment and Support Consortium (INTASC). This organization was instituted by the Council of Chief State School Officers (CCSSO), with the help of education schools and teacher unions, in order to establish standards for the preparation and certification of teachers, and the report was drafted by a committee headed by Linda Darling-Hammond, a prominent education professor. The opening paragraph of the report's preface is a strong statement of progressive beliefs:

> Efforts to restructure America's schools for the demands of a knowledge-based economy are redefining the mission of schooling and the job of teaching. Rather than merely "offering education," schools are now expected to ensure that all students learn and perform at high levels. Rather than merely "covering the curriculum," teachers are expected to find ways to support and connect with the needs of all learners. This new mission requires substantially more knowledge and skill of teachers and more student-centered approaches to organizing schools. These learner-centered approaches to teaching and schooling require, in turn, supportive policies for preparing, licensing, and certifying educators and for regulating and accrediting schools.[15]

The report then proceeds to assert ten principles that define the proposed standards for teacher certification, each of which comes with specifications for the kinds of knowledge, dispositions, and performances that a teacher needs to demonstrate in order to meet the standard. These principles alone make a clear statement of progressive values:

Principle #1: The teacher understands the central concepts, tools of inquiry, and structures of the discipline(s) he or she teaches and can create learning experiences that make these aspects of subject matter meaningful for students.

Principle #2: The teacher understands how children learn and develop, and can provide learning opportunities that support their intellectual, social, and personal development.

Principle #3: The teacher understands how students differ in their approaches to learning and creates instructional opportunities that are adapted to diverse learners.

Principle #4: The teacher understands and uses a variety of instructional strategies to encourage students' development of critical thinking, problem solving, and performance skills.

Principle #5: The teacher uses an understanding of individual and group motivation and behavior to create a learning environment that encourages positive social interaction, active engagement in learning, and self-motivation.

Principle #6: The teacher uses knowledge of effective verbal, nonverbal, and media communication techniques to foster active inquiry, collaboration, and supportive interaction in the classroom.

Principle #7: The teacher plans instruction based upon knowledge of subject matter, students, the community, and curriculum goals.

Principle #8: The teacher understands and uses formal and informal assessment strategies to evaluate and ensure the continuous intellectual, social, and physical development of the learner.

Principle #9: The teacher is a reflective practitioner who continually evaluates the effects of his/her choices and actions on others (students, parents, and other professionals in the learning community) and who actively seeks out opportunities to grow professionally.

Principle #10: The teacher fosters relationships with school colleagues, parents, and agencies in the larger community to support students' learning and well-being.[16]

Note that only parts of two of these principles (#1 and #7) focus on knowledge of subject matter. All of the others focus on classic progressive concerns: creating "learning experiences" (#1), understanding child development (#2) and student differences (#3), employing "instructional strategies" (#4), promoting "individual and group motivation" and "active engagement" (#5), fostering "active inquiry, collaboration, and supportive interaction" (#6), knowing students and community (#7), using assessment for "development of the learner" (#8), engaging in reflective practice (#9), and fostering relationships with all relevant actors "to support students' learning and well-being" (#10).

Because of the strong link between ed schools and progressive rhetoric, most insiders to the ed school culture are lacking in either the incentive to examine that culture's attachment to progressivism or the perspective required to analyze that attachment in light of possible alternatives. However, critics of American education schools—especially those from a conservative perspective—have both. As political opponents of the progressive agenda, they can spot progressive ideas a mile off, and they are eager to assert traditional methods as a more desirable alternative. In the absence of a literature critical of the progressive stance arising from within the ed school, therefore, I find it useful to draw from the literature produced by outsiders—many, but by no means all, of whom are politically conservative. As with any other sources, the analytical value of these texts comes not from the truthfulness of their depiction of the ed school, since critics are as capable of overstressing the negative side of this institution as ed professors are of overstressing the positive, but from their ability to bring out issues and data that otherwise would remain invisible. Like lawyers in an advocate-style judicial system, such as the one we have in the United States, these critics can be relied upon to dig out the dirt on the other side and to present the strongest arguments for their own side. This does not provide a balanced or fair portrait of the ed school, but it certainly brings up many of the things that ed professors can't see or would prefer to keep under wraps.

For example, insiders to the ed school wouldn't think of polling education professors in order to demonstrate the progressive cast of their beliefs about education and the gap between these beliefs and those held by average Americans. But this is what the Thomas B. Fordham Foundation did when it commissioned a poll by Public Agenda, an opinion research organization, in 1997. The foundation is headed by Chester Finn Jr., a former assistant secretary of education in the Reagan administration, who has been a long-time critic of the education establishment. The pollsters reached nine hundred randomly selected education professors by phone and then held focus group discussions involving forty of them. The final report was titled *Different Drummers: How Teachers of Teachers View Public Education.*[17] An article in *Education Week*[18] provides an apt summary of this study and two earlier studies by the same polling group.[19] The following excerpt provides a concise portrait of the progressive beliefs of the ed school faculty.

> Professors of education hold an idealistic view of public education that differs so markedly from the concerns of parents, taxpayers, teachers, and students that it amounts to "a kind of rarefied blindness," a report released last week says. . . .
>
> The disconnect between what education professors believe and the concerns expressed by parents, teachers, and students is "often staggering," the survey found.

The study paints a picture of a professoriate preparing teachers for an idealized world that prizes "learning how to learn" but disdains mastery of a core body of knowledge and gives short shrift to fundamentals such as classroom management.

In contrast, previous Public Agenda studies have found that the public wants schools to emphasize the basics: reading, writing, and mathematics, taught in orderly and disciplined classrooms. While Public Agenda is accustomed to identifying gaps between ordinary Americans and leaders on a variety of issues, the report says, "it is unusual to find disparities of this magnitude about such fundamental goals, and involving an issue—public education—that is so close to the public's heart. . . . "

Education professors, the report says, define the essence of teaching as showing students how to learn. To that end, they expressed an overwhelming preference for process over content.

When asked about teaching math or history, 86 percent said it was more important for students "to struggle with the process of seeking the right answers," while 12 percent considered it more important for students to end up knowing the correct answer.

"Giving people tools is probably more important than all of that information—which they can now get on a computer," one Boston professor said in a focus group.

Survey respondents also emphasized active learning, the survey found, with six in 10 saying that teachers faced with unruly classes have probably failed to make their lessons engaging enough.

Nearly 60 percent said intrinsic love of learning should motivate students, not the threat of failing a course or being held back a grade. They took a similarly dim view of academic competition as a way of motivating students; only 33 percent considered rewards such as honor rolls a valuable incentive to foster learning, while 64 percent said schools should avoid competition. "I don't like hearing about a kid who's high-achieving [and] doing things in the classroom for stars," one Chicago professor said.

Memorizing factual information and standardized testing also got low marks from the professors, 78 percent of whom called for less reliance on multiple-choice exams in schools. Nearly 80 percent endorsed the use of portfolios and other assessments considered to be more authentic measures of what students can do.

When asked to rate qualities that are "absolutely essential" in teachers, 84 percent said that teachers should be lifelong learners and constantly updating their skills. A far smaller proportion, 57 percent, agreed that teachers should be deeply knowledgeable about the content of the subjects they will be teaching.[20]

This contrast between the views of education professors and those of the public is somewhat exaggerated in the report. The polls do show that the public is more concerned about basic skills, standards, safety, and discipline than education professors. But they also show that 92 percent of the public feels that "schools should place much greater emphasis on making learning enjoyable and interesting to elementary schools students" (86 percent for high school students) and that 84 percent feel that "schools should put more emphasis on building self-esteem in elementary school students and helping them feel good about themselves" (81 percent for high school students)—both of which are classic concerns of progressive education.[21] This just demonstrates that if you are partisan, which the Fordham Foundation is, you can write questions to ask in an opinion poll and select answers to emphasize in your report on the poll that will make the target group look bad. But the point in reporting the poll results here is simply to confirm the obvious, that education professors do indeed espouse the principles of progressivism.

THE NATURE AND ROOTS OF THE
PROGRESSIVE VISION

The beliefs expressed by education professors in the Public Agenda study provide a capsule summary of the progressive vision, which E. D. Hirsch Jr. calls the ed school's "thoughtworld." "Within the educational community," he says, "there is currently no *thinkable* alternative. . . . Its foundational premise is that progressive principles are right."[22] In *The Schools We Need and Why We Don't Have Them,*[23] Hirsch develops an insightful analysis of the nature of this vision and its intellectual roots, which builds on his earlier book, *Cultural Literacy,* adopting a perspective that he defines as politically liberal and pedagogically conservative.[24] This analysis provides a useful starting place for us in exploring the reasons for the strong connection between progressivism and the education school. I begin with a look at progressivism as a theory of teaching and learning and then consider it as a set of values for social reform.

Progressivism as a Theory of Teaching and Learning

In part, progressivism constitutes an argument about the nature of teaching and learning, which is expressed as a theory of curriculum and a corresponding theory of pedagogy. Hirsch argues that the progressive approach to curriculum is best characterized as formalism, and its approach to pedagogy as naturalism. Let's consider each of these in turn.

CURRICULAR FORMALISM

Hirsch calls the progressive approach to curriculum "formalism," on the grounds that it concentrates on the form more than the substance of learning.

The evidence suggests that he's onto something here. As Dewey noted in the section from *The Child and the Curriculum* quoted earlier, progressive teaching starts not with the curriculum but with the child: "Not knowledge or information, but self-realization, is the goal." What this means is avoiding the traditional approach, which sees education as a transfer of curricular knowledge to students, and concentrating instead on fostering "students' development of critical thinking, problem solving, and performance skills," in the words of INTASC Principle #4. Instead of having students accumulate substantive knowledge, the focus is on having them accumulate learning skills that they can apply to knowledge acquisition in the future as needed; in short, the goal is learning to learn. As we saw in the poll of education professors, this means putting a priority on process over content, as in the preference for struggling to find answers rather than knowing the right answer. As one professor put it, "Giving people tools is probably more important than all of that information—which they can now get on a computer." This is the approach that Diane Ravitch was complaining about in a recent exchange in *Daedalus,* where she argued that progressivism has produced "the contentless curriculum."[25] Another participant in the exchange, Howard Gardner, gave the classic process-oriented progressive response: "I differ from Diane Ravitch, E. D. Hirsch, Jr., and doubtless many contributors to this volume in my belief that the particular topics or courses do not matter nearly so much as the ways of thinking that are (or are not) taught in those courses. Once equipped with these ways of thinking, students can go on to master whatever content they may wish; bereft of disciplined minds they can only continue to accrue what Alfred North Whitehead called 'inert knowledge.'"[26] There you have a concise depiction of the two views of curriculum. Progressives see the traditional curriculum as filled with "inert knowledge," and their opponents call the progressive curriculum "contentless."

PEDAGOGICAL NATURALISM

Hirsch calls the progressive approach to pedagogy "naturalistic," because he sees it grounded in "the belief that education is a natural process with its own inherent forms and rhythms, which may vary with each child, and is most effective when it is connected with natural, real-life goals and settings."[27] At the heart of this belief is a dedication to the notion that the child has a natural interest in learning. Thus the aim of progressive pedagogy is to foster and spur this interest in order to motivate students to pursue learning on their own, whereas the primary progressive critique of traditional curriculum-driven and teacher-centered pedagogy is that it stifles student interest and promotes disengagement from learning. Dewey put the progressive view this way: "The source of whatever is dead, mechanical, and formal in schools is found precisely in the subordination of the life and experience of the child to the curriculum. It is because of this that 'study' has become a synonym for what is irksome, and a lesson identical with a task."[28] Thus the teacher needs to be a coach for the students rather than their drillmaster, using intrinsic motivators that induce interest rather than extrinsic devices such as grades, competition, and external rewards and punishments (Dewey's "adventitious leverage," "factitious drill," and "artificial bribe"), and students need to be seen as active learners rather than passive recipients of knowledge. These ideas are embedded in INTASC principles #1, 4, 5, and 6.

Two important components of the naturalism inherent in progressive pedagogy, according to Hirsch, are developmentalism and holistic learning. If learning is natural, then teaching needs to adapt itself to the natural developmental capacities of the learner, which requires a careful effort to provide particular subject matter and skills only when they are appropriate for the student's stage of development. "Developmentally appropriate" practices and curricula are central to the progressive vision, as reflected in at least three of the INTASC principles (#2, 4, and 8). Closely related to this is the concern about adapting teaching to the particular development of the individual student (principle #3). The second key extension of the naturalistic approach to teaching is the idea that learning is most natural when it takes place in holistic form, where multiple domains of skill and knowledge are integrated into thematic units and projects instead of being taught as separate subjects. Thus the progressive passion for interdisciplinary studies, thematic units, and the project method.

Note that progressives see their naturalistic pedagogy as an attack on what they consider the formalism of traditional teaching, and thus when Hirsch uses the term *formalism* to characterize the progressive curriculum it is with deliberate irony. What progressives refer to as formalism is the way in which traditional education adheres rigidly to formal patterns of instruction: seeking to transmit highly structured knowledge by means of lecture and textbook directly to passive students, without taking into account the natural learning styles and interests of these students. Thus in the passage quoted above, Dewey equates the "formal" with the "dead" and the "mechanical" in schools. In other words, for progressives, formalism is non-naturalistic pedagogy; for Hirsch, formalism is non-substantive curriculum. The differences in the way Hirsch and the progressives use this term reflects the difference in the emphasis each places on one of the two components of teaching, with Hirsch stressing the importance of curriculum content and progressives stressing the importance of pedagogical technique.

ROOTS IN ROMANTICISM

Hirsch finds the roots of the progressive vision of education in European romanticism and its American heirs. He sees two romantic beliefs in particular lying at the heart of educational progressivism: "First, Romanticism believed that human nature is innately good, and should therefore be encouraged to take its natural course, unspoiled by the artificial impositions of social prejudice and convention. Second, Romanticism concluded that the child is neither a scaled-down, ignorant version of the adult nor a formless piece of clay in need of molding, rather, the child is a special being in its own right with unique, trustworthy—indeed holy—impulses that should be allowed to develop and run their course."[29] Closely linked to these beliefs is "the idea that civilization has a corrupting rather than a benign, uplifting, virtue-enhancing effect on the young child."[30] From this perspective, traditional education is not just an ineffective method of instruction but one that is misdirected and damaging, by seeking to impose a fixed body of knowledge on the child at the will of the teacher. The romantic alternative is a naturalistic pedagogy (which arises from the needs, interests, and capacities of the child and responds to the will of the child) and a skill-based curriculum (which focuses on providing the child with the learning skills that can be used to acquire whatever knowledge he or she desires).

Hirsch is not alone in seeing romanticism at the root of progressive education. David Cohen has analyzed the strong romantic tradition in American progressivism, which is expressed in a deep-seated aversion to formal schooling and all its accompaniments (teachers, texts, desks, and discipline) combined with a deep affection for a more spontaneous, natural, and self-directed form of education—a combination that is captured nicely in the title of Cohen's paper "Willard Waller: On Hating School and Loving Education."[31] Historian William Reese, in "The Origins of Progressive Education," sees the child-centered strand of progressivism arising from European romantics such as Rousseau and Wordsworth and their American heirs such as Emerson and Thoreau, filtering through the romantic ideas of European educators such as Pestalozzi and Froebel, and infusing the thought of American educational reformers from

Mann and Barnard through Parker, Sheldon, and Dewey: "Despite their many differences, advocates of a 'new education' insisted that young children, who should be educated in kindly and natural ways, learned best not through books but through sensory experience and contact with real objects."[32]

One other legacy of romanticism embedded in the progressive vision of education is a tendency toward anti-intellectualism. Reese argues that "an anti-intellectual strain was fundamental in many child-centered educators, who saw a broad array of sensory experiences as the basis of education and often emphasized transcendence, intuition, and feeling. They could ably cite key passages in the writings of European romantics which questioned the importance of books, textbooks, grammars, and catechism in the instruction of the young."[33] This is a common complaint in the critique of progressive education—visible in Hirsch[34] and Ravitch,[35] for example—but it is also found in the work of scholars such as Reese and Hofstadter.[36] Of course, as we saw in the previous chapter, it would be unfair to blame progressivism entirely for the lack of intellectual engagement in education schools. Recall the professor who told Ducharme, "I read *about* books more than I read books."[37] Sizer and Powell prefer to think of the issue among education professors as "*un-intellectualism*—not anti-intellectualism, as this assumes malice. . . . The unreflective, unquestioning (if frighteningly well-meaning) professor is still, alas, the rule."[38]

Progressivism as a Set of Social Values

Whereas some critics concentrate their attack on progressivism's theory of teaching and learning, others also focus on the social values it expresses. For example, in a critique of the standards for teacher education programs used by the National Council for Accreditation of Teacher Education (NCATE), J. E. Stone (a professor of education at East Tennessee State University, writing in a publication of the Fordham Foundation) sees these standards as infused with the social values that are part of the progressive vision: "NCATE's standards do not explicitly call for learner-centered teaching but they plainly adhere to a learner-centered vision of education. In this view, schooling cannot be expected to succeed without greater equity, diversity, and social justice in American society and thus teacher training must be infused with right-minded social and political values."[39] He gives examples from the standards that mandate a "global perspective" and "multicultural perspective."[40]

From a more sympathetic perspective, Sir Peter Newsam (former director of the Institute of Education at the University of London and education officer of

the Inner London education authority) provides a succinct summary of the social values inherent in the progressive educational vision in his entry on teaching and learning in the *Encarta Encyclopedia 2000:*

> So far as values are concerned, the progressive approach tends to see attempts to
> teach or improve these directly as less effective than creating schools which exemplify
> values of greatest relevance to the young. Hence the importance placed on the way
> individuals, adults and learners alike, are encouraged to behave towards each other.
> A disciplined environment, rather than being externally imposed, is a direct conse-
> quence of that process. Social values, cooperation rather than competition and equal
> value given to the efforts of the least as well as the most able, are emphasized. Finally,
> as a point of principle, it is assumed all can succeed at some level in some aspects of
> learning. As one 19-century educator insisted: "All can walk part of the way with ge-
> nius." Sharply differentiated forms of education, with children attending schools or
> classes confined to those with particular levels of aptitude, however assessed, are
> thought to conflict with this principle. By inducing a sense of failure in children al-
> located to what are seen, by others and themselves, as schools or classes with lower
> standards than others, general levels of achievement are thought to be depressed and
> an unmotivated and under-achieving group of children unnecessarily created.[41]

The values embedded in the progressive vision, therefore, encompass a set of
orientations and ideals that stretch beyond what is needed in order to promote
effective learning. They include a commitment to cooperation over competition in social relations, democratic decision making, social equality, educational success for all students, multiculturalism, and internationalism. At its
broadest, progressivism envisions the school as a model democratic community, an ideal that incorporates the possibility of making the reform of education a means for the reform of society as a whole around principles of social justice and democratic equality. Conservative critics take special note of these
political tendencies within progressivism.

HOW PROGRESSIVISM BECAME THE IDEOLOGY
OF THE EDUCATION PROFESSOR

Education professors have a longstanding, deeply rooted, and widely shared
rhetorical commitment to the progressive vision. Why is this the case? The
answer can be found in the convergence between the history of the education school and the history of the child-centered strand of progressivism during
the early twentieth century. Historical circumstances drew them together so

strongly that they became inseparable. As a result, progressivism became the ideology of the education professor.

Ed schools have their own legend about how this happened, which is a stirring tale about a marriage made in heaven, between an ideal that would save education and a stalwart champion that would fight the benighted forces of traditionalism to make this ideal a reality. As is the case with most legends, there is some truth in this account.

But here I want to tell a different story, one that arises from the history of the education school and the impact of this history on the institution's status and role. In this story, the union between progressivism and the ed school is not the result of mutual attraction but of something more enduring: mutual need. It was not a marriage of the strong but a wedding of the weak. Both were losers in their respective arenas: child-centered progressivism lost out in the struggle for control of American schools, and the education school lost out in the struggle for respect in American higher education. They needed each other, with one looking for a safe haven and the other looking for a righteous mission. As a result, education schools came to have a rhetorical commitment to progressivism that is so wide that, within these institutions, it is largely beyond challenge. At the same time, however, this progressive vision never came to dominate the practice of teaching and learning in schools—or even to reach deeply into the practice of teacher educators and researchers within ed schools themselves.

In order to examine the roots of the ed school's commitment to a particular form of progressivism, we first need to explore the history of the progressive education movement in the United States in the first half of the twentieth century. Only then can we understand the way that the institution and the ideology fell into each other's arms.

How Dewey Lost: A Short History of Progressive Education

When we try to explain the connection between progressivism and the education school, the first thing we need to recognize is that the progressive education movement in the United States was not a single entity. Lawrence Cremin, who wrote the definitive history of progressivism, warned in his preface that "the movement was marked from the very beginning by a pluralistic, frequently contradictory, character. The reader will search these pages in vain for any capsule definition of progressive education. None exists, and none ever will; for throughout its history progressive education meant different things to different people."[42] Herbert Kliebard, in his study of the subject (which provides the foundation for much of what follows in this section), calls the idea of a single progressive movement "not only vacuous but mischievous."[43] Historians have used a variety of schemes for sorting out the various tendencies within the movement. David Tyack talks about administrative and pedagogical progressives;[44] Robert Church and Michael Sedlak use the terms *conservative* and *liberal progressives;*[45] Kliebard defines three groupings, which he calls social efficiency, child development, and social reconstruction.[46] I will use the administrative and pedagogical labels, which seem to have the most currency,[47] with the understanding that the conservative and social efficiency groups fit more or less within the administrative category and the liberal and social reconstructionist groups fit roughly within the pedagogical, with child development straddling the two.

The second thing we need to recognize about the link between progressivism and the ed school is that the administrative progressives trounced their pedagogical counterparts. Ellen Lagemann explains this with admirable precision:

> I have often argued to students, only in part to be perverse, that one cannot understand the history of education in the United States during the twentieth century unless one realizes that Edward L. Thorndike won and John Dewey lost. The statement is too simple, of course, but nevertheless more true than untrue and useful for several reasons. First, it suggests that, even if Thorndike and Dewey both spoke and wrote in the "progressive" idiom, the differences of view that separated them were large and significant. Beyond that, it calls attention to differences in the way each man's ideas were received. If Dewey has been revered among some educators and his thought has had influence across a greater range of scholarly domains—philosophy, sociology, politics, and social psychology, among them—Thorndike's thought has been more influential within education. It helped to shape public school practice as well as scholarship about education.[48]

What this means for our purposes is that the pedagogical progressives had the most impact on educational rhetoric, whereas the administrative progressives had the most impact on the structure and practice of education in schools. A sign of the intellectual influence exerted by the pedagogical group is that their language has come to define what we now call progressivism, and the progressive ideology of the contemporary ed school is their legacy. At the same time, however, it was the administrative progressives who were most effective in putting their reforms to work in the daily life of schools.

PEDAGOGICAL PROGRESSIVES

We already know the aims and ideals of the pedagogical group, from our close examination of the ed school's progressive vision.[49] The focus of this strand of progressivism was on the teaching and learning process within the classroom. As we have seen, pedagogical progressives wanted to base instruction on the needs, interests, and developmental stage of the child; to develop a curriculum that focused on teaching students the skills they need in order to learn any subject instead of one focused on transmitting particular bodies of knowledge; to promote discovery and self-directed learning by the student through active engagement; to have students work on projects that express student purposes and that integrate the disciplines around socially relevant themes; and to promote values of community, cooperation, tolerance, justice, and democratic equality. As befits a movement driven by ideas and exerting its greatest impact on educational thought, it drew heavily from a wide array of intellectual precursors, including Jean-Jacques Rousseau, Friedrich Froebel, Heinrich Pestalozzi, Johann Herbart, Horace Mann, Edward Sheldon, and William James.

Major actors in the movement included Francis W. Parker, John Dewey, G. Stanley Hall, William Heard Kilpatrick, George S. Counts, Harold O. Rugg, and Boyd H. Bode. Hall's contribution was to develop the field of child study in psychology using scientific methods, which granted credibility to the idea of adapting education to the needs of the child, focusing on stages of development, and building education on the child's impulses and interests. Kilpatrick took the lead in promoting the project method, which came to embody many of the elements of the pedagogical progressive creed (the activity curriculum, the experience curriculum), and in the process helped make Teachers College the prime mover in the progressive movement. Counts was most strongly identified with the strand of pedagogical progressivism that Kliebard calls social reconstructionism, arguing forcefully for the role of educational reform in promoting social reform around values of democracy and social justice. Rugg wrote effectively in support of social reconstructionism and the child-centered school. Bode, like Dewey, found fault with both branches of progressivism (including criticism of the pedagogical progressives' overenthusiastic embrace of developmentalism and the project method), but reserved his most detailed and powerful critiques for the proposals of the administrative progressives.[50]

ADMINISTRATIVE PROGRESSIVES

What held the pedagogical progressives together was a common romantic vision, but the vision that held the administrative progressives together was strictly utilitarian. And whereas the former focused on teaching and learning in the classroom, the latter focused on governance and on the structure and purpose of the curriculum. Because of their utilitarian orientation, the administrative progressives did not draw from a long list of intellectual precursors like their pedagogical counterparts. These were men of action, and the actors they threw into the reformist fray were considerably greater in number than those mobilized by Dewey's side. In addition to Thorndike, high visibility members of this group in the first half of the twentieth century included David Snedden, Ross L. Finney, Edward A. Ross, Leonard Ayres, Charles Ellwood, Charles H. Judd, Ellwood P. Cubberley, Charles C. Peters, W. W. Charters, John Franklin Bobbitt, Charles Prosser, and, in conjunction with the pedagogical progressives, G. Stanley Hall.

The organizing principle of the diverse reform efforts that arose from this group was *social efficiency.* In one sense, this meant restructuring the governance and organization of schooling in order to make it run more efficiently, in line with business management practices (this was the era of the efficiency expert) and with demands for the prudent investment of public funds. A major thrust along these lines was to buffer the administration of schools from political pressures, which they proposed to do by having school boards elected at large rather than by district, and to centralize control in the hands of a small number of professional administrators. They sought to accomplish the latter by consolidating ward-level school boards into a single citywide board with a small number of members and by consolidating rural school districts into larger entities, with the new board then hiring a superintendent who was responsible for running the schools. Another related thrust was to attack the newly defined problem of "retardation," which referred to the large number of overage students who had been repeatedly denied promotion to the next grade. Administrative progressives argued that holding students back like this for reasons of academic failure was grossly inefficient, since in many districts it was taking the average student ten years to complete eight grades of schooling. Their proposed solution was social promotion, which allowed students to proceed through the grades by age rather than by academic merit.

In another sense, social efficiency meant reorganizing education in order to make it more efficient in meeting the needs of economy and society, by preparing students to play effective adult roles in work, family, and community. This utilitarian vision was strikingly different from the romantic perspective of the pedagogical progressives, who wanted schools to focus on the learning needs and experiences of students in the present rather than the future, as children rather than as apprentice adults. It led to the administrative progressives' most distinctive contribution to American education: scientific curriculum making. This notion of curriculum was grounded in the principle of *differentiation*. It started with the developmental differences in students at different points in their social and intellectual growth, as spelled out in the work of psychologists such as Hall, and with the differences in intellectual ability of students at the same age, as measured by the apparently objective methods of the new IQ testing movement. The idea then was to match these differences in the abilities of individual students with the different mental requirements of the vast array of occupational roles required by a complex industrial society. And the curriculum approach that linked these two came from the enormously influential learning theory of the psychologist Edward L. Thorndike.

According to Thorndike, skills learned in one kind of learning task did not carry over very well to other kinds of tasks. This was in direct opposition to nineteenth-century faculty psychology, the reigning rationale for the study of traditional academic disciplines, which argued that the disciplines were effective at training mental faculties and that these faculties could then be applied to a wide variety of substantive domains. It also contradicted the psychological theory of the pedagogical progressives, who put primary emphasis on students' learning to learn and saw subject matter as a secondary concern, valuable mostly as a medium for skill acquisition rather than as the substantive focus of learning. (There are striking similarities between the faculty psychology that supported learning of traditional academic subjects and the skill-oriented learning theory of the pedagogical progressives—which is ironic, since faculty psychology was the grounding for the classical curriculum that the pedagogical and administrative progressives so strongly opposed.)

Thorndike's view had enormous consequences for the curriculum. As Kliebard puts it, "If transfer from one task to another was much less than had been commonly believed, then the curriculum had to be so designed as to teach people specifically and directly those exact skills required for the tasks that lay before them in life."[51] Thus, in Thorndike's words, "no high school is successful which does not have in mind definitely the work in life its students will have to perform, and try to fit them for it."[52] This meant that a core curriculum, concentrated in a few academic disciplines, made no sense for schools, especially at the secondary level where students were getting closer to their adult roles. Instead you needed a vastly expanded array of curriculum options, differentiated both by student abilities and by projected future occupation and focused on the specific knowledge and skills that the student can handle and that the job requires. From this perspective, then, all education was vocational.

The two forms of progressivism, for all their differences, had several key elements in common that allowed them to join forces on occasion or at least tolerate each other. One was a shared belief in developmentalism, which led them to call for education that was adapted to the capacities of students at particular stages of intellectual and social growth, although they took off from this basic position in different directions. The administrative progressives combined developmental differences with same-age differences in ability to provide the rationale for a radically differentiated curriculum, whereas the pedagogical progressives used developmentalism as a basis for opposing a standardized curriculum and supporting a learning process shaped by individual student interest and initiative. The strongest bond between the two strands of progressivism, however, was their common dissatisfaction with, and active hostility toward, the traditional academic curriculum. In this attack on discipline-based school subjects, the two stood together, although the grounds for their attacks were quite different. Administrative progressives saw academic subjects as an impediment to the acquisition of the useful knowledge needed to play adult social and economic roles, but the pedagogical progressives saw these subjects as an imposition of adult structures of knowledge that would impede student interest and deter self-directed learning.

SETTING THE REFORM AGENDA WITH THE *CARDINAL PRINCIPLES* REPORT

In 1918, the U.S. Bureau of Education published a report by the Commission on the Reorganization of Secondary Education (appointed by the National Education Association), which constitutes the most comprehensive and authoritative expression of the curriculum reform principles of the administrative progressives. Known as *Cardinal Principles of Secondary Education,* the report has served over the years as a favorite punching bag for critics of progressivism. It's not hard to see why. The proposed curriculum was extraordinarily broad in scope. The commission announced the "main objectives of education" as: "1. Health. 2. Command of fundamental processes. 3. Worthy home membership. 4. Vocation. 5. Citizenship. 6. Worthy use of leisure. 7. Ethical character."[53] Only one of these, number 2, even obliquely refers to academic disciplines. The proposed curriculum is also highly differentiated and vocationally oriented: "The range of such curriculums should be as wide as the school can offer effectively. The basis of differentiation should be, in the broad sense of the term, vocational, thus justifying the names commonly given, such as agricultural, business, clerical, industrial, fine-arts, and household-arts curriculums. Provision should be made also for those having distinctively academic interests and needs."[54] For obvious reasons, critics love quoting that last sentence, with its grudging acceptance of academic learning as an added component of the curriculum.[55] In addition, the commission report supports social promotion of students, the retention of all students until age eighteen, and the establishment of the junior high school. The attraction of the latter institution was that it would permit schools to begin differentiating curriculum and sorting students around future social roles as early as grade 7.

The *Cardinal Principles* report displays the predilection of both progressive groups for developmentalism and their antagonism for traditional subjects, but otherwise the perspective of the pedagogical progressives is visible in the report in only the most marginal ways. Among the eight education professors who served on the twenty-eight-member commission was William Kilpatrick, the emerging leader of progressivism's romantic wing, but the commission was headed by Clarence Kingsley, a protégé of one of the leading administrative progressives, David Snedden. The term "interest" or "interests" (a favorite of the pedagogical progressives) appears no fewer than thirty-four times in the report. But most often the term is used to connect the societal interest with the individual interest in a manner that reinforces the report's basic focus of preparing students for useful adult roles. Overwhelmingly, therefore, the dominant theme of this report is social efficiency.[56]

THE IMPACT OF ADMINISTRATIVE PROGRESSIVES ON SCHOOLS BY 1940

If the *Cardinal Principles* represented a triumph for the administrative progressives in setting the reform agenda for the progressive movement, how successful was this group in implementing that agenda? Let's use 1940 as a cutoff, in order to focus on the impact of this movement during its prime—the period that is most relevant to formation of the education school and its commitment to the pedagogical progressive creed. In the larger cities, administrative progressives were enormously successful in centralizing control of schools in the hands of a small, elite school board that was buffered from politics, and also in lodging daily management of the schools in a bureaucracy staffed with professional administrators. Movement in this direction was much slower in rural areas, but here too the trend toward consolidation into ever larger districts continued throughout the twentieth century. Between 1932, when the federal government began collecting information about such things, and 1940, the number of school districts in the United States declined by 10,000.[57] Another sign of the impact of the administrative progressives was the growth of social promotion. For example, in Philadelphia the average annual rate at which students were forced to repeat a grade in the first eight grades fell from 18 percent in 1908 to 2 percent in 1945, while the nonpromotion rate for high school students fell from 23 percent to 15 percent.[58]

The impact of the administrative progressives on the curriculum was more mixed than on governance and promotion, but it was still substantial. One area of impact was the effort to transform traditional disciplinary subjects (math, science, history, and English) into a form that was less narrowly academic and more broadly aligned with the diffuse social-efficiency aims of *Cardinal Principles*. The most successful change along these lines was the reconstruction of history as social studies, but other successes included the invention and dissemination of general math and general science. Other signs of the impact of the social efficiency agenda were the sharp decline in classical languages and the more moderate but still significant drop in modern language enrollments.[59]

But the biggest impact was in the shift toward a curriculum that was vocational in purpose and differentiated in structure. As David Angus and Jeffrey Mirel show in their study of high school course enrollments in the twentieth century, most courses that students were taking in the 1930s were still nominally in traditional academic subjects rather than in the new vocational, health, and home economics courses.[60] But these academic courses themselves had already undergone transformation into a social efficiency form, such as social studies and general science, and the purpose of the whole curriculum was now increasingly recast as an effort to prepare students for their vocational roles as workers and homemakers, whatever the particular course title. Most important of all, Angus and Mirel found that the curriculum was increasingly being expanded to provide a wide array of academic and nonacademic courses at multiple ability levels, which were intended to meet the needs of students with widely differing occupational trajectories and academic skills. This differentiation of the curriculum, with accompanying segregation of studies by gender and social class, was the most striking and enduring of the consequences of the social efficiency agenda for schools.

Some of these changes were welcomed by pedagogical progressives. Social promotion was right in line with their concern about ranking, competition, and extrinsic rewards; and the effort to broaden academic subjects beyond narrow disciplinary limits loosened the boundaries that these subjects placed on teacher discretion, thus potentially allowing teachers to open up the classroom to the interests and initiative of the students.

But the main thrust of the social efficiency curriculum, with its emphasis on vocational training and differentiated outcomes, was diametrically opposite to the core principles of the pedagogical progressives. It mandated exactly the kind of top-down curriculum that the latter abhorred, imposed on students in order to serve society's need for particular skills and knowledge and forcing them spend their time in schools becoming socialized for the adult social roles they will play. This puts priority on learning particular subject matter instead of learning to learn; it elevates the interests of society and of school administrators over the interests of students; it makes the classroom a preparation for adulthood rather than an exploration of childhood; and, in the name of these social benefits, it risks extinguishing the child's engagement in learning and curiosity about the world. It was, in short, exactly the kind of curriculum that Dewey deplored, "externally presented material, conceived and generated in standpoints and attitudes remote from the child, and developed in motives alien to him."[61]

Not only did the social efficiency curriculum threaten the kind of natural learning process treasured by the pedagogical progressives, but it also threatened the values of social justice and egalitarian community that were central to their beliefs. This curriculum was radical in its challenge to traditional notions of academic education, but it was profoundly conservative in its embrace of the existing social order and in its eagerness to prepare students for predetermined positions within that order.[62] It introduced tracking and ability grouping into American schools; it introduced ability testing and guidance as ways of sorting students into the appropriate classes; and it institutionalized the educational reproduction of social inequality by creating a system in which educational differences followed from and in turn reinforced differences in class, gender, and race.

THE IMPACT OF PEDAGOGICAL PROGRESSIVES ON SCHOOLS

While the administrative progressives enjoyed considerable and enduring success in implementing their program, pedagogical progressives did not. In general, the inroads they made on practice were small and fleeting. Larry Cuban and Arthur Zilversmit are two historians who have examined data on teaching practices before World War II, and both found that child-centered education had an impact on the classroom that was modest at best. Cuban looked at data on teaching in a variety of districts, including Denver, Washington, D.C., and

New York City,[63] and Zilversmit looked at school districts in the Chicago area.[64]

Cuban's operational definition of progressive (by which both he and Zilversmit mean child-centered) instruction is generous in that it allows him to place a teacher's practice in this category as long as it conforms some of the time to one or more behavioral proxies for progressive teaching practices. These include class arrangement (students sitting in clusters), grouping (students working in small groups), talk (students initiating interactions), activities (students working on projects or other activities), and movement (students moving away from desks).[65] Using these criteria, he found, for example, that in New York City from 1920 to 1940, "no more than an estimated one of four elementary teachers, and an even smaller fraction of high school teachers, adopted progressive teaching practices, broadly defined, and used them to varying degrees in the classroom."[66] The most frequent visible signs of progressive teaching were activity and movement.[67]

Zilversmit summarizes the findings of his study for the early years with this assessment: "Despite the impassioned discussions of progressive education in the 1920s and 1930s, despite the marked progressivism of a few school districts and the increasing importance of progressive ideas in state education departments and teachers' colleges, it is clear that by 1940 progressive education had not significantly altered the broad pattern of American education. The call for a child-centered school had, for the most part, been ignored."[68] In general, he concludes—paralleling the view expressed by Dewey himself looking back on the progressive movement from the perspective of the 1950s—that "the ultimate failure was that so much of progressivism's apparent success was rhetorical. While some schools and individual teachers had heeded Dewey's call for a more child-centered school, most had given only lip service to these ideas while continuing older practices."[69] Schools that adopted progressive teaching with any depth and seriousness were few, and these efforts usually did not last. Private progressive schools popped up, flourished for a while, and then typically reverted to type when the founder died or moved on. Public school systems that took the plunge likewise slipped back to a more traditional academic curriculum over time.

EXPLAINING THORNDIKE'S VICTORY

Why did the administrative progressives have a larger impact on schools than their pedagogical counterparts during the first half of the twentieth century? First, their reform message appealed to people in power. Business and political leaders were attracted to a mode of educational reform that promised to eliminate waste, to organize and manage schools more efficiently, to tailor instruction to the needs of employers, to Americanize the children of immigrants, and to provide students with the skills and attitudes they would need to accept and perform their future roles in society. For people who could make these reforms happen, this was the right message at the right time.

Second, the utilitarian quality of the administrative progressive agenda made it easier to sell than the romantic vision of their pedagogical counterparts. They were offering a way to make schools work better in serving society's needs, whereas the pedagogical progressives were offering a way to make learning more natural, more intrinsically engaging, more authentic. In a contest between utility and romance, utility is usually going to win: it promises to give us something we need rather than merely something we might like.

Third, the administrative progressives argued that their agenda stood on the authority of science. The pedagogical progressives also drew on science in making their claims (for example, Dewey published a book in 1929 called *The Sources of a Science of Education*), but they had a harder time demonstrating the empirical effectiveness of such diffuse notions as child-centered instruction and the project method. Meanwhile the social efficiency leaders adeptly deployed data from a flood of tests and statistics and school surveys to "prove" the value of their reforms.

Fourth, as Lagemann points out, Dewey lost the battle for the schools in part because he retired early from the field.[70] His direct involvement in schools lasted only eight years, from the founding of the Laboratory School in 1896 until the time he left Chicago in 1904 and entered the philosophy department at Columbia. After that, his work on education was spun out of memory and woven into theory, giving it an abstract and academic air, and these qualities became an enduring legacy for the pedagogical progressives. In contrast, the administrative progressives were deeply involved in the schools as administrators, policymakers, curriculum developers, educational researchers, and teacher educators. Empirically grounded, personally engaged, and resolutely practical, they enjoyed enormous credibility in promoting their reform agenda. Under these circumstances, it should be no surprise that Dewey's main effect was on educational rhetoric while Thorndike's main effect was on educational practice.

Finally, the administrative progressives' focus on the management of schools and the structure of the curriculum gave them an important power advantage over the pedagogical progressives, who focused on teachers and their practice in the classroom. Teachers were in a weak position to effect change in the face of opponents who were school administrators and educational policymakers. This was especially true when the latter had managed to define the administrative and curriculum structures within which teachers had to function. Even teachers who really wanted to carry out child-centered instruction in their classrooms found themselves confined within a bureaucratic school system that had mandated a differentiated and vocationally oriented curriculum unconducive to this kind of teaching. Under these circumstances, it is no surprise that teachers were more likely to adopt some rhetoric from pedagogical progressivism and to inject some token activity and movement into their classrooms than they were to implement the full Deweyan agenda.

How the Rhetoric of Pedagogical
Progressivism Came to Rest at the Ed School

If administrative progressivism won the fight for control of the schools, how did pedagogical progressivism come to win the struggle for the heart of the ed school? The education business was booming in the early twentieth century, and the various entities that were to become education schools were in a state of rapid expansion. As we saw in chapter 2, normal schools were in the midst of a transition into teachers colleges. This meant changing from an anomalous institution—part high school, part trade school, and part junior college—into an entity that was modeled after the liberal arts college, complete with disciplinary departments and bachelor's degrees, but with a mission as a professional school for teachers. However, two forms of market pressure compromised the identity of the new colleges as professional schools—pressure from school districts and the state to produce an ever larger number of teachers at high speed and low cost, and pressure from student consumers to offer educational programs beyond teacher preparation in order to open up social opportunity—and these pressures dragged down the quality of their professional programs and diffused their institutional mission.

At the same time, university departments and (later) schools of education were expanding as well. These units first emerged late in the nineteenth century as an extension of philosophy departments, offering courses that were "usually general and often theoretical."[71] The emphasis was on broad issues in education from disciplinary perspectives, including philosophy, history, sociology, and psychology. Around the turn of the twentieth century, they began to provide programs of systematic professional preparation for high school teachers (who were reluctant to attend normal schools, where the focus was on elementary teaching), and they gradually added two other functions as well, preparing school administrators and carrying out educational research.[72] The growth of these new functions was strongly spurred by the educational reform efforts of the administrative progressives, many of whom were professors at these schools (including Thorndike, Snedden, Bobbitt, Judd, and Cubberley).

A NEW SOCIAL EFFICIENCY ROLE FOR THE ED SCHOOL

Michael Katz argues that this transition put a severe strain on the identity of the university education school as it moved from "theory to survey."[73] Instead of seeking to establish theoretical accounts of education, the professors at these institutions turned instead to carrying out a series of school surveys. These surveys, a major tool of the administrative progressive movement, were detailed statistical descriptions of the practices in individual school systems, whose aim was to demonstrate the social inefficiency of these systems and thus provide the basis for an effort to reform them. This change reflected a shift in orientation from thinking of education as an intellectual discipline, with its own theoretical stance that gives it the ability to stand back and capture education as a whole, to thinking of it as a domain of institutional responsibility, which required professors to survey the field and catalogue its various parts and practices. Parallel to this intellectual change came an organizational change, as "the frame of reference for the development of programs and course offerings became the separate occupational divisions of the educational bureaucracy rather than a theoretical conception embracing the total educational enterprise and the interrelation of its parts."[74]

As a result, in the 1920s education came to separate itself from the disciplines and define itself as a professional school, parallel to medicine and law in the university's structure. This outcome seems obvious and natural to us now. What else would an education school be but a professional school organized around the occupational roles in the field? But Katz points out the enormous costs that this change wrought in the nature of the institution, as it abandoned its position as the conscience of the educational system to become the system's servant, and abandoned its role as synthesizer of knowledge about education to become a collector of facts. "Lost, in the first place, was the normative orientation. The point of reference became the field of education as it existed rather than as it should exist. Lost, in the second place, was all opportunity to create a coherent or unified conception of the world of education. Education became a fragmented series of specialties with no internal logic."[75]

Education schools fumbled around in an effort to recapture some form of critical perspective and intellectual coherence, and the result was the creation of educational "foundations" (history, philosophy, and sociology of education). This, however, has turned out to be an inadequate solution. As new areas of specialization, foundations did not enhance intellectual and programmatic coherence but instead fostered further fragmentation; and as intellectual backwaters (credible in neither the disciplinary nor professional domains), foundations provided no basis for developing an effective critical perspective. As Katz concludes, "The occupational frame of reference, in fact, simply reinforces the status quo. Schools of education become so intricately meshed with the structure of education as it exists that they reinforce that structure and become incapable of initiating change."[76]

Thus by the 1920s teachers colleges and university-based schools of education were beginning to converge on a common organizational model. Both their instructional programs and their faculty's intellectual efforts were organized around occupational roles in the educational bureaucracies (school teachers, administrators, counselors, psychologists, and university administrators), while the disciplines and the big issues were confined to the foundations ghetto. In universities, these organizational units were usually known as schools or colleges of education. As teachers colleges continued their evolution into all-purpose state colleges and regional universities in the next several decades, education there also became just one among many program areas, increasingly contained within this same sort of professional-school structure.

THE ATTRACTIONS OF DEWEY FOR EDUCATION PROFESSORS

As a result of all these changes, both in the larger progressive reform movement and in the evolution of the education school, American education professors in the 1930s found themselves in an increasingly uncomfortable position. Administrative progressives had succeeded in transforming the organization of schools and the school curriculum, and in the process they had also reconstructed the organization and curriculum of the ed school. The result was that education professors were left with a role that was now clearly defined but not very attractive: to prepare teachers and other educators for the various roles in the new structure of schooling, and (for those in university settings) to carry out research and development activities in support of the same structure. It was a job, to be sure, but it wasn't much of a mission. It presented the education professor as a functionary, a cog in the new social-efficiency education machine, but this left the professor with nothing to profess. Administrative progressivism promised a cold and scientific kind of educational efficiency. This was cause enough for some professors; recall that many of the administrative progressives were themselves education professors, most of them found in programs such as administration, educational psychology, and testing. Yet for most of the faculty, especially those involved in curriculum and instruction and teacher education, this was not the kind of cause that made them want to jump out of bed in the morning and race into work.

As Katz points out, their work no longer involved generating an overarching vision of education as a whole, and it no longer permitted them to carry out a role as social reformers who could promote educational change as a way to create a more just world. They had been able to play this kind of prominent and consequential mission in early days of the progressive education movement at the start of the century, which was one of the factors that drew such strong support for the movement from teacher educators. In the context of the larger history of education professors in the United States, in which they never received much respect, early progressivism granted them a temporary measure of status and influence that was striking, and this made them take the loss of these benefits particularly hard. For within the new professional school of education in the 1920s and 1930s, the function of education professors was merely to train students who could adapt to and comply with the new socially efficient structure of education.

In view of the downscaled and deskilled role of the education faculty, it is easy to understand why the success of administrative progressivism reinforced their attraction to pedagogical progressivism. It was a vision of education that could really get an education professor's blood pumping. Pedagogical progressivism proposed to do a lot more than just make schools efficient. It called for turning education upside down, by having the purposes and interests of the student drive the curriculum rather than forcing the curriculum onto the student. It offered a way to free schools from artificial constraints and rigid disciplines and unleash the student's natural impulse to learn. It proposed to re-create the classroom as a model democratic community of learners, which could become a way to reduce injustice and enhance democratic equality in the larger society.

The need for this kind of pedagogical vision for schools seemed stronger in the interwar years than it did at the start of the century, when progressivism was just beginning to stretch its wings. As Cuban shows, the administrative progressives may have transformed the structure of American education, but the old traditional pedagogy was continuing to operate largely undeterred within the new scientific curriculum. Classroom instruction continued to be teacher centered and textbook based, aimed at delivering prescribed subject matter to passive students. The differentiation and vocationalism of the new social-efficiency curriculum only exacerbated the elements that made schools closed to child-centered, interest-based, naturalistic, and intrinsically engaging instruction. Pedagogical progressivism explicitly warned against this kind of schooling. It warned that paying too much attention to the efficient delivery of subject matter would stifle the interest of students and keep them from learning to learn. It warned that sorting students and differentiating their access to knowledge would block the great learning potential that is present in all students. And it warned that if you try to force students to adapt to adult roles instead of dealing with their needs and interests as children, you will encourage them to reject rather than to embrace education.

So the professors found that the old enemy—traditional pedagogy—was still alive and well and that administrative progressive reform had produced new instructional problems, both of which begged for the remedy offered by child-centered education. This situation is a common one in the history of American education. Every reform movement leaves part of the original mission unaccomplished and simultaneously creates new educational problems that demand their own resolution; thus one spell of reform provokes another, in an unending chain of problem solving and problem making. For that reason, educational reform (in the words of Elmore and McLaughlin) has always been "steady work."[77]

Pedagogical progressivism, therefore, may have lost the fight to shape practice in schools and even in ed schools; but the vision was still alive, and in the ed school it found an ideological safe haven. It offered most education professors the mission they needed in order to infuse meaning into their newly redefined work as teacher educators and functionaries in the educational machine. They did their teaching and research within the structure defined by Thorndike, but their hearts and minds belonged to Dewey. Not for nothing has Dewey's picture been found on the wall in so many ed school offices for so many years.

This rhetorical entrenchment of pedagogical progressivism within the education school posed no serious threat to the accomplishments of the administrative progressives. Early on, the two groups in the progressive movement had in effect divided the territory between themselves, with one taking the ground and the other taking the air: The administrative progressives focused on organization and the pedagogues on rhetoric. As Lagemann suggests, it probably all started when Dewey left the lab school for the philosophy department. The control of the administrative progressives over organization, curriculum, and practice in schools was so secure that they could afford to have faculty members in education schools spouting the creed of child-centered instruction. The professors could teach the language of Dewey to teacher candidates, employ it in decorating their scholarship, and talk it up in their workshops in schools. Teachers too could come to talk the talk of pedagogical progressivism, but, like the professors, they also had to work within the differentiated and vocationally oriented structure of schooling created by the administrative progressives, so the consequences for this structure were minimal.

The persistence of a harmlessly rhetorical form of pedagogical progressivism within the education school also proved useful to the newly established administrative progressive order in schools by providing it with much-needed ideological cover. Social-efficiency education, when examined closely from the perspective of American traditions of democratic equality and individual opportunity, was not an attractive sight. As a social process, it sorted students into ability groups based in part on social origins, provided them with access only to the knowledge deemed within their ability, and then sent them off to particular positions in the pyramid of jobs based on their academic attainments. As an educational process, it was mechanistic, alienating, and dull, with a dumbed-down curriculum and a disengaging pedagogy. This was a coldly utilitarian and socially reproductive vision of schooling, and the offer it made to students—learn a skill and take your place in the workforce—was hard to get excited about and easy to refuse. Into this efficient and heartless environment, the romantic educational vision of the pedagogical progressives introduced welcome elements, such as natural learning, student-centered teaching, interest-based curriculum, and possibilities for personal fulfillment and social improvement. Having education schools imbue student teachers with commitment to this kind of engaging and optimistic form of teaching and learning helped make the whole prospect of social-efficiency education seem more promising and engaging.

PROGRESSIVISM AND PROFESSIONALISM

At the turn of the twentieth century, one institution took the lead in defining the role of the education school and maintained its leadership for many of the next hundred years: Teachers College. Much of this was due to the leadership of its dean from 1897 to 1927, James Earl Russell, and a key to Russell's formula for the education school was, in Cremin's view, a fruitful union between progressivism and professionalism:

Thus did Russell merge the professionalism and progressivism that had been instrumental in the founding of the college into a full-fledged reformist philosophy of teacher preparation. It was a merger of prodigious significance for American education. For in progressivism teachers soon found that they had an ideology that dignified in the noblest terms their own quest for status, while in professionalism progressives had the key to their demand for scientifically trained pedagogues who could bring into being a new society "more worthy, lovely, and harmonious." The merger colored the whole subsequent history of progressive education, and goes far in explaining Teachers College's meteoric rise to pre-eminence during the years of Russell's administration.[78]

There are two interesting ambiguities in this passage that are important for our story. First, Cremin points to the role of progressivism in establishing the professionalism of teachers, but in my view it played a more substantial role in establishing the professionalism of teacher educators and other education school professors. After all, it was Teachers College that experienced the "meteoric rise" after the advent of progressivism and not the teaching profession. Then as now, education professors desperately needed some sort of status prop, and the progressive ideology helped supply it. Progressivism provides a wonderful combination of noble aims and scientific methods, which correspond to the two defining characteristics of a true profession, high ideals of public service and clinically effective methods. TC professors were scorned by their Columbia colleagues across 120th Street (known as "the widest street in America"). "Little wonder that professors of education, ever under attack for having no real content to teach, saw in [progressivism's] science the great panacea for their field."[79] Attaching themselves to progressivism, with its high public visibility and professionalizing potential, was and is of great benefit to their professional standing.

A second ambiguity in the quoted passage is the question of which progressivism he is talking about. Recall that Cremin refused to define progressivism because of "its pluralistic, frequently contradictory, character," and that Teachers College was well represented in both camps, with Dewey[80] and Kilpatrick on one side and Thorndike and Snedden on the other. Here Cremin seems to refer to both of the main strands of the movement, the pedagogical progressives for their noble aims and the administrative progressives for their scientific approach. This shows the way in which each side was able to draw from the strength of the other for its own benefit, albeit disingenuously, each choosing to define the progressive camp broadly or narrowly as the occasion warranted. As I've already pointed out, the administrators liked to draw on the pedagogues' high-minded child-centered naturalism as useful cover for their essentially mechanistic and socially reproductive approach to education. But at the same time, the pedagogues liked to draw on the administrators' strong suit—the authority of science—from time to time, as useful cover for their fundamentally romantic vision of education. The argument that the child-centered approach to teaching and learning was grounded in solid scientific evidence was a prop to the credibility of the professors promoting this view, and it helped give them an aura of professionalism that was useful in reinforcing their standing with university colleagues and the public.

At this point I want to shift focus from the historical context of the first forty years of the twentieth century, when the meaning of progressive education was hotly contested, to the present, and therefore I would like to abandon the somewhat cumbersome term "pedagogical progressive" to define the child-centered vision of education. Although this strand of progressivism failed to have the impact it sought on schools, it was extraordinarily effective in the rhetorical realm, where it succeeded in taking full ownership of the progressive label. In part this rhetorical success was due to its practical failure. By the 1940s, administrative progressivism constituted the facts on the ground in American education, and, like most successful reforms, it thus quickly became invisible. Differentiation and vocationalism became part of what Tyack and Cuban call the "grammar of schooling,"[81] and as such they were no longer a matter open to contest or worthy of comment. At the same time, the pedagogical progressives in education schools continued to promote their vision relentlessly, a pattern that has persisted to the present day, and for good reason. Without constant repetition, the ideas would have disappeared, since they had not become embedded in the organization and practice of schools but existed only in the rhetorical effusions of education schools. However, the persistent chatter from pedagogical progressives, combined with the smug silence of their old administrative opponents, has allowed the former to redefine the language of the debate in their own favor. Progressivism now means child-centered instruction, and I will now go back to using the term in this manner.

Other Reasons for the Ed School's Ties to Progressivism

Building on the foundation of the preceding historical analysis of progressivism and the education school, let's consider several other factors that have reinforced the connection between the two.

CONTENT, PROCESS, AND PROGRESSIVISM

As we saw in chapter 2, one chronic structural problem facing the education school is that responsibility for subject matter knowledge has come to reside in the hands of others; this has been another important factor in reinforcing the ed school's attachment to the progressive ideology. Teachers teach subject matter, and teacher educators teach teachers how to teach subject matter, but definitive expertise in subject matter itself is held by professors in the respective disciplines: math, English, the natural sciences, history, and the social sciences. Since education schools have no control over instructional content, they concentrate their energies on the domain that is left to them, instructional process. And progressivism is the educational vision that focuses on process—that, in fact, elevates process into a high art and the essence of good teaching.

The separation of subject matter from teacher preparation was not always the case. In nineteenth-century normal schools, where all students were (or at least said they were) preparing to become teachers, and where all faculty were teacher educators, faculty members taught both subject matter knowledge and pedagogical knowledge. The two forms of knowledge were integrated into a single curriculum, which was under the control of the normal school faculty. But as normal schools evolved into teachers colleges, state colleges, and state universities during the twentieth century, disciplinary departments developed full organizational and intellectual separation from the education faculty. And where education schools emerged within existing universities, this segregation of content from teacher preparation was present from the very beginning.

In some ways the gradual segregation of the two forms of knowledge appears to be an artifact of a particular set of historical contingencies, as market pressure from the normal school's consumers led it to abandon its distinctive professional mission and transform itself into a full-service university, with teacher preparation as just one of many curricular options. If there had been stronger control of these schools by government and less leverage in the hands of the students, the government could have held the normal school to its professional mission. Consider, for example, the case of the community college. Apparently having learned their lesson from the example of the normal school, the fifty states have for the most part refused to allow this most recent addition to American higher education to follow the path of the land grant college and normal school by reconstructing itself in the model of the university. Instead, community colleges typically remain restricted to offering associate degrees.

In other ways, however, the separation of content from pedagogy seems an inevitable consequence of the growing specialization of knowledge both inside and outside the academy. Within individual disciplines, specialization has developed well past the point where a scholar can attain credible expertise in anything more than a fraction of the field. Under such circumstances, it is unlikely that, for example, a science educator on the faculty of an education school, whose job is to prepare science teachers for the schools, could at the same time be a credible expert in physics or biology or chemistry. Even if the normal school had survived as a separate institution with a purely professional mission, its science, math, social studies, and English professors would by no means be considered comparable to their counterparts in the disciplines, and the teachers who graduated from these institutions would correctly be considered even weaker in subject matter knowledge than the graduates of today's university-based education schools.

This separation of education professors from subject matter expertise leaves them in a bind professionally, and progressivism seemed to provide a way out. They don't have the depth of knowledge in the school subjects that their disciplinary colleagues across campus do, but progressivism says they don't need it. It is not important for a teacher to be loaded with authoritative knowledge and ready to transmit this knowledge to the student; that is the approach in traditional pedagogy, which only alienates students and impedes their learning. Instead, what is really important is for the teacher to be skillful in spurring the curiosity and desire of students to pursue learning for their own purposes and on their own initiative. Students need teachers who can help them learn how to learn. The subject matter deployed as part of progressive teaching is only a means to that end. Once students acquire the appropriate learning skills, they will be able to learn all the subject matter they need without having to depend on the expertise of the teacher in that particular subject. Since the teacher doesn't need this kind of subject matter expertise to the same degree as required by the traditional model, neither does the teacher educator. But the teacher educator must be expert in the theory and practice of promoting student engagement in the learning process, and progressivism is a comprehensive, philosophically grounded, and even arguably scientific system that supplies just that expertise. In this way, then, progressivism appeared to be the answer to the chronic knowledge problem facing education professors.

Of course, this is not an answer that satisfies their critics or earns them respect with colleagues in the disciplines. Both ridicule education professors for being all process and no content, for teaching classes in erasing blackboards and taking attendance. For most people outside the education school, knowing how to teach means knowing the subject you are teaching. As I argued in chapter 3, this view is only a half truth. You need to know the subject to teach it; but, for example, just because you know how to read doesn't mean that you know how to teach a group of children to read—especially how to do so with some degree of effectiveness and efficiency for students who have a wide range of abilities and social backgrounds. However, even if you acknowledge that knowing how to teach is a critically important form of expertise, and that being able to teach this skill, as teacher educators must, likewise constitutes an important form of expertise, it is still hard to convince people that this process knowledge is in any way equal to the content knowledge of the disciplinary professor. And often progressivism is not much help in this regard, since its blithe disregard for subject matter makes it too easy to caricature as a system of education without a curriculum and a system of learning without a teacher.

Into this breach stepped Lee Shulman, a teacher educator at Stanford, who in a series of essays in the 1980s responded to the chronic question about both teachers and education professors—what, if anything, is their area of expertise?—with his own ingenious answer: pedagogical content knowledge.[82] In setting out to establish the nature of the knowledge base for teaching, he listed seven kinds of knowledge: (1) content knowledge, (2) general pedagogical knowledge, (3) curriculum knowledge, (4) pedagogical content knowledge, (5) knowledge of learners and their characteristics, (6) knowledge of educational contexts, and (7) knowledge of educational ends, purposes, and values.[83] In an earlier paper he defined the type of knowledge occupying the central position in this scheme, pedagogical content knowledge, as "the particular form of content knowledge than embodies the aspects of content most germane to its teachability," in other words "the ways of representing and formulating the subject that make it comprehensible to others."[84] Here is how he explained the significance of this form of knowledge: "Among these categories, pedagogical content knowledge is of special interest because it identifies the distinctive bodies of knowledge for teaching. It represents the blending of content and pedagogy into an understanding of how particular topics, problems, or issues are organized, represented, and adapted to the diverse interests and abilities of learners, and presented for instruction. Pedagogical content knowledge is the category most likely to distinguish the understanding of the content specialist from that of the pedagogue."[85]

Shulman developed this concept expressly for the purpose of establishing the contours of the knowledge base for teaching, but he wrote about it in two journals and a book that are aimed primarily at education professors, and it may be the latter who are the biggest beneficiaries of this invention. Pedagogical content knowledge provides education professors with a distinctive form of expertise (defined as knowledge and not as mere skill) that is crucial for effective teaching—expertise that we have and professors in the disciplines do not. Notice that he frames it in a way that neatly responds to the standard criticism of progressive teaching—all pedagogical process and no curriculum content—by equally weighting both pedagogy and content. He even argues that the present-day education professor is the true heir to the spirit of the university, pointing out that the medieval university was in effect a normal school, whose primary function was to produce teachers, whose highest degrees (master's and doctorate) were designations for master teachers, and whose oral examinations were demonstrations of the candidate's ability to teach his subject effectively.[86] And he does this without abandoning his commitment to the progressive ideal. In a footnote, he cautions: "The rhetoric of the analysis . . . is not meant to suggest that education is reduced to knowledge transmission, the conveying of information from an active teacher to a passive learner, and that information is viewed as product rather than process. My conception of teaching is not limited to direct instruction. Indeed, my affinity for discovery learning and inquiry teaching is both enthusiastic and ancient."[87]

So we education professors can hold onto our progressive credo while simultaneously acquiring an apparently credible form of knowledge that is distinctly our own. Which would resolve the expertise problem of the education professors—if, in fact, this newly defined form of knowledge actually exists. What's not clear, however, is whether it does. When you examine closely the seven forms of knowledge that make up the teacher knowledge base, it starts to look as if pedagogical content knowledge is actually just the combination of the other six. If it is "the ways of representing and formulating the subject that make it comprehensible to others," then it involves drawing together what the teacher knows about subject matter, context, curriculum, learners, educational aims, and general pedagogy in order to accomplish this. If so, then pedagogical content knowledge is not a distinctive form of knowledge for teachers but the sum of all the other knowledges, all of which are at least shared with, if not owned by, other occupational groups (like faculty in the disciplines, psychologists, curriculum developers, and so on). Instead of being a newly discovered form of knowledge in its own right, it may just be another label for all the things involved in teaching effectively. In this sense, then, we may be justified in reading Shulman's account of pedagogical content knowledge as an adept rhetorical move in the status politics of teaching and teacher education:

Wouldn't it be nice, he may be saying, if there were a distinctive form of expertise that belonged to teachers and education professors? If it existed, wouldn't it look something like this?

Progressivism, then, fills an important need for education professors by providing us with a rationale for focusing on the process we know rather than the content we don't. In turn, pedagogical content knowledge fills an important need for us by responding to the critique of progressivism as process-happy with an apparently new and distinctive form of expertise that incorporates both process and content.

There is, however, another way of interpreting Shulman's concept that is complementary to this rhetorical reading. As Jeffrey Mirel[88] has suggested to me, maybe pedagogical content knowledge is not only a way for Shulman to give rhetorical cover to education professors, allowing them to represent themselves to the world as people with a substantive area of expertise, but also a way for him to advocate injecting subject matter into the work of education professors, by doing so under cover of the progressive passion for pedagogy. Arguing straight out for taking subject matter seriously in education schools would have been counterproductive in two ways. It would undercut education professors' claim of professional autonomy by making them dependent on the disciplines that own the various subject matters, and it would ask them to violate their progressive principles by asserting that the content of the curriculum is essential and is not just a mechanism for acquiring learning skills. But by representing his proposal as pedagogical content knowledge, he could show it as a distinctive property of education professors and as a natural extension of their pedagogically focused progressive creed; and he could do so without seeming to introduce anything new into the world of the ed school, since, after all, it has been present since the middle ages as a central element of teacher preparation.

THE ED SCHOOL'S ATTACHMENT TO USABLE LEARNING

If one reason for the education school's attachment to progressivism is this institution's alienation from educational content, another is its alienation from educational exchange value. Institutionally, the normal school was a latecomer to American higher education. First came the private colleges, founded in the colonial and early national period, then the flagship state universities, which began appearing in the early nineteenth century, then the land-grant state universities in the mid-nineteenth century. By the time normal schools were evolving into state colleges and universities in the mid-twentieth century, the hierarchy of higher education was well established, and there was no room at the top for the new arrivals. Also well established were the rules of the academic credentials market, which naturally favored the older players. What consumers were seeking and universities were selling was the exchange value of education more than its use value. Students wanted a degree that would open the doors of social opportunity, which they could cash in for a good job and a comfortable life, and the kind of degree that accomplished this for them came from the institutions with the highest reputation. In market terms, it was the relative scarcity of the credential that gave it value more than the quality of learning that was required to obtain it.

The former normal schools were too lowbrow to be in strong demand and too accessible to be in short supply, so they were unable to offer credentials with high exchange value. Education schools that developed within existing universities were also short on exchange value in comparison to other colleges in the same institution. Part of this was a case of low status by association—association with the former normals, with the semiprofession of teaching, and with the disproportionately female and working-class students who entered it. Part of it was the result of the soft and applied knowledge produced by educational researchers, which was unable to enhance the education school's institutional prestige and social influence in the way that hard and pure knowledge did for other fields.

In short, the low status of the education school prevented it from offering credentials of high exchange value. At the same time, its role as a professional school compelled it, unlike the more privileged parts of higher education, to take the use value of its education seriously. Both by default and by design, education schools have historically concentrated their efforts on providing useful knowledge and skills to prospective and practicing teachers in order to enable them to teach effectively. They are in a position where they need to be concerned about the quality and depth of the learning of their own student-teachers, and where they also need to be concerned about the quality and depth of the learning skills that these teachers will engender in their own elementary and secondary classrooms. Under these circumstances, they are likely to be antagonistic toward formalistic modes of schooling that discount or deter what they consider authentic learning by students. This includes the kind of exchange-value-driven educational consumerism that I have written about elsewhere, in which students concentrate on accumulating grades, credits, and degrees for the extrinsic rewards they bring instead of pursuing education for the intrinsic value of the learning it provides.[89] This antagonism is also directed toward the kind of teaching that goes through the motions of delivering a set curriculum to the students by talk and text and then assumes that learning will follow.

The alternative to this kind of formalistic teaching and learning is a classroom in which students are deeply engaged in pursuing their own interest in the world and in which teachers focus on spurring students' intrinsic motivation to learn. And an approach to education that captures this vision is progressivism. This ideology responds perfectly to the conditions of learning that are both forced on and embraced by education professors. Given where they are, they have to take learning—as a process if not as a content—seriously, and progressivism provides a pedagogy for doing so; given where they want to be, they need an approach that elevates their work into a worthy mission, and progressivism provides an educational ideal that seems worth pursuing.

THE ED SCHOOL'S AFFINITY FOR THE DISADVANTAGED

One final factor that attracts education professors to progressivism is a shared concern for the underdog. Progressivism takes a reform position toward education. It sees traditional education as the status quo that needs to be overthrown, and given its failure in bringing about this change thus far, the reformist stance has become something like a permanent posture for its adherents. Progressivism adopts the perspective of the student, whom it sees as the put-upon object of the existing educational system, ordered around by teachers and forced to ingest an unpalatable curriculum. In particular it sees itself taking the side of those students who—for reasons of race, gender, class, and culture—are less willing and able to play the current academic game and thus experience the largest rate of failure in the current system. These values of progressivism resonate with those of us on the faculties of ed schools. We may come from more privileged social backgrounds than many of the students in the schools, and we may have done better in school. But as education professors, we have empathy for students who don't succeed in the current educational system, and our own history as victims makes us natural advocates for the downtrodden. Progressivism provides a vision of an alternative approach to education that seems to respond to our experience as well as theirs.

History threw the education school and progressivism into each other's arms, and mutual need, born of mutual impairment, has kept them locked together. An accumulation of social and historical factors has so reinforced the strength of this bond that it is hard for education professors to view education any other way. At the same time, the strength of the bond between ed schools and progressivism, the dominance of progressive rhetoric in educational discourse, and the usefulness of progressivism as a foil for proponents of traditional education have in combination led some critics to conclude mistakenly that ed school progressivism has ruined American schools. Their error in this regard is two-fold—in taking us education professors at our word, instead of examining our modest impact on practice, and in attributing substantial power to us, instead of considering how little power we can generate from our lowly status. In the final chapter, I explore these issues and their implications.

Chapter 8 The Trouble with Ed Schools: Little Harm, Little Help

Education schools are the objects of attack from all quarters.[1] Everyone likes to pick on them: teachers, administrators, policymakers, education bureaucrats, conservatives, liberals, academics in the disciplines, and even their own faculty and students. And as you, the reader, have seen, this book is no exception. Apparently, finding something good to say about this institution is difficult even for someone like me, who has been an insider to the ed school for many years and is deeply involved (perhaps I should say implicated) in its programs and research efforts. But just because it is difficult to say good things about ed schools doesn't mean that such a task is impossible or entirely without merit.

Part of the trouble with ed schools is that picking on them is far too easy. As the ninety-seven-pound weaklings of American higher education, they pose no threat of retaliation. Their low status makes them defenseless, which means they get blamed for things they didn't do, and it also makes them unsympathetic, which means no one is willing to see things from their point of view.

What I have tried to do in this book is restore a little balance to our understanding of the ed school. I have not been shy about criticizing the institution I inhabit; in fact, many of my colleagues in the ed school community are likely to consider this account unfair and unkind, as just another effort to kick sand in their faces. But at the same time, I have taken pains to show the difficulties involved in trying to carry out the ed school's basic mandate, difficulties that are vastly in excess of anything required in programs across campus that have far higher academic standing; and I have showed how the ed school's long history of being besieged by market pressures and status politics has exacerbated these difficulties. These parts of the book are likely to strike the ed school's critics as just another effort to justify this institution and rationalize its failures.

Balance, it seems, is unwelcome on both sides of this debate. Insiders want to praise the ed school and show how its progressive vision is the cure for what ails American education, and outsiders want to defame the ed school and show how it and its ideology are the source of infection. Neither side is interested in considering that the other may have a point, and therefore neither is likely to be pleased with my approach to the subject. Instead, I am resigned to the prospect that many readers will draw quite selectively from this book in order to support their own entrenched positions at one pole or the other. I provide plenty of evidence for both. There is much to respect and much to ridicule in the work we do in education schools, and the powerful pull of these two extremes makes it difficult to maintain a position that is anywhere near the middle.

As you have seen in the preceding chapters, my own position is not in the middle of this debate either; instead, it alternates between both ends. The argument in this book is balanced only in the sense that it validates elements of the depiction of the ed school at both poles of the current discourse on the subject. In the end, therefore, my position is not so much balanced as profoundly ambivalent. My analysis of this institution as a historian and sociologist, combined with my experience in it as a teacher and researcher, lead me to this position, which has been reinforced rather than resolved by the act of writing this book. In some ways the work done by ed schools is necessary, admirable, and even noble, while at the same time in other ways it is counterproductive, reprehensible, and even laughable. I have not sought to reconcile these elements or to propose solutions for the trouble with ed schools; instead, I have aimed to complicate, clarify, and explain these characteristics, and to demonstrate why a solution to the ed school problem has been so difficult to attain.

The institutional terrain assigned to the ed school—education—is hard to manage effectively. First, it's huge. In 1999, the total number of students in the United States, from kindergarten through graduate school, was about 67 million, or one-quarter of the entire population.[2] Second, it comes with great responsibility and little control. If the educational system were to fail in fulfilling its social functions, the consequences would be devastating, both for individuals (who would lose the ability to thrive or even survive in a complex social structure) and for society (which would lose the capable personnel it needs in order to reproduce itself). But whereas all parts of the university help sustain the educational system, only the education school is charged with this responsibility as the central element of its institutional mission. When things go wrong with education, the ed school takes the blame. Third, the education-support roles that the ed school is asked to play are particularly demanding. As I showed in chapters 3, 4, and 5, each of these roles—preparing teachers, producing educational research, and preparing educational researchers—poses its own special problems of practice for the education faculty. Not only are education schools asked to carry out forms of professional preparation and knowledge production that are particularly demanding, but they are also expected to do so under conditions that are unusually trying. As I pointed out in my short history of the ed school in chapter 2, these institutions have long had to work in a situation characterized by high market pressure and low status.

So ed schools have to do a tough job under difficult conditions. I would love to be able to say that they have risen to this challenge and done the job well. However, as we have seen, too often this is not the case. Ed schools are indeed weak institutions. They are weak for good reasons, which I have tried to spell out in this book, but they are nonetheless weak. Contrary to what many critics say, the causes of this weakness are neither the ed school's negligence nor its sheer incompetence. I would challenge anyone among the institution's most ardent critics to try doing this kind of work under the conditions that ed schools have traditionally operated in and to do so at a level that is beyond reproach. But, then again, those of us who work in these beleaguered institutions can hardly take great pride in our accomplishments.

As I have shown, the weaknesses are real. Teacher education programs continue to be intellectually unstimulating and academically undemanding, and their impact on professional practice in schools is remarkably slight in comparison to the powerful inertia of traditional practice and the powerful culture of the school. Educational research struggles to attain even modest levels of coherence and credibility, and as a result it is not a major factor in the formulation of educational policy. Education professors have trouble gaining respect, which undermines their effectiveness in preparing teachers, producing research, and preparing future professors. The culture of the ed school is dominated by an unreflective romantic attachment to the rhetoric of pedagogical progressivism, which further undercuts the institution's credibility and underscores its ineffectuality. And the ed school's programs, research, and ideology all serve to support its longstanding reputation for being an anti-intellectual backwater in the intellectual culture of the university.

THE GOOD NEWS: ED SCHOOLS ARE TOO WEAK TO DO MUCH HARM TO AMERICAN EDUCATION

In light of the ed school's many failings, it is not surprising that critics often identify it as a prime source of the problems with American schools. But here I have some good news to report: The ed school is simply too weak to perpetrate such a crime. Institutionally it is clearly implicated in the work of schools, and rhetorically it provides support for some of the problems in schools, so it can't claim to be innocent of their failings. But if a fair-minded jury examined the evidence for the charge that the ed school has ruined public education, it would find enough room for doubt to render a verdict of not guilty.

For many critics this charge rests to a considerable extent on the ed school's deep attachment to progressive ideas. These ideas are dangerously wrong, they say, and the ed school has done its damage to the schools by forcing these ideas into the classroom through the media of teacher education and educational research. They see this impact occurring in two main areas. Ed school progressivism, they argue, has directly undermined the *content of the curriculum* in schools, promoting activity and skill training over the acquisition of substantive knowledge; and it has also undermined the *commonality of the curriculum*, promoting differentiated access to knowledge and thus sharply increased social inequality. In exploring this indictment of the ed school, I draw on two prominent books that make this case with vigor, *The Schools We Need and Why We Don't Have Them,* by E. D. Hirsch Jr., and *Left Back: A Century of Failed School Reforms,* by Diane Ravitch.[3]

Undermining Academic Content

On the issue of the ed school's role in undermining content, no one has been more effective than Hirsch, who, as we saw in the previous chapter, sees the root of the problem in what he calls the formalism and naturalism of the progressive approach to education. His reaction to the progressives' formalism—their love affair with the learning process—is to assert that learning has to be about something, namely the subject matter in the school curriculum: "It is a fallacy, then, to claim that the schools should or could teach all-purpose reading, thinking, and learning skills. But paradoxically, adequate attention to the transmission of broad general knowledge actually does lead to general intellectual skills. The paradox is quite stunning. Our emphasis on formal skills has resulted in students who are deficient in formal skills, whereas an appropriate emphasis on transmitting knowledge results in students who actually possess the skills that are sought by American educators—skills such as critical thinking and learning to learn."[4] In response to the progressive vision of a naturalistic pedagogy, Hirsch argues that there is nothing necessarily natural about the kind of learning we need children to carry out in school. Children learn spoken language on their own through informal interaction with family and friends, he acknowledges, but learning to read is something quite different, since it requires systematic instruction in order to accomplish it effectively and efficiently. He argues that learning is too important to be left to the discretion of minors, that developmentalism leads to delaying and differentiating students' access to knowledge, and that holistic, project-based instruction fails to establish a solid basis for learning in the individual disciplines.

This critique makes a lot of sense to me. There is indeed something dangerous about the way pedagogical progressives emphasize process over content, treating curriculum as an open category to be filled by whatever substantive knowledge is convenient in order to teach students what really matters, which is the skill to learn on their own. It is true, as progressives claim, that learning how to learn enables you to acquire any knowledge you want, but Hirsch is convincing in arguing that accumulating broad forms of knowledge is essential to the acquisition of these learning skills. Also, as he notes, many of the things we want and need children to learn are not the kinds of things they can acquire easily through informal means, and they may well not be things that children would choose to learn at this point in their lives. The most efficient way to make these kinds of learning happen is through systematic instruction of students in content that adults decide is necessary.

If we were to follow the lead of the progressives and try to implement the progressive vision in the full and unhybridized form that pervades the rhetoric of education schools, we might well bring about some of the damage to education that Hirsch and others warn us about. Fortunately, however, the carriers of this belief system, education professors, don't have the academic credibility or professional clout to make this happen. In short, we could do some real damage to the schools if we were able to put their romantic ideology into practice, but we're too weak to do so.

Hirsch is more effective in explaining the potential damage that progressive ideas might have on the content of the curriculum than in demonstrating that they actually have had this effect. The problem is in trying to show that the ed school—the sad sack of American higher education—had the muscle to inflict so much damage. Hirsch acknowledges the weakness of ed schools; in fact, he emphasizes the issue. But he tries to spin the weakness of ed schools into a form of strength. After detailing how education professors are held in low esteem by their colleagues at the university, he argues: "But the plight of education schools in the universities is counterbalanced by their enormous importance in the sphere of teacher certification and their huge ideological influence in the nation's schools. It is never a healthy circumstance when people who are held in low esteem exercise dominant influence in an important sphere. The connection of power with resentment is deadly. The educational community's identification of knowledge with 'elitism' . . . is a strategy born more of hostility than of rational principle."[5] He suggests two factors that give ed schools the leverage to suppress academic learning in American classrooms: their structural role in certifying teachers and their ideological dominance in the education community. Let's consider each of these in turn.

THE ED SCHOOL'S CONTROL OF TEACHER CERTIFICATION

Ed schools do occupy the central position in the structure for certifying teachers, which potentially gives them considerable power, and they use this position to try to convert their student-teachers to the progressive view of teaching—as an inquiry-based, child-centered, and activity-oriented practice aimed at promoting learning skills rather than at transmitting an academic curriculum. However, as we have seen, there are several factors that severely undercut that power. For one thing, there are several ways in which prospective teachers can get into the classroom without first passing through an ed school teacher education program; these include pursuing one of several different alternative certification programs and also getting hired with little or no formal training by means of a temporary, provisional, or emergency license.[6]

But the most important factor that belies the ed school's importance in teacher education is the consistent finding in the research on teacher education that these programs exert remarkably little impact on the way their graduates teach. In a review of the literature on teacher change, Richardson and Placier report that teacher education programs are more effective at moving "students to the point of indicating on a short-answer or multiple-choice test that they have acquired academic knowledge about teaching and learning" than at changing their fundamental views about teaching: "What we see expressed in these current studies of teacher education is the difficulty in changing the type of tacit beliefs and understandings that lie buried in a person's being. These cognitions and beliefs drive everyday classroom practice within local contexts."[7] One study after another reported that "students did not change their beliefs and assumptions about good teaching during the course of their teacher education programs"; instead, studies found that "the novices' perspectives tended to solidify rather than change over the course of the student teaching experiences."[8]

In chapter 3 we saw some of the reasons for this. Prospective teachers learn about teaching from a sixteen- or seventeen-year apprenticeship of observation as students, which provides them with a powerful attachment to an image of teaching that several years in a teacher preparation program can do little to change.[9] Compounding this resistance to the teacher ed message is the strong belief among prospective teachers and the public at large that teaching is natural and easy and therefore does not require extensive professional training. Finally, student and novice teachers are quickly drawn into the culture of practice in the schools, which to them represents the compelling "practical" story about teaching in contrast with the less useful "theoretical" version they get in the ed school.

So, contrary to Hirsch's claim, the ed school's structural position as the conduit for teacher preparation and certification has not given it the kind of power that would be required to divert schools from academic learning to the progressive focus on learning to learn. But what about its ideological position as the mother church of the progressive creed?

THE ED SCHOOL'S CONTROL OF EDUCATIONAL RHETORIC

Here Hirsch is on stronger ground. As I suggested in the previous chapter, the primary accomplishment of the ed school's pedagogical progressives in the first half of the twentieth century was to gain hegemony over educational discourse in the United States. About this point there doesn't seem to be much disagreement. Here, for example, is the way Cremin opens the concluding chapter of his classic history of progressivism:

> There is a "conventional wisdom," to borrow from John Kenneth Galbraith, in education as well as economics, and by the end of World War II progressivism had come to be that conventional wisdom. Discussions of educational policy were liberally

spiced with phrases like "recognizing individual differences," "personality development," "the whole child," "social and emotional growth," "creative self-expression,"
"the needs of learners," "intrinsic motivation," "persistent life situations," "bridging
the gap between home and school," "teaching children, not subjects," "adjusting the
school to the child," "real life experiences," "teacher-pupil relationships," and "staff
planning." Such phrases were a cant, to be sure, the peculiar jargon of the pedagogues. But they were more than that, for they signified that Dewey's forecast of a
day when *progressive* education would eventually be accepted as *good* education had
now finally come to pass.[10]

The dominance of this progressive cant in education has continued to the
present. Recall, for example, the language in the ten INTASC principles for
teacher education, which capture most of the sense and repeat many of the
phrases in Cremin's list. If every profession has its jargon, then the language of
pedagogical progressivism has become and remained the jargon of American
education, and the ed school is where this language is cultivated and dissemi-
nated. Hirsch is thus correct in noting the ideological dominance of the ed
school, but this does not mean that the ed school killed off academic learning
in the schools. It tried to do so, but it failed. If you look closely at most of the
claims people make about the dominance of ed school progressivism over
American education, you find that the strongest evidence for this is found in
rhetoric rather than practice. Consider the Cremin quote. The last sentence
sounds like a claim that pedagogical progressivism took over the schools, but in
the context of his book he is really only saying that it took over our ideas about
what "would finally be accepted as good education." As Michael Katz has
noted, Cremin's book is "an intellectual history of progressive thought" and not
an effort to "relate theory to action."[11] It focuses on the emergence of progressive ideas and the men who developed and promoted these ideas, but it tells us
little about what kind of teaching and learning was going on in schools during
this period.

Consider another example, Jeanne S. Chall's *The Academic Achievement
Challenge,* in which she mounts a book-length attack on progressivism for
undermining academic achievement in schools. Early on, she asserts: "An overview of the history of American public education in the twentieth century
reveals a general movement, until quite recently, away from a classic, teacher-
centered approach to a more open, student-centered one. There have been attempts, from time to time, to bring education back to a more teacher-centered
focus, but these attempts have been largely unavailing so far."[12] Chall's book
provides a useful analysis of the central differences between progressive and tra-

ditional ideas about pedagogy and curriculum, which I drew upon in my previous chapter, but it never demonstrates that the former actually established itself in school practice at the expense of the latter.

In chapter 7, titled "Student-Centered Education: From Theory to Practice," Chall seeks to address this issue directly. She begins by noting that "some researchers have found that progressive education was not as widely implemented in practice as was thought earlier," citing in particular the work of Goodlad and Cuban.[13] She then goes on to say, "And yet, it would seem that most schools were influenced in some ways by progressive education. This influence was reflected by their accepting certain concepts and beliefs from progressive education without necessarily implementing the broader program."[14] This is hardly a strong claim about the impact of progressivism on practice, is it? She talks about how "it would seem" progressivism had an impact "in some ways," especially given that the impact was primarily on "accepting certain concepts and beliefs" rather than "implementing the broader program." In the rest of the chapter she does little to show the effect of theory on practice, presenting instead a series of examples that for the most part demonstrate the way educators talk about schooling, using progressive ideas such as "readiness," "naturalness," and "the whole child."

The evidence that pedagogical progressivism did indeed have a major impact on practice in schools is scant. In the last chapter, I talked about the findings of the historical accounts by Larry Cuban and Arthur Zilversmit, which showed that progressive ideas had only a minimal effect on teaching practice up through the middle of the twentieth century.[15] Now let's consider some evidence about its effect on practice closer to the present.

John Goodlad, while dean of the Graduate School of Education at University of California, Los Angeles, conducted a massive study of schools in the early 1980s that included observations in more than one thousand classrooms in thirty-eight elementary and secondary schools in all regions of the United States. Published as *A Place Called School* in 1983, the book presents a portrait of teaching that fits the traditional model much better than the progressive model. Here are his conclusions about what goes on inside classrooms:

> First, the dominant pattern of classroom organization is a group to which the teacher most frequently relates as a whole . . . .
>
> Second, each student essentially works and achieves alone within a group setting. . . .
>
> Third, the teacher is the central figure in determining the activities, as well as the tone, of the classroom. . . .

Fourth, the domination of the teacher is obvious in the conduct of instruction. . . .

Fifth, there is a paucity of praise and correction of students' performance, as well as of teacher guidance in how to do better next time. . . .

Sixth, students generally engage in a rather narrow range of classroom activities—listening to teachers, writing answers to questions, and taking tests and quizzes. . . .

Seventh, the patterns summarized above describe early elementary classes less well than they do classes in higher grades. . . .

Eighth, large percentages of the students we surveyed appeared to be passively content with classroom life. . . .

Ninth, even in the early elementary years there was strong evidence of students not having time to finish their lessons or not understanding what the teacher wanted them to do.[16]

If you are dedicated to the principles of pedagogical progressivism—as Goodlad is—this depiction of traditional patterns of teaching in American classrooms in the 1980s is quite depressing, especially in light of the long-standing rhetorical commitment of education schools to child-centered pedagogy.

Consider another example, turning this time to a case study of a single classroom. David Cohen examined the practice of a California second grade teacher, dubbed Mrs. Oublier, who "eagerly embraced change" in her teaching practice by adopting a reform framework for math education.[17] This framework arose from progressive principles that were spelled out by the National Council of Teachers of Mathematics and that gained strong support from state education officials. The aim of the reform was to move from a traditional approach to math, which relies on doing worksheets and "memorizing facts and procedures," to a progressive approach that focused on student engagement, connecting concepts to students' own ideas and experience, and enlisting them in active participation in mathematical thinking.[18] The results of this "Revolution in One Classroom" (the title of the paper) were mixed at best. As Cohen puts it, "the mixture of new mathematical ideas and materials with old mathematical knowledge and pedagogy permeated Mrs. O's teaching."[19] She bought into the reform ideas, "but it is one thing to embrace a doctrine of instruction, and quite another to weave it into one's practice."[20] For example, she reorganized the class into groups of four in order to facilitate the kind of cooperative learning that was central to the reform approach, "but the instructional discourse that she established cut across the grain of this organization. The class was conducted in a highly structured and classically teacher-centered fashion."[21] Cohen concludes: "As Mrs. O revolutionized her math teaching, then, she worked with quite conventional materials: A teacher-centered conception of instructional discourse; a rigid approach to classroom management; and a traditional conception of mathematical knowledge."[22] This, therefore, is a case that shows how progressive rhetoric can thrive while traditional practice persists.

In spite of the evidence about the large gap between progressive rhetoric and classroom reality in American schools, conservative critics continue to produce studies that purport to show how the dominance of progressive cant among educators has ruined schools. All they can really show, however, is that ed school professors have managed to have an impact on the thinking of teachers, but showing an impact on teacher practice in the classroom is quite another thing.

For example, the Manhattan Institute, a conservative think tank, published a report in 2002 that presents the results of a study of teachers' educational philosophies and their attitudes toward methods of instruction.[23] The researchers surveyed 403 fourth grade teachers and 806 eighth grade teachers and then followed up with focus groups. They found that 55 percent of fourth grade teachers and 57 percent of eight grade teachers preferred student-directed learning as opposed to 40 and 37 percent respectively favoring teacher-centered methods.[24] Of the teachers for each grade, 74 and 76 percent agreed with the philosophy that "learning how to learn is most important for students," compared with 15 and 13 percent who agreed that "it is most important to teach students specific information and skills."[25] Only a quarter of the teachers said they grade students based on "whether the student got the right answer," as compared to grading based on "whether the student approached the task in a creative and thoughtful way" or "how hard the student tried";[26] and a little more than half of the teachers favored cooperative learning and small groups, compared with between a quarter and a third who favored whole group instruction.[27]

In the foreword, the ubiquitous Chester E. Finn Jr. (the president of the Thomas B. Fordham Foundation) correctly traces these ideas back to education schools: "One should by no means castigate teachers, much less the conscientious instructors who cooperated with this survey, for harboring wrong attitudes or using ill-chosen methods. They are what they are. They are what they've been told to be by those who trained them yesterday and supervise them today. For the most part, I believe, the attitudes, expectations and priorities of teachers, as well as the methods they employ when the door is closed, reflect above all the influence of their ed school professors and their mentors and peers within the education profession."[28] All we need to do to confirm this point is to observe how closely the opinions of the teachers track the opinions of the ed school professors displayed in the survey I drew upon in chapter 7—a survey which, not coincidentally, was sponsored by Finn's foundation.

The problem is that Finn and the author of the report want to conclude from the study that teacher attitudes (about which they have evidence) have translated into teacher practices (about which they have none). The report's title is *What Do Teachers Teach?*—which is misleading, to say the least, since the study does not tell us what teachers teach but only what teachers believe. As we have seen from Goodlad's observations of actual practice in classrooms and from the case of Mrs. Oublier, "harboring" particular "attitudes" does not necessarily lead to "using" the corresponding "methods." The education writer for the *Washington Post,* Jay Mathews, picks up on this point in his own analysis of the study. His comments are telling, since he is a vigorous supporter of a strong academic curriculum for the schools, as shown in his support for standards and testing[29] and in his book *Class Struggle,*[30] about the benefits of organizing high schools around advanced placement courses:

> I have seen other surveys that reflect this majority commitment to the ideals of educational theorist John Dewey, a squishy-brained dreamer to standards advocates like Finn. But I have come to think this is just a reflex, probably the result, as Finn argues, of what is taught in education schools. It does not say much about how most of those Dewey fans conduct themselves in the classroom. I have yet to observe a teacher who is not putting considerable emphasis on specific information and skills. Just how successful they are is another matter, but if you know of a study that shows that Dewey's principles are actually practiced in any serious way in many American classrooms, I would like to see it, because it conflicts with what I have found.[31]

Differentiating Access to Knowledge

In *Left Back,* historian Diane Ravitch argues, parallel to Hirsch, that over the course of the twentieth century ed school progressivism undermined the academic content of the curriculum in American schools. But she emphasizes another related aspect of its negative impact on learning, the way progressivism produced a differentiated access to knowledge and thereby destroyed the democratic promise inherent in public education:

> The aim of this book is to trace the origins of America's seemingly permanent debate about school standards, curricula, and methods. In particular, it recounts the story of unrelenting attacks on the academic mission of the schools. As enrollments in school increased in the early twentieth century, there was a decided split between those who believed that a liberal education (that is, an academic curriculum) should be given to

all students and those who wanted such studies taught only to the college-bound elite. The latter group, based primarily in the schools of education, identified itself with the new progressive education movement and dominated the education profession in its formative years.

. . . Curricular differentiation meant an academic education for some, a nonacademic education for others. . . . Such policies, packaged in rhetoric about democracy and "meeting the needs of the individual child," encouraged racial and social stratification in American schools. This book will argue that this stratification not only was profoundly undemocratic but was harmful, both to the children involved and to American society.[32]

Curriculum in American schools is indeed differentiated, especially at the secondary level; on that point there is wide agreement. Students are exposed to different kinds of knowledge, and this differentiation takes three forms: tracking within schools, ability grouping within classrooms, and tracking between schools. Secondary schools in general practice curriculum tracking. In one form, an individual subject like English is offered in different classes that are stratified by level of difficulty, such as advanced placement (at the top), college prep, general track, and remedial. Tracking also occurs between subjects in a sequence, as in math, where some students never go beyond pre-algebra while others go all the way to calculus, or in science, where the spectrum runs from general science to physics. In addition, tracking occurs across whole domains of knowledge, with some students focusing on special education or vocational education at the bottom of the hierarchy while most end up at some level of study within the academic domain. Within individual classes, especially in the elementary grades, students are customarily sorted into ability groups for core subjects like reading and math, where each group works at a different pace and frequently uses different curriculum materials. Finally, students in different schools often face different levels of difficulty in the same subject and the same track or ability group.

Ravitch's concern about this differentiated curriculum, similar to the concern expressed by Hirsch in an earlier book, the bestseller *Cultural Literacy*,[33] is that it prevents students from acquiring the common body of knowledge that they need in order to function effectively as citizens in a democracy. This body of knowledge, she says, is found in the academic curriculum, which she defines as "the systematic study of language and literature, science and mathematics, history, the arts, and foreign languages; these studies, commonly described today as a 'liberal education,' convey important knowledge and skills, cultivate aesthetic imagination, and teach students to think critically and reflectively about the world in which they live."[34] The problem with ed school progressivism, she argues, is not only that it undercuts the academic curriculum in general in favor of vocational and student-initiated studies, but that it limits access to this rich resource to only a few of the most privileged students in the top tracks and at the best schools. For the less privileged students, the curriculum becomes diffused, dumbed down, vocationalized, and socially limiting.

This is a familiar argument in the research literature in education, but it has usually come from the political left. An entire body of work known as social reproduction theory emerged in the 1960s, which argued that schooling serves to reproduce social inequality by sorting students according to their social origins, tracking them into stratified classes that give them access to different levels of knowledge, and then channeling them into jobs at different levels in the stratified occupational structure, with the result that students from the various social classes and ethnic groups end up in positions similar to the ones occupied by their parents. The fact that schools do this sorting overtly through the criterion of academic merit (test scores, grades, etc.) rather than social origins only makes the process worse, since it convinces both the winners and the losers that they got what they deserved in proportion to their academic abilities. Prominent examples from this literature include Samuel Bowles and Herbert Gintis on the overall framework of social reproduction, Jeannie Oakes on the structure of tracking within schools, and Jean Anyon on tracking between schools.[35] The difference in *Left Back* is that Ravitch does not present the pattern of stratified learning and stratified social outcomes as the result of the basic inequality in the structure of American society, but instead as the result of misguided curriculum ideas promulgated by ed school progressives. On this point we disagree. She portrays the whole progressive movement as the cause of the problem, whereas I lay the blame primarily on the administrative progressives.

ADMINISTRATIVE PROGRESSIVES DID IT

Curriculum differentiation arises from two central principles of the administrative progressives—developmentalism and social efficiency. According to the developmental approach, education can be effective only if it is tailored to the developmental needs of the individual student. From this perspective, a common academic curriculum is counterproductive, since it fails to take into account what kind of learning students will be able to accomplish in light of their cognitive capabilities at a given point. Pitching the curriculum too fast or too slow, too high or too low for a particular student will produce frustration and failure rather than learning. Therefore, you need to assess a student's level of learning through systematic testing and then assign that student to the appropriate curriculum. And as a practical matter, since individualized instruction is unrealistic in a classroom of twenty-five or thirty students, this means assigning each student to an appropriate ability group or tracked class along with other students who are at approximately the same developmental level.

The principle of social efficiency operates at two levels in the administrative progressive approach to curriculum. At the societal level, social efficiency means that schools need to produce graduates who are capable of filling the full array of occupational positions in a complex social structure if the society is going to function efficiently. Since different jobs require substantially different kinds of knowledge and skill, schools need to differentiate the curriculum in a way that approximately matches the differential knowledge requirements of these jobs. Under these circumstances a common academic curriculum is dysfunctional, both because the commonality of learning fails to meet the needs of a differentiated society and because the academic nature of learning fails to prepare students for the practical demands of work. At the school level, social efficiency means that schools need to organize themselves in a manner that allows them to manage this complex instructional task efficiently. You have a heterogeneous collection of students, who need to be assigned into grades by age and then assigned into ability groups and tracks by development level. To do this you need a system of testing and a stratified array of course options, whose number and distribution are a function of the capabilities of the students and the capacities of the staff. Since this system embeds ability in track level more than grade level, and since students tend to stay in the same track during their school careers, you need social promotion in order to keep students moving through the grades and out the door.

Pedagogical progressives shared with administrative progressives a concern for the developmental needs of the child, but instead of using developmentalism as a reason for building a complex stratified curriculum structure, they used it as a reason for deconstructing formal curriculum entirely. For them the key was to put the stress on student interest and initiative, both of which were suppressed by formal curriculum, and to shift the focus from mastering bodies of knowledge to learning how to learn, which meant discounting content in favor of process. At the same time, pedagogical progressives saw social efficiency in a very different light from their administrative counterparts. If they used the concept at all, it was in reference to the need for education to be practical in the broadest sense of the word, providing usable knowledge and skill that would help people function in the world. This reinforced their hostility to the traditional academic curriculum, which they shared with the other progressives (about which I'll say more below). But they were adamantly opposed to the notion of tracking. This went directly against their commitment to equality and social justice, it threatened to squash all hope of engaging student interest and engendering student initiative, and it reified formal curriculum at the expense of pedagogical process.

Note that the administrative progressives' devotion to developmentalism and social efficiency led not only to a curriculum that was differentiated but also to one whose academic content was substantially lower than before. If you need to adjust school subjects to the capacities of students and to the requirements of the job market, and if most students have modest capacities and most jobs have modest skill requirements, then you need only a few classes that provide a rigorous academic content for the college-bound elite, while most students need classes that are less academic, less demanding, and better suited to their modest future roles in society. This is a straightforward prescription for diluting academic content. As a result, the administrative progressives were responsible for turning the meat of academic subjects into meatloaf, with such inventions as social studies, general science, and home economics. Recall the recommendations of the *Cardinal Principles* report, the canonical statement of the administrative progressive view of the curriculum, which defined the seven goals of education as almost everything but academic learning,[36] and recall how explicit the report was on the centrality of vocational studies and the marginality of the academic.[37] Therefore, on the charge that ed school progressives ruined schools by eradicating academic content, I say they tried but failed. On the charge that they ruined schools by differentiating the curriculum, I say, flat out, they didn't do it; in fact, they were philosophically opposed to this effort. The real culprits in both cases were the administrative progressives, who had motive and opportunity and whose guilt is well supported by the evidence.

Critics who are concerned about the way American schools have come to play down academic learning and play up curriculum differentiation should be looking for a more powerful and persuasive cause than the lowly ed school. I have already suggested one, the administrative progressives, who, as school administrators and professors of administration, were in a strong position to push for changes in the curriculum and who had goals that were congruent with a vocationalized and differentiated approach to learning. But they couldn't have done it alone. Top-down reforms don't work very well in an organizational setting that is as loosely coupled as the American school system. Reforms from above usually make headway only if they resonate with and are reinforced by demand from below. In that light, let me suggest another cause of these educational ailments: consumerism.

CONSUMERISM DID IT

In the discussion of the evolution of the normal school in chapter 2, I talked about two kinds of goals for education that shaped that evolution: social efficiency and social mobility. Both also apply to education at the elementary and secondary levels.[38] From the perspective of the social-efficiency goal, schooling is a mechanism for providing society with productive workers, giving them the knowledge and skill they need in order to work effectively in the various jobs in the occupational structure. This is the basic principle that motivated the work of the administrative progressives and that continues to infuse the work of their modern-day heirs in the standards movement. From the perspective of the social-mobility goal, schooling is a mechanism for providing individual students with the credentials they need in order to compete effectively for desirable social positions. In their similarities and in their differences, these two goals help explain both the decline in academic content and the growth in the differentiated form of the curriculum in twentieth-century American education.

For both goals, the ideal school curriculum is differentiated and stratified. For efficiency purposes, you need to have the skill training in school parallel the skills required in the economy, and thus the shape of the curriculum should mimic the shape of the occupational structure, with its division of labor and hierarchy of rewards. For mobility purposes, you need to have a system of schooling that supplies some students with more educational advantages than others, so that the former will qualify for positions at a higher level than the latter. From both perspectives, a common academic curriculum for all students is counterproductive, since it stands in the way of the sorting and selecting of students that both find so important. Therefore, the differentiation of the curriculum that took place in the early twentieth century and has continued to the present is the result of not only administrative design but also consumer demand. Educational consumers—students and their families—demanded and flocked to programs that broke up the common curriculum into an array of sharply unequal options, allowing some people to get ahead and others to reinforce an already advantaged position. Thus the inequality of offerings that Ravitch rightly identifies as undemocratic was an essential requirement if the schools were going to serve the mobility needs of their consumers.

If consumerism therefore helped create and sustain the differentiation of the curriculum that was being put forward by the administrative progressives, it also pushed to dumb down the academic content of the curriculum. From the social-efficiency perspective, education is a public good, in which investment in the education of other people's children pays off for society as a whole in the form of higher productivity and economic growth. But from the social-mobility perspective, education is a private good, a commodity whose benefits accrue only to the individual who owns it. The point of education from this angle, therefore, is to enhance the social position of the credential holder in relation to everyone else, the public interest be damned: Let other consumers take care of themselves. The consequences for learning are substantial. For the consumer, learning is at best a side effect of education; the main effect is the credential. The point of going to school is to obtain grades, credits, and degrees that will translate into social position; if you get an education along the way, that's okay too. But, like any other consumer, the educational consumer has a strong incentive to get the maximum benefit from a commodity while investing the minimum amount of time, effort, and money to obtain it. In school this translates into strong consumer pressure to lower academic standards, reduce requirements, and minimize the amount of learning that is needed in order to attain a particular level of credential, such as a high school diploma or college degree. The result is the familiar situation in schools in which students bargain to get more credit for less learning.[39]

As I have shown elsewhere,[40] consumerism has been a powerful force shaping American education in the twentieth century, gradually subordinating other goals, including social efficiency and another purpose, democratic equality. Backed by the market power that comes from mobilized consumers and by the political clout that comes from citizens voting their consumer interest, educational consumerism in the United States has exerted an enormous impact on schools. It has increased inequality by stratifying the curriculum, reduced learning by bargaining down content, and increased costs by extending the demand for educational credentials well beyond the social requirement for human capital. Therefore, if anyone wants to explain major problems with American education, they would be best advised to look to consumers and administrators, who have had the power to effect changes in schools, rather than to progressive-minded ed school professors, who have not.

PROGRESSIVE RHETORIC DIDN'T DO IT, BUT IT *WAS* AN ACCESSORY

Contrary to the claims of its conservative critics, the ed school has not done much damage to American schools, but, as I pointed out above, this wasn't for lack of desire. The absence of solid evidence to support the charge that it played

a direct role in undermining academic content or in differentiating and voca-
tionalizing the curriculum doesn't relieve it of being charged as an accessory. After all, the ed school's pedagogical progressivism did manage to establish its
hegemony in the realm of educational rhetoric, and this makes the ed school
complicit in these two educational misdeeds. Let's consider the impact of the
ed school's progressive rhetoric on each.

First, there is the matter of academic content. Progressive rhetoric has taken
a strong and consistent position over the years that the traditional academic
content of the school curriculum has to go. From the perspective of the pedagogical progressives, everything about this curriculum is counterproductive to
authentic learning. As a fixed body of knowledge determined by adults and imposed on the classroom, it stifles student interest and initiative by compelling
the teacher to become an authoritarian agent of transmission and the student
to become a passive or resistant object. They have seen this curriculum as irrelevant to the student's real-world needs for useful knowledge and as an impediment to the student's willingness to embrace learning.

But the pedagogical progressives have not only opposed the traditional academic curriculum, they have also opposed having any particular body of
knowledge as the central focus of classroom learning. William Heard Kilpatrick, the man who took the lead of the pedagogical progressives during their
formative period in the 1920s and 1930s, asserted simply that "subject matter is
primarily means, not primarily ends."[41] Kliebard captures Kilpatrick's position
nicely: "Attacking what he liked to call the 'cold storage' view of knowledge,
Kilpatrick proposed instead a curriculum which deemphasized the acquisition
of knowledge in favor of a curriculum which was synonymous with purposeful
activity."[42] With its emphasis on process over content, the activity-curriculum
rhetoric of the pedagogical progressives, then, provided a philosophical rationale for the dumbing down of content, which was already being put in place by
the administrative progressives and educational consumers for their own reasons. Ed school progressives were not in a position to put their own approach
into practice in the schools, but their rhetoric gave permission for both the assault on the academic curriculum and the installation of a diluted and vocationalized alternative.

There is also the matter of curriculum differentiation. Here the story is a bit
more complex. Pedagogical progressives have generally taken a strong position
in favor of education for democracy and equality, which put them at odds with
the stratified vision of school and society that emerged both from administrative progressives and from educational consumers. This democratic view of ed-

ucation was central to the work of Dewey and Counts, but it also provided an important rationale for Kilpatrick's work. For example, in his seminal essay "The Project Method," he argued that "as the purposeful act is . . . the typical unit of the worthy life in a democratic society, so also should it be made the typical unit of school procedure," since, in its absence, the student is faced with "servile acceptance of others' purposes."[43]

However, in spite of their opposition to the idea of stratified schooling, the pedagogical progressives in the ed school did not launch an all-out assault on the stratified curriculum that developed during the first half of the twentieth century. One reason for this was ideological. Since they dismissed curriculum as a matter of secondary importance and asserted the primacy of pedagogical process, the precise form of the curriculum at this point was not terribly important to them. Curriculum served as a background resource, to be drawn upon as needed to supply material for classroom forays in inquiry learning that originated in the interest and experience of the students. Any old curriculum could serve this purpose. The differentiated curriculum of the administrative progressives was thus only a matter of background noise, easily ignored. Curriculum became a problem only at the point when it imposed itself on the learning process in the late twentieth century, through the standards movement and its fixed requirements for knowledge acquisition backed up by high-stakes testing, a reform that has stirred strong opposition from ed school progressives. Another reason for this was structural. As noted, education professors by the 1940s found themselves trapped in the role of supplying teachers and administrators for a stratified system of schooling that was not of their making. The administrative progressives had established this system, and the pedagogical progressives in the ed school had no power to do anything but adapt to it and prepare people to enter it. These same conditions continue to shape the way ed schools approach their work; let me explain.

ED SCHOOLS DIDN'T EVEN DO IT TO THEMSELVES

Although the rhetoric of ed schools is unrelentingly progressive, their practice is not. At these institutions both the production of research and the preparation of teachers take place under a veneer of pedagogical progressivism, but in each case the internal machinery supports the operation of the social-efficiency structure of schooling, with one supplying its technology and the other its technicians.

First, consider the *practice of research*. At the end of her authoritative history of American educational research, Ellen Condliffe Lagemann concludes that this research took an early direction whose legacy for education is "deeply troubling":

> To look at the history of education research is to discover a field that was really quite shapeless circa 1890 and quite well shaped by roughly 1920. By that date, research in education had become more technical than liberal. It was more narrowly instrumental than genuinely investigatory in an open-ended, playful way. The field's applied emphasis had resulted in the marginalization of most subject matter that did not appear to be immediately "relevant" to the professional concerns of school administrators and, to an extent, teachers. Useable knowledge, quite narrowly defined, had become the sine qua non of educational study. Equally important, the psychology that had come to stand at the core of educational scholarship was not only excessively and narrowly behaviorist, but also distinctly more individualistic than social.[44]

What emerged from this foundation was the tradition of research on teacher effectiveness that became the dominant form of educational research in the twentieth century, as Alan Tom and Lee Shulman show in their respective surveys of the subject.[45] Work in that tradition focused on establishing the causal connection between particular actions by the teacher and student achievement on subject matter tests. This kind of technical, instrumental, and behaviorist research was far removed from the humanist, exploratory, and interest-based vision of education that was promoted in progressive rhetoric, but it fit comfortably within the structure of socially efficient education that was put in place by the administrative progressives. Likewise, its concentrated focus on the teacher flew in the face of the progressive rhetoric of child-centered education, but it accorded well with the reality of teacher-centered practice in public school classrooms.

By the end of the century, this type of work was under fire from other researchers, who advanced alternative forms of research that were less prescriptive and more interpretive, and that fostered a pedagogy that was more progressive.[46] But a good case can be made that the instrumental approach is still alive and well and continues to occupy a strong position in the field. In his review of the research literature Robert Floden finds considerable "evidence that research on teaching effects is vital and highly regarded."[47] A key reason for this is that "many policymakers and funding agencies are now asking researchers for more evidence regarding effects on student learning. Although the complexity of the education system often makes such effects difficult to identify, the demands for evidence will encourage investigators to contrive research designs that will deliver."[48] The No Child Left Behind Act (PL 107–10), signed into federal law in

2001, included language mandating scientifically based research to support programs with proven effectiveness, which led to the establishment of guidelines for authoritative research about effective methods in the Education Department's What Works Clearinghouse,[49] and which also quickly prompted the education research community to come up with its own defense of *Scientific Research in Education*.[50]

This is a good case for showing how it is that structural imperatives trump rhetorical commitments for educational researchers. As ed professors we may prefer the progressive approach to teaching and learning, but all of the mandates and incentives from policymakers, school administrators, and funding agencies line up behind a demand for research that shows "what works"[51]—in particular what techniques and curricula demonstrably raise the scores of students in tests of academic achievement. Throughout the twentieth century, progressive-minded researchers have dutifully lined up to play a supporting role in this effort.

We can see a similar pattern in the *practice of teacher preparation*. As the university education school, in its formative phase in the early twentieth century, adapted itself organizationally to the emerging structure of professional roles in the school systems created by the administrative progressives, it traded critical distance for lasting functionality. As Michael Katz suggested, education professors could have treated their field as a discipline, establishing for themselves a role in generating innovative ideas about education and in providing independent criticism of the way things are done in schools.[52] But this would have meant ceding the main work of preparing educational practitioners to the teachers colleges, thus permanently confining university ed schools to the margins of the burgeoning educational enterprise. So instead, the education faculty adopted the model of the professional school, organized around the production of practitioners for the socially efficient school system, a strategy that opened up large and lasting opportunities for creating faculty positions and attracting research dollars. This gave ed schools a sizeable, visible, and enduring role in the vast arena of public education, but it locked them firmly in place within the existing educational structure. Their critical stance toward education was reduced to a pedagogical progressivism that necessarily remained primarily rhetorical, while they focused their instructional efforts on preparing students to work in the real world of schools.

Thus in the preparation of teachers as well in the production of research, structural realities triumphed over rhetorical ideals for the American ed school. As ed professors, we may prefer to produce teachers who will carry out the progressive ideal of student-centered, integrated, and inquiry-based learning, but we have accommodated ourselves, however reluctantly, to the role pushed on us, which is to prepare teachers who will fit into the existing pattern of teacher-centered, differentiated, and curriculum-driven instruction in schools.

One useful way to think about this tension between rhetoric and practice in teacher education is to consider it in light of two archetypal approaches to professional education identified by Mary Kennedy.[53] In examining practices in a wide array of professional education programs, she finds that some programs focus on giving professionals specific knowledge about what works whereas others focus on giving them general skills for figuring out problems on their own: "One [strategy] is to develop, codify, and give to students as much knowledge as possible—knowledge about every conceivable situation they might ever encounter—so that they will be prepared for the maximum possible variety of situations. The other strategy is to prepare students to think on their feet, giving them both reasoning skills and strategies for analyzing and interpreting new situations, until they are sufficiently flexible and adaptable to accommodate the variety of situations they are likely to encounter."[54] Medicine and engineering adopt the first approach, law and architecture the second.

For our purposes, what is most interesting about these approaches to professional education is the way they parallel the old debate between traditional and progressive approaches to teaching. Thus for teacher preparation, the progressive approach is to lead teachers to become reflective practitioners, in Schön's phrase,[55] rather than storehouses of professional knowledge. This is Dewey's argument in the essay "The Relation of Theory to Practice in Education"[56] and it has been the argument of progressive writers on the subject ever since.[57] Although teacher educators talk longingly about the reflective approach to professional preparation, their practice heads the other way. As Kennedy explains, "Teacher preparation has not concentrated on codified, prescriptive knowledge to the degree that medicine and engineering have, but it tends to lean in this direction more than in the direction of independent thought and analysis. Teacher education courses are organized around disciplines, called *foundations,* and around techniques of practice, usually called *methods.*"[58] This knowledge-based tendency in the practice of teacher education is in turn grounded in the instrumental knowledge produced by educational researchers: "Now, a body of research findings on effective teacher behaviors has developed that could form the basis for a more prescriptive teacher education curriculum (Brophy & Good, 1986; Gage, 1977, 1985; B. O. Smith, 1980. Watts, 1982). In light of these new findings, teacher education is experiencing a new movement toward codified and more prescriptive content in its curriculum (Evertson, Hawley, & Zlotnick, 1984; Gage, 1985; Gideonse, 1986)."[59]

Education professors, therefore, are a bundle of contradictions. We retain our rhetorical commitment to progressivism, but our work as researchers and teacher educators bespeaks a practical commitment to instrumentalism. We talk about inquiry, but we do what works. As a result, we can be attacked for inconsistency, but we can't be blamed for imposing progressivism on schools when we can't even implement it in our own practice.

ED SCHOOLS ARE EASY TO BLAME, BUT THE FAULT LIES ELSEWHERE

Ed schools are an obvious and easy target for anyone who wants to place blame for problems with American education. They're obvious because they are so clearly in the middle of things, preparing teachers and producing research, purveying the talk that educators talk. They're easy because their social standing is so low, because their progressive rhetoric is so close to self-parody, and because their weakness leaves them in no position to fight back effectively.

The problem with this situation, as I have been pointing out repeatedly, is that blaming ed schools for these problems is simply wrong. We education professors love to talk like John Dewey, but, like everyone else in education, we walk in the path of Edward Thorndike. If our progressive rhetoric were faithfully put into practice in American classrooms, the impact on teaching and learning might well be negative in significant ways. I agree with critics that the progressive emphasis on classroom process over curriculum content and on discovery by students over instruction by teachers could indeed be harmful to teaching and learning. But these critics can relax. Our impact has been minimal. The mistake that the critics have made is in taking us at our word instead of watching us in action, in listening to teachers talk about their practice instead of observing what they do in the classroom.

If critics paid less attention to educational speech and more attention to educational behavior, they would notice something striking: The educational traditionalists have already won.[60] Instruction in American schools is overwhelmingly teacher-centered; classroom management is the teacher's top priority; traditional school subjects dominate the curriculum; textbooks and teacher talk are the primary means of delivering this curriculum; learning consists of recalling what texts and teachers say; tests measure how much of this students have learned; and the tests drive the classroom process. In short, traditional methods of teaching and learning are in control of American education. The progressives lost.

Of course, the more thoughtful critics blame ed schools for more than promoting progressive methods. As we saw with E. D. Hirsch and Diane Ravitch (who call themselves liberal traditionalists, emphasizing a belief in liberal education and traditional subject matter),[61] they charge that ed schools are undermining the educational foundation of democracy, by discounting academic learning and by differentiating access to knowledge. These are serious charges, and the evidence suggests that both of these tendencies are present in American schools. But, as I have shown, ed schools were not in a position to bring about these outcomes. Instead, the two factors that were directly responsible for dumbing down learning and stratifying curriculum were administrative progressivism and consumerism.

THE BAD NEWS: ED SCHOOLS ARE ALSO
TOO WEAK TO PROVIDE MUCH HELP FOR
AMERICAN EDUCATION

The good news about ed schools is that they are not powerful enough to do much harm to American education, despite all the heinous crimes that are often attributed to them. But the bad news is that they are also not powerful enough to do much good for a system of schooling that could really use their help. As we have seen, the central functions of the research-oriented ed school—teacher education, knowledge production, and researcher training— are extraordinarily difficult, and thus it is not surprising, though nonetheless disappointing, that the ed school does not carry them out very well. To fail at an important and difficult task carries a certain nobility, but it would be more gratifying for those of us who work within this institution—and a lot more helpful for American schools and American society—if the ed school were actually to succeed. I won't recap the trials of carrying out these functions; instead I will focus on several areas where ed schools are well positioned to make a significant contribution but where their lowly status and their attachment to the romantic rhetoric of progressivism are likely to vitiate that contribution. One such area is the need for clarity in the current debate over major issues of educational reform, including standards, vouchers, and teacher training; another is the need for greater use value for the learning fostered and knowledge produced in universities; a third is the need for a closer connection between theory and practice in education at all levels.

Contributing to Current Debates
about Educational Policy

One would logically expect that, given its institutional position, the ed school would be the obvious place to turn for advice about important issues in the current politics of American education. But then that would only happen if one could ignore all its troubles, which is simply impossible. Consider a series of prominent issues facing American education at the start of the twenty-first century.

STANDARDS

The most durable and consequential reform movement at the turn of this century is the one that seeks to impose standards on the schools. The primary issue in this movement is to hold schools accountable for producing a desired level of academic performance, and the mechanisms it has introduced to carry out this goal are both numerous and varied. There are efforts to establish curriculum guidelines for subject coverage, grade by grade, in each of the fifty states, and efforts to set standards for achievement at crucial points during students' elementary and secondary careers through some form of standardized testing. States issue report cards for local school districts and individual schools, the federal government issues comparisons of performance across states, and international bodies make comparisons across countries. Professional groups for each of the major subject areas are involved.

A bewildering collection of acronyms provide a shorthand for all the entities involved. Focusing on testing are NAEP (National Assessment of Educational Progress), ETS (Educational Testing Service), ACT (American College Test), and TIMSS (Third International Mathematics and Science Study); focusing on teachers and teacher education are NEA (National Education Association), AFT (American Federation of Teachers), NBPTS (National Board for Professional Teaching Standards), NCATE (National Council for Accreditation of Teacher Education), TEAC (Teacher Education Accreditation Council), NCTAF (National Commission on Teaching and America's Future), and NCREST (National Center for Restructuring Education, Schools, and Teaching); at the interstate level we have NGA (National Governors Association), CCSSO (Council of Chief State School Officers), and INTASC (Interstate New Teacher Assessment and Support Consortium). And this doesn't even count all the standards-oriented organizations that have been established by the various interest groups, political organizations, and think tanks.

In any other country but the United States, you would naturally expect that education schools would be welcome to join these other groups in the conversation about educational standards, drawing on their experience and expertise to make a significant contribution by sorting through the complex issues that arise from all that reform activity. But, as we have seen, there are several factors that limit the credibility of ed schools around issues of standards in this country. First, for many supporters of standards, ed schools represent the problem and not the solution. It is the latter's perceived lack of standards for teaching and learning that has been stated as a primary reason for the necessity of a standards movement.[62] Second, the research carried out by ed schools is seen as having only limited ability to shed light on these problems, because of questions about its validity and reliability. But most of all, the problem is that too many people in the standards movement feel that they already know what the ed schools will say on the subject: Education professors will spout the usual line of progressive ideology. We will say that the standards movement will kill off students' interest and stifle their motivation to learn; that it will substitute formal learning for authentic learning; that it will reinforce extrinsic rewards at the expense of intrinsic rewards for learning; and that the real solution to the learning problem in American schools is to move in the direction of student-centered, inquiry-based, experience-rich pedagogy, as we have been recommending for nearly the past hundred years to little effect.

The sad thing about the way the standards movement bypasses the ed school is that the latter really does have something valuable to offer. The progressive critique of the standards movement exposes some significant problems that this movement can and does generate for teaching and learning in schools. For example, the standards movement does raise incentives to learn, but it manages this by emphasizing the punitive over the positive—increasing the consequences of failure for the student and the school without doing much to increase the rewards for success—and by emphasizing the extrinsic over the intrinsic. As a result, it may improve short-term performance on tests, but at the cost of killing off student interest in books and learning in the long run. It is easy to ridicule a progressive like Kilpatrick, but the questions he asks in the middle of his "Project Method" seem apt ones to direct toward the standards movement: "How many children at the close of a course decisively shut the book and say, 'Thank gracious, I am through with that!' How many people 'get an education' and yet hate books and hate to learn?"[63] Moreover, though the standards movement may increase the performance of the least able teachers, by compelling them to hew closely to a prescriptive curriculum guide and teach to a high-stakes test, this may end up stifling the initiative and spirit of the most talented teachers, thus restricting the possibilities of learning in their classrooms and even driving these teachers out of the profession.

Ed school professors are indeed making these kinds of cogent critiques of the standards movement right now, but these arguments are largely falling on deaf ears. We've said it all too often before. Our credibility is undermined by the sense that we are reciting a creed rather than analyzing a particular form of practice. We often sound as if we are attacking academic learning in general rather than critiquing a particular way of establishing curriculum guidelines; as if we are opposing any form of performance goals for teaching and learning rather than opposing particular forms of high-stakes testing; and as if we are resisting any effort to limit teacher autonomy or student initiative rather than resisting only those limits that might undermine a student's engagement in learning.

SCHOOL CHOICE

Another major reform issue at the turn of the century revolves around proposals for school choice, charter schools, and school vouchers. The basic idea behind the various forms of the choice concept is to loosen the current monopoly of the local public school district over the form and delivery of education, and to vest some degree of discretion over which school to attend and some degree of control over this school with the families of students. The roots and goals of the movement are complex. Alternatively, it is a political reform, aimed at reducing the role of government and increasing individual liberty; an ideological reform, aimed at replacing democratic politics with capitalist markets as the principle of control for schools; an organizational reform, aimed at replacing a dysfunctional school bureaucracy with a lean, efficient, and responsive mode of local school management; a consumerist reform, aimed at replacing both politics and bureaucracy in schools by making the educational consumer king; a social justice reform, aimed at giving minority inner-city parents a way out of school systems that are failing to educate their children; and a pedagogical reform, aimed at liberating schools from domination by educational ideas that are—take your pick—too progressive or liberal-humanist or racist or multicultural or monocultural or traditional, in favor of educational approaches that meet the needs of particular communities and subcultures.

Ed schools bring a lot of expertise to this issue. As the primary place where professional educators are trained and educational research is carried out, they know a lot about how schools work, how they are organized and governed, how they are managed, and how well or badly they educate students. Drawing on this expertise, education professors have been weighing in on the debates about school choice from the very beginning. But several familiar factors undermine the credibility and effectiveness of our intervention. There is the old problem of the questionable validity and reliability of educational research upon which professors draw for authority in the debate. And there is another old problem, the education professors' status deficiency, which often makes anyone else more credible on educational issues.

However, the biggest problem affecting the credibility of our views on this issue is our identification with the educational establishment. This identification is puzzling to most education faculty members. We see ourselves as progressive reformers who are constantly storming the gates of the education establishment, demanding student-centered reforms that never seem to be welcomed into the fundamental practice of the schools. Our link to the status quo is a consequence of the problem that Michael Katz identified in the direction taken by the university ed school early in its history.[64] In the period before the Second World War, the ed school evolved from its role as a critical commentator on education to a role as a cog in the educational machinery, when it took on the job of preparing people to fill the various professional positions within the existing structure of schools. This functionality gave the ed school an enduring place in the university, but that put it in a weak position to act as an agent for reform. The progressive culture of the ed school is in many ways only a veneer covering an institutional structure that is deeply embedded in the existing organization and governance of schooling, and this makes it look, to the public and the policymaker alike, as part of the problem that the choice movement is trying to cure. The fact that education professors overwhelmingly stand in opposition to school choice in most of its forms does nothing to disabuse outsiders of this opinion.

TEACHER EDUCATION

The debate about reforming teacher education poses a similar challenge to the credibility of the ed school. The issues underlying the debate include a concern for improving the quality of teachers recruited to and retained in the profession and a concern for improving the knowledge and skill of teachers, on the theory that any improvement in student learning is only going to be possible if preceded by changes in the recruitment and preparation of teachers. On one side is a group of reformers who argue for establishing alternative forms of teacher certification. Approaches along these lines include reducing certification requirements; shifting requirements away from the ed school and toward subject area departments; establishing programs of teacher preparation in independent agencies, such as Teach For America; allowing alternative routes to certification that are faster and involve less coursework; and ending state certification entirely, leaving it up to school systems to hire anyone they consider a qualified teacher. On the other side are groups like NCATE, INTASC, NBPTS, and NCTAF, who seek to fortify and extend the existing system for preparing and certifying teachers. These groups advocate measures such as defining the kinds of knowledge and skill that prospective teachers need to acquire in order to teach effectively; using program accreditation to make sure that teacher education programs focus on transmitting these capabilities; using testing and the certification process to make sure that prospective teachers demonstrate competency in these areas before entering the classroom; and using board certification to set standards for optimal practice among practicing teachers.

As the primary locus of teacher preparation currently, ed schools are both naturally expert and naturally suspect in speaking on these issues. Who knows more about teacher education? And yet who has more incentive to preserve the ed school's role in it? As a result, the proponents of alternative routes for teacher certification are almost entirely drawn from groups outside the ed school, whereas the supporters of reinforced preparation of teachers within the current structure are almost entirely drawn from the ed school community. Those in the alternative routes camp can therefore easily discount the ideas on teacher education coming from the ed school, which is seen both as partisan and as part of the problem.

Producing Use Value over Exchange Value

There is another area in which the ed school could be in a good position to contribute something important to American education but probably won't—by modeling a way that universities can focus on enhancing the use value of student learning and of the research knowledge that the ed school produces. A good case can be made for the proposition that American education—particularly higher education—has long placed a greater emphasis on the exchange value of the educational experience than on its use value. That is, what consumers have sought and universities have sold in the educational marketplace is not the content of the education received at the university (what the student actually learns there) but the form of this education (what the student can get in exchange for a university degree). From this perspective, the key educational product is usable credentials rather than usable knowledge.[65]

The evidence supporting this conclusion is strong. Schools and colleges award degrees based on credit hours that students have accumulated (seat time) rather than on the particular quantity of knowledge that these students actually acquired along the way. (American education has always been reluctant to demand that students prove what they have learned in order to be awarded a diploma.) Employers screen potential employees based on what degrees they have earned rather than on what they know or what they can do, blandly assuming that credentials certify competence without ever trying to validate this assumption. (How many employers ask, or care, about what a student learned in tenth-grade plane geometry class? Or what a B+ in a college course on colonial history shows about a candidate's ability to be an effective mid-level manager?) And students, knowing both of these facts, tend to focus their energy less on learning content than on acquiring the necessary educational commodities (grades, credits, degrees) that can be cashed in for a good job.

One result of this is that universities have a strong incentive to promote research more than teaching, for publications raise the visibility and prestige of the institution much more effectively than does instruction (which is less visible and more difficult to measure). And a prestigious faculty raises the exchange value of the university's diploma, independently of whatever is learned in the process of acquiring this diploma.

The process of marketing the university degree is not one that leaves an honored position for the ed school. Since the latter's primary form of knowledge production is focused on soft knowledge about practical problems—the production of nonauthoritative use value—it is not in a good position to contribute to the university's marketing effort (which relies heavily on the more prestigious work in hard/pure disciplinary fields). And since the ed school's primary instructional programs focus on providing students with useful knowledge and skill for application in low-status professions in schools, and since its own institutional prestige is low, it is not in a position to offer credentials with high exchange value that will add to the university's luster.

From this perspective, then, there is little that the education school can do that will boost the marketability of the university degree, but instead it seems to exert a steady downward drag on this degree's exchange value. As a result, the ed school is useful to have around, as a way of increasing enrollments and supporting academic departments, but it is also somewhat embarrassing, because of the way it potentially undercuts the university's reputation for high academic standards and high-status knowledge.

What all of this suggests is that education schools are not at all well positioned to play the university status game. They are in a true no-win situation: Education schools serve the wrong clientele and produce the wrong knowledge; they bear the mark of their modest origins and their traditionally weak programs; and yet they are pressured by everyone from their graduates' employers to their university colleagues to stay the way they are. If we didn't have education schools, we would probably want to invent them in much their current form, since they fulfill so many needs for so many constituencies.

But consider for a moment what would happen if we decide to abandon the status perspective in establishing the value of higher education, the perspective that American universities and their customers cling to so obsessively. What if we choose to focus on the social role of the education school rather than its social position in the academic firmament? What if we examine what this institution does rather than how it is viewed? What if we consider the possibility that the education school—toiling away in the dark basement of academic ignominy—in an odd way has actually been liberated by this condition from the constraints of academic status attainment? Is it possible that the ed school may have actually stumbled on a form of academic practice that could serve as a useful model for the rest of the university?

Perhaps not, given the continuing all-too-obvious weaknesses of this institution. But what does seem to be true is that the ed school, through the peculiar contingencies of its history, occupies a unique position within American higher education from which we can gain insight into some of the key problems facing the university in the twenty-first century. It is a useful construct in a kind of discrepant case analysis—something on the order of an anti-college—which allows us to think about what a university college might look like that was not obsessed with the status game and the marketing of exchange value. Such an institution might well decide to do a lot of what education schools currently try to do. Ironically, in light of the chronic trouble with ed schools, these schools may in some ways (even if by accident) be better positioned to meet the environmental demands of this decade than are many of those other colleges that draw more respect. Let me explain.

First a disclaimer: The university status game is as American as the dream of getting ahead, so raw credentialism is not likely to go away soon. Neither is it likely that the university will stop selling degrees on the basis of institutional prestige or grounding this prestige in the production of abstract research rather than instruction in usable knowledge. In the current political and fiscal environment, however, there is an increasing danger that someone will stand up and make a persuasive case that the emperor is wearing no clothes: that there is no necessary connection between university degrees and student knowledge or between professorial production and public benefit; that students need to learn something when they are in the university; that the content of what they learn should have some form of intrinsic value; that professors need to work on developing ideas that have a degree of practical significance; and that the whole university enterprise needs to find ways to justify the huge public and private investment that it currently requires.

There is an element of the confidence game in the market-based pattern of academic life, since the whole structure depends on a network of interlocking beliefs that are tenuous at best: the belief that graduates of prestigious universities know more and can do more than other graduates; the belief that prestigious faculty make for a good university; and the belief that prestigious research makes for a good faculty. The problem is, of course, that when confidence in any of these beliefs is shaken, the whole structure can come tumbling down. And when it does, the only recourse is to rebuild on the basis of substance rather than reputation, demonstrations of competence rather than symbols of merit.

By all accounts, this dreaded moment is at hand. There are currently a large number of looming challenges to the credibility of the current pattern of university life, and not all are coming from conservatives. While the latter are primarily concerned about radical professors and multicultural curriculum, the kind of challenges I am referring to derive from sources that are more structural than ideological. One such source is the current fiscal crisis of state and local governments. Another is the growing political demand for accountability and utility. A third is the intensification of competition in higher education.

With the relentless demand for lower taxes and reduced public services that characterizes American political life in the new century, the university is hard pressed to justify a high level of public funding on grounds of prestige alone. Instead, it is increasingly being asked to demonstrate the dividends that it returns on the public funds invested in it. State governments are demanding that universities produce measurable beneficial outcomes for students, businesses, and other taxpaying members of the community. And, by withholding higher state subsidies, states are throwing universities into a highly competitive situation in which they vie with other institutions in their market area to see who can attract the most student tuition dollars and the most outside research grants and who can keep the tightest control over internal costs.

In this kind of environment, education schools actually have a certain advantage over many other colleges and departments in the university. Unlike other colleges across campus, they offer traditionally low-cost programs that are explicitly designed to be useful, both to students and to the community. They give students practical preparation for and access to a large sector of employment opportunities. Their research focuses on the problems and needs of education, an area about which Americans worry a great deal. They offer consulting services and policy advice to teachers, schools, and school systems trying to work their way through the array of pressing problems facing them. In short, their teaching, research, and service activities are all potentially useful to students and community alike. How many colleges of arts and letters can say the same?

However, before we get carried away with the counterintuitive notion that ed schools might serve as a model for a university under fire, we need to consider that these browbeaten institutions are still not likely to have much success or gain much credit for their efforts to serve useful social purposes, in spite of the current political saliency of such efforts. No one has ever gone broke in American education betting on the value of educational form over educational content, and no one has gotten rich selling education with low-brow use value. We have always measured the performance of educational institutions by their ability to open social opportunities for their graduates rather than their ability to provide usable knowledge. Doing the right thing—by focusing on social need and useful learning in a market-driven and consumer-oriented educational environment like this one—is more likely to draw punishment than reward. A good example of this is the difficulty that faces any units within the university that try to walk the border between theory and practice.

Working the Border between Theory and Practice

Ed schools provide a potentially priceless service by focusing their energies, both as educators and as researchers, in working the border between theory and practice. This is not a common situation for an American educational institution, in part because such a balance is difficult to maintain, and in part because those who try are resoundingly punished for their efforts.

Traditionally, the university's peculiar area of expertise is theory. Removed from the press of events and from the concern for the particular, the university professor's intellectual contribution arises from the ongoing effort to generalize and explain, to construct theory. In contrast, the public school is a realm of practice. Confronted with a relentless demand to do something right now to meet the special needs of a particular group of students, teachers have to focus on constructing an effective mode of practice in the classroom. The situation, however, is more complicated than this. For the university is also a realm of social practice, as faculty members work at developing their professorial craft, and instructional practice in the school is in turn guided by theory, since teaching without theoretical backing would be nothing but mindless activity. So the difference between the two institutional realms is more a matter of emphasis (with the university focusing more on theory and the school on practice) and of context (with the university leaning toward the universal and the school toward the particular).

A primary function of the education school is to provide a border crossing between these two countries, each with its own distinctive language and culture and with its own peculiar social structure. When an ed school is working well, it presents a model of fluid interaction between university and school and encourages others on both sides of the divide to follow suit. What this means intellectually is that an ed school must be proficient at developing both theoretical and practical understandings of education and must work vigorously to establish viable links between the two. The ideal is to encourage the development of teachers and other educators who are truly "reflective practitioners,"[66] able to draw on theory to inform their instructional practice. The flip side of this aim is to encourage university professors to become practice-oriented theoreticians, able to draw on issues from practice in their theory building and to produce theories with potential use value.

That is the ideal. But no one would argue that education schools (or any other groups, for that matter) come close to meeting this ideal. The natural tendency (as we saw in the case of doctoral programs in ed schools) is to fall on one side of the border or the other with only weak crossover ability, rather than to hold the middle ground and retain the ability to work well in both domains. The history of the Holmes Group in the 1980s and 1990s is instructive on this point. The deans at leading ed schools, who constituted the membership of the Holmes Group, gave lip service to the ideal spelled out here, but in practice they have expressed total confusion on the subject. In the group's first report (*Tomorrow's Schools*), they argued that the ed school should ground itself thoroughly in the prestige and the scientific knowledge-building of the university and then seek to export both to the schools.[67] But in the third and final report (*Tomorrow's Schools of Education*), they reversed themselves by arguing that the ed school should turn its back on the academic life of the university and bury itself in the world of daily practice within the public school classroom.[68] So in less than a decade, the deans shifted from a position of intellectual imperialism to one of anti-intellectual populism.

At one level, the zigzagging course followed by the Holmes Group just reinforces the standard view that ed schools really don't know what they are doing or where they are going. But at another level, it serves to demonstrate just how difficult it is for an institution to position itself on the border between theory and practice, between the university and the world outside. Life is much more comfortable and responsibilities are much more clear-cut on one side or the other.

Because of their location in the university and their identification with the primary and secondary schools, ed schools have had no real choice over the years but to keep working along the border, but this has meant that they have continued to draw unrelenting fire from both sides. Professors dismiss them as unscholarly and untheoretical while school people dismiss them as impractical and irrelevant. From the university's perspective, colleges of education are trade schools, which supply vocational training but no academic curriculum; however, students complain that ed school courses are too abstract and academic, and they demand more field experience and fewer course requirements. On the one side, ed school research is seen as too soft, too applied, and totally lacking in academic rigor; but on the other side, it is seen as serving only a university agenda and being largely useless to the schools.

Of course, it may be that both sides are right. Attend enough annual meetings of the American Educational Research Association, and you may conclude that the work produced by educational researchers is often lacking in both intellectual merit and practical application. But there is something noble and necessary about the way that the denizens of ed schools continue their quixotic quest for a workable balance between theory and practice. If only others in the academy would try this vigorously (and, one can only hope, more successfully) to accomplish the marriage of academic elegance and social impact.

The Trouble with Ed Schools Revisited

So where does this leave us in thinking about the poor beleaguered ed school? And what lessons, if any, can be learned from its checkered history?

GUILTY, AS REQUESTED

One lesson is that these institutions really are weak in a number of ways but that much of this weakness is the result of the fact that ed schools did what was demanded of them. They provided mass programs of teacher preparation that did not cost much money or require much time. They put teachers in empty classrooms and drew students into the university. They tried to serve the needs of practitioners in the field. And for all this, they have been soundly punished—by academics and educators and the public alike.

Of course, while the historical adaptability of the ed school is understandable, it is not exactly honorable. Giving in to all of the pressures placed on it allowed the ed school to establish itself as the central institution for preparing the country's teachers and to secure itself a place within the hallowed halls of the university. These outcomes, however, were achieved at considerable cost. Instructionally, ed schools too often provide an academically thin and professionally ineffective form of preparation for teachers, which is not adequate to the urgent needs of American education. And intellectually, they too often provide a form of knowledge production that is neither scholarly nor useful.

STATUS MATTERS

Another lesson is that it doesn't pay to be a parvenu in the university status order. A key to the trouble with ed schools is that history assigned them a lowly location in the academic hierarchy, and this means that no one is willing to cut them a break. As Joanies-come-lately to the university, ed schools carry the indelible stigma of the normal school and of the working-class women who have entered the semiprofession of teaching, about which Americans are so ambivalent. Much of the scorn that has rained on the ed school is the result of its lowly status rather than any demonstrable deficiencies in the actual educational role it has played.

But much of this scorn has been well grounded. Institutional status has a circular quality about it, which means that predictions of high or low institutional quality become self-fulfilling. The high standing of the university provides it with a protective cover beneath which excellent teaching and research can potentially incubate and prosper (even if this opportunity is often sacrificed on the altar of credentialism). The umbrella of high status allows institutions the time and space to work things out in relative privacy, without being subjected to unwanted interventions or corrosive criticism. At the same time, however, the education school is clearly lacking such an umbrella. Its low social standing denies it adequate protection and therefore subjects its programs and research to an acid rain of extramural criticism and meddling intervention that never gives it the chance to grow.

BEING RIGHT IS NO EXCUSE

In some ways, ed schools have been doing things right. They have wrestled vig-orously (if not always to good effect) with the problems of public education, an area that is of deep concern to most citizens. This has meant tackling social problems of great complexity and great practical importance, but unfortu-nately the university does not place much value on the production of this kind of messy, indeterminate, soft, and applied knowledge. It has taken on the diffi-cult task of trying to prepare people for a remarkably complex job that most people consider easy, without even being granted adequate control over the preparation process.

Oddly enough, the rest of the university could learn a lot from the example of the ed school. The question, however, is whether they will see this example as positive or negative. If academics consider this story in light of the current po-litical and fiscal climate, then the ed school could serve as a model, which illus-trates how the university can meet growing public expectations for it to teach things that students need to know and to generate knowledge that produces benefits for the community.

But it seems more likely that academics will consider this story a cautionary tale about how risky and unrewarding such a strategy can be. After all, educa-tion schools have demonstrated that they are neither very successful at accom-plishing the marriage of theory and practice nor well rewarded for trying. In fact, the odor of failure and disrespect continues to linger in the air around these institutions. In light of such considerations, academics are likely to feel more comfortable placing their chips in the university's traditional confidence game, continuing to bet on the pursuit of academic status and market educa-tional credentials. And from this perspective, the example of the ed school is one they should studiously avoid.

Notes

CHAPTER 1: INTRODUCTION

1. Bebow, 2003.
2. Bebow, 2003.
3. Rose and Gallup, 2001.
4. Koerner, 1963, pp. 17–18.
5. Koerner, 1963, p. xii.
6. Koerner, 1963, p. xii.
7. Warren, 1985, p. 5.
8. Lanier & Little, 1986.
9. Lanier & Little, 1986, p. 530.
10. Lanier & Little, 1986, p. 531.
11. Lanier & Little, 1986, p. 535, quoting Ducharme & Agne, 1982, p. 33.
12. Lanier & Little, 1986, p. 540.
13. Lanier & Little, 1986, p. 549.
14. The Holmes Partnership defines itself as "a network of universities, schools, community agencies and national professional organizations working in partnership to create high quality professional development and significant school renewal to improve teaching and learning for all children" (Holmes Partnership, 2003).
15. In recent years, Randall Collins (*The Credential Society*) has been the most prominent sociologist pursuing this line of argument. Other people working

in this vein include Ivar Berg (*Education and Jobs: The Great Training Robbery*), Lester Thurow and other economists (in work on the labor queue and job signaling), Michael W. Sedlak (*Selling Students Short*), and David Brown (*Degrees of Control*). My own work has also focused on these issues—in a 1988 book (*The Making of an American High School: The Credentials Market and the Central High School of Philadelphia, 1838–1939*) and my 1997 book (*How to Succeed in School without Really Learning: The Credentials Race in American Education*).

16. There is a small and eclectic but intellectually rich literature to draw upon for support of this argument about the peculiar role that education schools are called upon to play. For example, there are Dan Lortie (*Schoolteacher*), Willard Waller (*The Sociology of Teaching*), Philip Cusick (*The Educational System*), David Cohen ("Teaching Practice"), and John Dewey ("The Relation of Theory to Practice in Education") on the distinctive nature of teaching as a practice. There is Arlie Hochschild (*The Managed Heart*) on the nature of emotional labor. And there is Tony Becher (*Academic Tribes and Territories*) on the different epistemological and organizational structures of knowledge production in different academic fields.

17. Consider, for example, the studies by Abbott (1988), Larson (1977), and Witz (1992).

18. See Trow (1988) and Jencks & Riesman (1968).

CHAPTER 2: TEACHER ED IN THE PAST

1. This chapter is a revised version of a paper that was previously published under the title "The Lowly Status of Teacher Education in the U.S.: The Impact of Markets and the Implications for Reform" in Nobuo K. Shimihara and Ivan Z. Holowinsky, eds., *Teacher Education in Industrialized Nations* (New York: Garland, 1995), pp. 41–85. Reprinted by permission. I first explored ideas about the relationship between markets and teacher education in a lecture delivered at the conference Continuity and Change in Teacher Education (University of Western Ontario, 1991) and in an article for *Kappan* (1994). An early version of this chapter was presented at the Rutgers International Seminar on Education in 1994. I am grateful to William Firestone for his helpful comments at that seminar. I am particularly grateful to Andrew Gitlin for his insights about many of the issues raised in this chapter, which emerged during our intensive collaboration on a paper about the early history of teacher education; that paper was presented at the annual meeting of the American Educational Research Association in New Orleans, 1994.

2. Books: Borrowman, 1953; Clifford & Guthrie, 1988; Herbst, 1989a; Goodlad, Soder, & Sirotnik, 1990a; Levin, 1994. Articles: Borrowman, 1971; Urban, 1990; Warren, 1985; Johnson, 1987; Clifford, 1986; Herbst, 1980 and 1989b. Chapters in books: Clifford & Guthrie, 1988; Johnson, 1989; Herbst, 1989b; Ginsburg, 1988; Liston & Zeichner, 1991; Tom, 1984; Goodlad, 1990.

3. Weber, 1968; Collins, 1979; Marx, 1867–94/1967.

4. I am grateful to Tom Popkewitz for clarifying the difference between my use of the term and the usage in contemporary critical theory.

5. Labaree, 1988.

6. Trow, 1988, and, for example, Collins, 1979, and Brown, 1995.

7. Warren, 1985, p. 7; Sedlak & Schlossman, 1986, table 11.
8. Quoted in Sedlak, 1989, p. 261.
9. Sedlak, 1989, p. 262.
10. Some assign this honor to Samuel Hall, who founded a normal school in 1823 in Concord, Vermont (Borrowman, 1971).
11. Borrowman, 1965, p. 65.
12. Borrowman, 1971, p. 71.
13. Elsbree, 1939, p. 152.
14. Borrowman, 1971, p. 70.
15. Sedlak, 1989, p. 266; the quotation is from Cook, 1927, p. 3.
16. Sedlak, 1989, p. 266.
17. Herbst, 1989a.
18. None of this should be taken to mean that the normal school failed to provide anyone with an adequate professional education. As I have suggested elsewhere (Labaree, 1997a, chap. 7), a small number of women and men in the nineteenth century acquired an educational preparation at the normal school that served them very well in their later careers.
19. See Labaree (1997a) for a full description of the social efficiency and social mobility functions.
20. Hartz, 1955, p. 62.
21. Trow, 1988, p. 17.
22. Trow, 1988, p. 17.
23. As Brown (1995) has shown, this situation was faced by all institutions of higher education in the United States in the late nineteenth century.
24. Collins, 1979, p. 119.
25. Herbst, 1989b, p. 219.
26. Herbst, 1989a, p. 129.
27. Altenbaugh & Underwood, 1990, p. 164.
28. Herbst, 1980, p. 227; quoted in Altenbaugh & Underwood, 1990, p. 143.
29. Herbst, 1989a, p. 6.
30. Herbst, 1989a, p. 135.
31. In spite of all these pressures, however, the normal school provided a significant boost to the job prospects of a small number of its students (mostly women) who ended up pursuing extended careers in education. These alumnae looked back on their normal school experience with fondness and gratitude. (See Labaree, 1997a, chap. 7.)
32. Johnson, 1989, p. 243; quoted in Altenbaugh & Underwood, 1990, p. 149.
33. Altenbaugh & Underwood, 1990, p. 149.
34. Altenbaugh & Underwood, 1990, p. 150.
35. For a fascinating case study of the role that the market played in the evolution of normal schools in Pennsylvania, see Eisenmann (1990).
36. See Labaree (1997a), chap. 9, for a discussion of the many constituencies that benefited from the evolution of the normal school, and that continue to benefit from the role played by the university-based education school.
37. Borrowman, 1971, pp. 71–72.

38. For close examination of the causes and effects of commodification on American education and the impact of the social mobility goal on educational institutions, see Labaree (1988); Collins (1979); Goldman & Tickamyer (1984); and Green (1980).

39. Lanier & Little, 1986; Goodlad, 1990.

40. Herbst, 1989a.

41. Herbst, 1989a, p. 4.

42. Powell, 1980. I discuss the evolution of the ed school within existing universities in chapters 6 and 7.

43. Goodlad, 1990.

44. For a perceptive analysis of the tension between "the academic and the vocational" within university-based schools of education, see chapter 3 of Clifford & Guthrie, 1988.

45. Lanier & Little, 1986, p. 530.

46. National Center for Education Statistics, 1992, table 4; Clifford & Guthrie, 1988, p. 21.

CHAPTER 3: TEACHER ED IN THE PRESENT

1. An early version of this chapter was presented at the PACT (Professional Actions and Cultures of Teaching) Conference in Hong Kong (January 13–14, 1999) and at the International Conference on "The New Professionalism in Teaching: Teacher Education and Teacher Development in a Changing World," sponsored by the Chinese University of Hong Kong (January 15–17, 1999). I am grateful to the students in my fall 1998 doctoral seminar for their helpful comments on an earlier version of this paper. A short version appeared in the *Journal of Teacher Education* (Labaree, 2000a); reprinted by permission.

2. Cohen, 1988, p. 55.

3. Cohen, 1988, p. 57.

4. Fenstermacher, 1990.

5. Dewey, 1933, p. 35; quoted in Jackson, 1986, p. 81.

6. Waller, 1932/1965, pp. 195–96.

7. Cusick, 1992, p. 46.

8. Waller, 1932/1965, p. 196.

9. Sedlak et al., 1986.

10. Powell, Farrar, & Cohen, 1985.

11. Labaree, 1997a.

12. Waller, 1932/1965, p. 383.

13. I am grateful to Brian Vance and other members of my fall 1998 doctoral seminar for reminding me of the potential differences in the teacher-student relationship that arise in educational systems driven by external examinations.

14. Parsons, 1951.

15. Fenstermacher, 1990, p. 137.

16. Dewey, 1904/1964, p. 319.

17. Freedman, 1990, pp. 29–30.

18. I owe thanks to two members of my doctoral seminar—Jo Lesser and Dana Sammons—for pointing out that the emotional link between teachers and students can undermine learning as well as promote it.

19. Hochschild, 1983, p. 147.
20. Hochschild, 1983, p. 35.
21. Waller, 1932/1965, p. 375.
22. Waller, 1932/1965, pp. 383–84.
23. Cohen, 1989.
24. Britzman, 1986, p. 449.
25. Lortie 1975, p. 74.
26. Britzman, 1986, p. 451.
27. Britzman, 1986, p. 451.
28. U.S. Dept. of Education, 1986.
29. U.S. Dept. of Education, 1986, p. v; emphasis in original.
30. U.S. Dept. of Education, 1986, p. 34.
31. U.S. Dept. of Education, 1986, p. 19.
32. U.S. Dept. of Education, 1986, p. 50.
33. Lortie, 1975; Jackson, 1986; Floden & Clark, 1988; Cohen, 1988.
34. Labaree, 1997a, chap. 1.
35. Lortie, 1975, pp. 61–62.
36. Lortie, 1975, p. 62.
37. Fenstermacher, 1990, p. 136.
38. Fenstermacher, 1990, p. 136.

CHAPTER 4: THE PECULIAR PROBLEMS OF DOING EDUCATIONAL RESEARCH

1. An early version of this chapter was presented at the annual PACT (Professional Actions and Cultures of Teaching) Conference (May 1997, Oslo, Norway) and also at the Sixth National Conference in Educational Research (May 1997, Oslo, Norway). I am grateful to the following colleagues at these two conferences for their helpful comments: Andrew Gitlin, Ivor Goodson, Andy Hargreaves, Kirste Klette, Nobuo Shimihara, and Arild Tjeldvoll. I am also grateful to the three *ER* reviewers and Robert Donmoyer, whose comments on an earlier draft proved very helpful. An early version appeared in *Educational Researcher* (Labaree, 1998); reprinted by permission.
2. Becher, 1989.
3. Kuhn, 1970.
4. Labaree, 1997a; 1997b.
5. Shulman, 1986.
6. Toulmin, 1972; Donmoyer, 1985.
7. Merton, 1968.
8. Toulmin, 1972; Donmoyer, 1985.
9. Gage, 1989; National Research Council, 2002.
10. Howe & Eisenhart, 1990.
11. Erickson, 1986.
12. Peshkin, 1993.
13. Berliner, 2002.
14. Berliner, 2002, p. 18.

15. For more on the impact of this distinction between exchange value and use value, see Collins (1979) and Berg (1971). I have developed this argument at greater length in Labaree, 1997a & 1997b.
16. Becher, 1989.
17. Rhoades, 1990.
18. Rhoades, 1990, p. 197.
19. Rhoades, 1990, p. 203.
20. Trow, 1988.
21. Brown, 1995.
22. Cohen & Garet, 1975; Lindblom & Cohen, 1979.
23. For example, see American Educational Research Association (2002), Gage (1963), Travers (1973), Wittrock (1986), Houston (1990), Sikula (1996), Richardson (2001).
24. Gage, 1996, p. 5.
25. Labaree, 1997a, chap. 6. Without acknowledging this, the Holmes Group began to back away from its early embrace of the natural science model for educational research in its second report (Holmes Group, 1990) and dropped it entirely in its third report (Holmes Group, 1995). See Labaree (1995) for a discussion of the sharp changes in argument and rhetoric that characterize these three reports.
26. Judge, 1982.
27. Clifford & Guthrie, 1988.
28. Labaree, 1997b.
29. For example, see Howe (1985).

CHAPTER 5: THE PECULIAR PROBLEMS OF PREPARING EDUCATIONAL RESEARCHERS

1. A very early version of this chapter was presented in a faculty seminar at the College of Education, Michigan State University, November 2000. A later version was presented at a meeting of the NAE-SSRC Joint Committee on Education Research, Social Science Research Council, New York City, June 2002. I benefited considerably from the comments and suggestions I received on both occasions. Other versions were presented at the annual meeting of the American Educational Research Association, April 2003, and the Committee on Research in Education (National Research Council) workshop in November 2003. I am grateful to my doctoral students at MSU, who taught me more about preparing educational researchers than I have been able to put into writing in this book or put into practice in my own teaching. I also appreciate the richly constructive critical comments I received from anonymous reviewers at *Educational Researcher*. A version appeared in *Educational Researcher* (Labaree, 2003); reprinted by permission.
2. Glazer, 1974.
3. Paul & Marfo, 2001.
4. Young, 2001; Metz, 2001; Page, 2001; Pallas, 2001.
5. Wilson, Floden, & Ferrini-Mundy, 2002; Florio-Ruane, 2002; Fenstermacher, 2002; Popkewitz, 2002.
6. National Research Council, 2002, p. 92.
7. National Research Council, 2002, pp. 92–93.

8. NCES, 1998, calculated from table 213.

9. NCES, 1998, table 299.

10. Neumann, Pallas, & Peterson, 1999.

11. Cronbach and Suppes, 1969, p. 215.

12. Neumann, Pallas, & Peterson, 1999.

13. Neumann, Pallas, & Peterson, 1999.

14. GRE Board, 1999, table 1.

15. GRE Board, 1999, footnote, table 4.

16. Calculated from the table on the *U.S. News* (2001) website.

17. The number of graduates from the top education schools is calculated from the table on the *U.S. News* (2000) website, reporting data from 1999; and the total number of education doctorates comes from the *Chronicle of Higher Education* (1999), reporting data from 1998.

18. Neumann, Pallas, & Peterson, 1999, p. 259.

19. Neumann, Pallas, & Peterson, 1999, p. 251.

20. One obvious response to the cultural conflict within doctoral programs in education, then, would be to develop programs that are more nearly bicultural, where the teacher perspective is respected and reinforced and where the research perspective is offered as an additional way to understand education rather than as a preferred substitute. This is what Neumann, Pallas, and Peterson (1999) propose.

21. Tom, 1984.

22. Cohen, 1988; Fenstermacher, 1990; Tom, 1984.

23. Booth, Colomb, & Williams, 1995, sec. 4.1.2.

24. Consider an example. In my teaching I have used a book by Timothy Lensmire, *When Children Write* (1994), which emerged from a dissertation written when the author was a doctoral student at MSU. In it, he talks about his effort to introduce into a fifth grade class a version of writing workshop, which is a form of teaching writing that encourages teachers to act as facilitators, spurring students to write about issues of their own choosing and to present this work to their classmates. Lensmire recounts how this method backfired on him, when some students used writing to assert their status superiority over others, by placing classmates into stories within which they were made to suffer humiliation. The book explores what the experience shows about the nature of teaching: in particular, how a teacher can balance a dedication to student-centered pedagogy in the pursuit of progressive principles with the unavoidable need to exercise power in the classroom in pursuit of moral principles. However, a remarkably common response to this book, by teachers and former teachers who read it in a graduate class, is to condemn the author for bad teaching. The teacher should never have allowed something like this to happen, they say; he should have defined acceptable limits ahead of time, and then none of this would have happened. And furthermore, they ask, why write about an educational failure like this? First he should have gotten this writing workshop thing right and then written about it; that would have been a book worth reading.

25. Cochran-Smith & Lytle, 1990; 1999.

26. Mills, 2002; Stringer & Guba, 1999.

27. Anderson, 2002.

28. Metz & Page, 2002.
29. Metz & Page, 2002, p. 26.
30. Hochschild, 1983.
31. Peshkin, 1993, p. 24.
32. Peshkin, 1993, p. 24.
33. Britzman, 1986; Lortie, 1975.
34. Neumann, Pallas, & Peterson, 1999.
35. Turner, 1960, p. 83.
36. Turner, 1960, p. 85.
37. I have discussed these issues in detail elsewhere; see Labaree (1997a, 2000b).
38. Koerner, 1963.
39. Kramer, 1991.
40. Koerner, 1963, p. 18.
41. Goodlad, 1990, pp. 267–68.
42. Even in the absence of such technology, education schools have been creative about undercutting the academic standards of their competitors in the effort to draw tuition dollars. For example, at least one institution in Michigan (the School of Education at Grand Valley State University) makes school districts an offer that is hard to refuse. The district provides professional development courses for its teachers, designed and taught by school district staff; the education school offers master's credit for these courses and collects tuition, sharing a portion of the take with the district on a sliding scale based on enrollment. (School of Education, n.d., ca. 1998).

CHAPTER 6: STATUS DILEMMAS OF EDUCATION PROFESSORS

1. I am grateful to Tom Bird, Jeff Mirel, Lynn Fendler, and Barbara Beatty for their very helpful comments on early versions of this chapter.
2. NCES, 2002, calculated from table 235.
3. NCES, 2002, table 236.
4. Lanier & Little, 1986.
5. Ducharme & Agne, 1989.
6. Ducharme & Agne, 1989, p. 67.
7. Guba & Clark, 1978, tables 1 and 2.
8. Goodlad, 1990.
9. Fairweather, 2002, tables 1 and 2.
10. Fairweather, 1996, tables 2.5 and 2.6.
11. Lasley, 1986, inside cover.
12. Quoted in Ducharme, 1993, p. 4.
13. Sizer & Powell, 1969, p. 61.
14. Koerner, 1963, pp. 17–18.
15. Counelis, 1969.
16. Bagley, 1975.
17. AACTE, 1987, 1988.
18. Wisniewski & Ducharme, 1989.

19. Ducharme, 1993.
20. Shen, 1999.
21. Howey & Zimpher, 1990.
22. Ducharme, 1993, p. 13.
23. Ducharme, 1993, p. 52.
24. Ducharme, 1993, p. 57.
25. Ducharme, 1993, p. 58.
26. Ducharme, 1993, p. 64.
27. Ducharme, 1993, p. 105.
28. Ducharme, 1993, p. 106.
29. Ducharme, 1993, p. 106.
30. Ducharme, 1993, p. vii.
31. Ducharme, 1993, p. 13.
32. Ducharme, 1993, p. 17.
33. Ducharme, 1993, p. 112.
34. Ducharme, 1993, p. viii.
35. Ducharme, 1993, p. viii.
36. Ducharme, 1993, p. ix.
37. E.g., C. Sykes, 1988.
38. *Chronicle of Higher Education,* 2002, p. 31.
39. NCES, 2002, table 236.
40. Fairweather, 1994, calculated from table 5.
41. NCES, 2002, table 262.
42. Guba & Clark, 1978, table 2.
43. Lanier & Little, 1986, p. 530.
44. Judge, 1982; Goodlad, 1990; Clifford & Guthrie, 1988.
45. Holmes Group, 1986.
46. Clifford & Guthrie, 1988.
47. Just to make things more confusing, the Holmes Group issued another report in 1995 (*Tomorrow's Schools of Education*), in which it effectively renounced the university-based reform strategy defined in *Tomorrow's Teachers* and embraced a school-based and teacher-oriented approach that closely resembles the argument laid out in *Ed School.* See my analysis of this dramatic turnaround (Labaree, 1995b). In spite of this reversal of positions, the Holmes Group's first report remains an important and influential statement about how to resolve teacher education's status problem by drawing on the resources of the university.
48. One high-visibility proposal for the reform of teacher education in recent years is the one put forward by John Goodlad in *Teachers for Our Nation's Schools* (1990), with two supporting volumes (Goodlad, Soder, & Sirotnik, 1990a, 1990b). On the issues that divide *Tomorrow's Teachers* and *Ed School,* Goodlad tends to take a middle road. As a result, his book is less useful for this discussion than the other two, since they provide a clear set of alternatives.
49. Holmes Group, 1986, p. 6.
50. Holmes Group, 1986, pp. 25–26.

51. Holmes Group, 1986, p. ix.
52. Holmes Group, 1986, p. 20.
53. Holmes Group, 1986, pp. 62–63.
54. Holmes Group, 1986, p. 52.
55. Witz (1992) provides a discussion of the various defensive strategies adopted by semipro-fessional occupations seeking to close off competition from below.
56. See my detailed analysis of this question in Labaree, 1997a, chap. 6.
57. Clifford & Guthrie, 1988, p. 3.
58. Clifford & Guthrie, 1988, p. 3.
59. Clifford & Guthrie, 1988, p. 325.
60. See my discussion of this issue in more detail in Labaree, 1997a, chap. 6.
61. Clifford & Guthrie, 1988, pp. 349–50.

CHAPTER 7: THE ED SCHOOL'S ROMANCE WITH PROGRESSIVISM

1. I am deeply grateful to the following colleagues for the insightful critical readings they gave of earlier versions of this chapter: Tom Bird, Jeff Mirel, Lynn Fendler, Barbara Beatty, E. D. Hirsch, and Diane Ravitch. I presented a short version of this chapter and chapter 8 at the annual conference on educational policy at the Brookings Institution, Washington, D.C., May 2003. This was published in the Brookings Papers on Education Policy, 2004 (Labaree, 2004); reprinted by permission. An even shorter version was presented in a keynote address at the annual meeting of the International Standing Conference for the History of Education in São Paulo, August 2003. I am grateful to the participants at both conferences for their helpful comments.
2. Dewey, 1902/1990.
3. Dewey, 1902/1990.
4. Silberman, 1970.
5. Jackson, 1986.
6. Stevenson & Stigler, 1992.
7. Sfard, 1998.
8. Dewey, 1902/1990, pp. 185–87.
9. Dewey, 1902/1990, pp. 202–5.
10. Dewey, 1902/1990, p. 205. Diane Ravitch captures this aspect of Dewey's rhetoric nicely: "With the perspective of time, it is striking to recognize that John Dewey was locked in dualisms, the famous 'either-ors' that he so often wrote about. He frequently described opposing tendencies in education (school and society, the child and the curriculum, interest and effort, experience and education) and claimed that he wanted to reconcile these dualisms. However, he never presented them as equally compelling alternatives, so it was scarcely surprising that his followers unfailingly chose society, not the school; the child, not the curriculum; interest, not effort; experience, not subject matter" (Ravitch, 2000, p. 309).
11. Chall, 2000.
12. Chall, 2000, p. 29.
13. Chall, 2000, pp. 187–92.

14. Cremin, 1961, p. 328.
15. INTASC, 1992, preface.
16. INTASC, 1992.
17. Public Agenda, 1997b.
18. Bradley, 1997.
19. Public Agenda, 1994, 1997a.
20. Bradley, 1997.
21. Public Agenda, 1994, p. 43.
22. Hirsch, 1996, p. 69; emphasis in original.
23. Hirsch, 1996.
24. Hirsch, 1988.
25. Ravitch, 2002, p. 15.
26. Gardner, 2002, p. 24.
27. Hirsch, 1996, p. 218.
28. Dewey, 1902/1990, p. 187.
29. Hirsch, 1996, p. 74.
30. Hirsch, 1996, p. 75.
31. Cohen, 1989.
32. Reese, 2001, p. 411.
33. Reese, 2001, p. 19.
34. Hirsch, 1996.
35. Ravitch, 2000.
36. Hofstadter, 1962.
37. Ducharme, 1993, p. 106.
38. Sizer & Powell, 1969, p. 73.
39. Stone, 1999, p. 209.
40. Stone, 1999, p. 203.
41. Newsam, 1999.
42. Cremin, 1961, p. x.
43. Kliebard, 1986, p. xi.
44. Tyack, 1974.
45. Church & Sedlak, 1976.
46. Kliebard, 1986.
47. See for example, Rury, 2002.
48. Lagemann, 1989, p. 185.
49. This brief summary of the history of the two main strands of progressive education in the United States draws from the extensive existing historical literature on the subject. The major source is Kliebard (1986), but I also draw from Tyack (1974), Cremin (1961), and Rury (2002).
50. Kliebard, 1986.
51. Kliebard, 1986, p. 108.
52. Quoted in Kliebard, 1986, p. 109.
53. Commission on Reorganization, 1918, pp. 10–11.
54. Commission on Reorganization, 1918, p. 22.

55. E.g., Hofstadter, 1962, p. 336.

56. Kliebard, 1986, p. 114; Ravitch, 2000, p. 128.

57. Bureau of the Census, 1975, table H 412.

58. Board of Public Education (Philadelphia), 1908–1945.

59. Krug, 1964, 1972.

60. Angus & Mirel, 1999.

61. Dewey, 1902/1990, p. 205.

62. Cremin, 1961; Church & Sedlak, 1976; Ravitch, 2000; Rury, 2002.

63. Cuban, 1993.

64. Zilversmit, 1993.

65. Cuban, 1993, table 2.1.

66. Cuban, 1993, p. 75.

67. Cuban, 1993, figures 2.1 and 2.2.

68. Zilversmit, 1993, p. 34.

69. Zilversmit, 1993, p. 168.

70. Lagemann, 1989.

71. Katz, 1966, p. 326.

72. Powell, 1976.

73. Katz, 1966.

74. Katz, 1966, p. 328.

75. Katz, 1966, p. 332.

76. Katz, 1966, p. 334.

77. Elmore & McLaughlin, 1988.

78. Cremin, 1961, p. 175.

79. Cremin, 1961, p. 200.

80. Dewey's primary focus at Columbia was the philosophy department, but he maintained connections with people at Teachers College as well.

81. Tyack & Cuban, 1995.

82. Shulman 1986b, 1987; Wilson, Richert, & Shulman, 1987.

83. Shulman, 1987, p. 8.

84. Shulman, 1986b, p. 9.

85. Shulman, 1986b, p. 8.

86. Shulman, 1986b.

87. Shulman, 1986b, p. 7.

88. Phone conversation, December 14, 2002.

89. Labaree, 1997a.

CHAPTER 8: THE TROUBLE WITH ED SCHOOLS

1. I am grateful to the following colleagues for the insightful critical comments they gave me on earlier drafts of this chapter: Tom Bird, Lynn Fendler, Barbara Beatty, E. D. Hirsch, and Diane Ravitch. I presented a short version of this chapter and chapter 7 at the annual conference on educational policy at the Brookings Institution, Washington, D.C., May 2003. This was published in the Brookings Papers on Education Policy, 2004

(Labaree, 2004); reprinted by permission. I am grateful to the participants at the conference for their helpful comments.

2. NCES, 2002, computed from tables 37, 63, and 191.

3. Hirsch, 1996; Ravitch, 2000.

4. Hirsch, 1996, p. 219.

5. Hirsch, 1996, pp. 115–16.

6. According to one report, more than one-quarter of teachers are not fully licensed (NCTAF, 1996, p. 15).

7. Richardson & Placier, 2002, p. 915.

8. Richardson & Placier, 2002, p. 915.

9. Lortie, 1975.

10. Cremin, 1961, p. 328; emphasis in original.

11. Katz, 1975, p. 117.

12. Chall, 2000, p. 35.

13. Goodlad, 1983; Cuban, 1993.

14. Chall, 2000, p. 114.

15. Cuban, 1993; Zilversmit, 1993.

16. Goodlad, 1983, pp. 123–24.

17. Cohen, 1990, p. 312.

18. Cohen, 1990, p. 311.

19. Cohen, 1990, p. 313.

20. Cohen, 1990, p. 314.

21. Cohen, 1990, p. 320.

22. Cohen, 1990, p. 324.

23. Barnes, 2002.

24. Barnes, 2002, p. 4.

25. Barnes, 2002, p. 5.

26. Barnes, 2002, p. 6.

27. Barnes, 2002, p. 7.

28. Barnes, 2002, p. v.

29. Mathews, 2002a.

30. Mathews, 1998.

31. Mathews, 2002b.

32. Ravitch, 2000, pp. 14–15.

33. Hirsch, 1988.

34. Ravitch, 2000, p. 15.

35. Bowles & Gintis, 1976; Oakes, 1985; Anyon, 1981.

36. Commission on Reorganization, 1918, pp. 10–11.

37. Commission on Reorganization, 1918, p. 22.

38. For a full account of the origins and consequences of these two goals (plus a third, democratic equality) for American education, see Labaree (1997a, chap. 1), from which this section is drawn.

39. Sedlak et al., 1986; Powell, Farrar, & Cohen, 1985.

40. Labaree, 1997a.

41. Quoted in Kliebard, 1986, p. 167.

42. Kliebard, 1986, p. 166.

43. Kilpatrick, 1918, p. 3 of web version of paper.

44. Lagemann, 2000, p. 236.

45. Tom, 1984; Shulman, 1986.

46. Hamilton and McWilliam, 2001.

47. Floden, 2001, p. 13.

48. Floden, 2001, pp. 13–14.

49. What Works Clearinghouse, http://w-w-c.org.

50. National Research Council, 2002.

51. This is the title of a booklet summarizing research about teaching and learning that was widely distributed by the U.S. Department of Education in 1986 (U.S. Dept. of Ed, 1986). It is also the name given to a website (the What Works Clearinghouse) established by the department in 2002 for the purpose of promoting science-based standards for evaluation of educational research (http://w-w-c.org).

52. Katz, 1966.

53. Kennedy, 1990.

54. Kennedy, 1990, p. 813.

55. Schön, 1983.

56. Dewey, 1904/1964.

57. Kennedy cites as examples Schwab, 1978; and Liston & Zeichner, 1987.

58. Kennedy, 1990, p. 815; emphasis in original.

59. Kennedy, 1990, p. 815.

60. I am grateful to my colleague Tom Bird (2003) for forcefully pointing this out to me in his comments on an earlier version of this chapter.

61. Ravitch, 2000, p. 464.

62. E.g., Finn, 2002; Hirsch, 1996; Ravitch, 2000; Sowell, 1993.

63. Kilpatrick, 1918, p. 5.

64. Katz, 1966.

65. Collins, 1979; Labaree, 1997a.

66. Schön, 1983.

67. Holmes Group, 1986.

68. Holmes Group, 1995.

References

Abbott, Andrew. 1988. *The system of professions*. Chicago: University of Chicago Press.

Altenbaugh, Richard J., and Kathleen Underwood. 1990. The evolution of normal schools. In John I. Goodlad, Roger Soder, and Kenneth A. Sirotnik, eds., *Places where teachers are taught*, 136–86. San Francisco: Jossey-Bass.

American Association for Colleges of Teacher Education. 1988. *RATE I: Teaching teachers: Facts and figures*. Washington, D.C.: AACTE.

American Association for Colleges of Teacher Education. 1987. *RATE I: Teaching teachers: Facts and figures*. Washington, D.C.: AACTE.

American Educational Research Association. 2002. *Annual meeting program*. Washington, D.C.: AERA.

Anderson, Gary L. 2002. Reflecting on research for doctoral students in education. *Educational Researcher* 31(7): 22–25.

Angus, David L., and Jeffrey E. Mirel, 1999. *The failed promise of the American high school, 1890–1995*. New York: Teachers College Press.

Anyon, Jean. 1981. Social class and school knowledge. *Curriculum Inquiry* 11: 3–42.

Bagley, Ayers. 1975. *The professor of education: An assessment of conditions*. Minneapolis, Minn.: Society of Professors of Education.

Barnes, Christopher. 2002. *What do teachers teach? A survey of America's fourth and eighth grade teachers*. New York: Manhattan Institute.

Bebow, John. 2003. He has $300 million for Detroit: Bob Thompson challenges establishment by exhausting fortune to build schools. *Detroit News,* February 16.

Becher, Tony. 1989. *Academic tribes and territories: Intellectual inquiry and the cultures of the disciplines.* Bristol, Pa.: Open University Press.

Berg, Ivar. 1971. *Education and jobs: The great training robbery.* Boston: Beacon.

Berliner, David C. 2002. Educational research: The hardest science of all. *Educational Researcher* 31(8): 18–20.

Bestor, Arthur. 1953. *Educational wastelands: The retreat from learning in our public schools.* Urbana: University of Illinois Press.

Bird, Thomas. 2003. Personal letter, January 8.

Board of Public Education (Philadelphia). 1908–1945. *Annual Reports.* Philadelphia: by the Board.

Booth, Wayne C., Gregory G. Colomb, and Joseph M. Williams. 1995. *The craft of research.* Chicago: University of Chicago Press.

Borrowman, Merle L. 1971. Teachers, education of: History. In L. C. Deighton, *Encyclopedia of Education,* vol. 9, 71–79. New York: Macmillan.

———, ed. 1965. *Teacher education in America: A documentary history.* New York: Teachers College Press.

———. 1953. *The liberal and technical in teacher education: A historical survey of American thought.* New York: Teachers College Press.

Bowles, Samuel, and Herbert Gintis. 1976. *Schooling in capitalist America.* New York: Basic Books.

Bradley, Ann. 1997. Professors' attitudes out of sync, study says. *Education Week,* October 29.

Britzman, Deborah P. 1986. Cultural myths in the making of a teacher: Biography and social structure in teacher education. *Harvard Educational Review* 56(4): 442–56.

Brown, David K. 1995. *Degrees of control: A sociology of educational expansionism and occupational credentialism.* New York: Teachers College Press.

Bureau of the Census. 1975. *Historical Statistics of the United States.* Washington, D.C.: U.S. Government Printing Office.

Chall, Jeanne S. 2000. *The academic achievement challenge: What really works in the classroom?* New York: Guilford.

Chronicle of Higher Education. 2002. *Almanac, 2002–3,* 49(1), August 30.

Chronicle of Higher Education. 1999. Facts and figures: Earned doctorates. November 26. Retrieved September 15, 2000, from http://chronicle.com/weekly/v46/i14/stats/4614_doctorates.htm.

Church, Robert L., and Michael W. Sedlak. 1976. *Education in the United States.* New York: Free Press.

Clifford, Geraldine Joncich. 1986. The formative years of schools of education in America: A five-institution analysis. *American Journal of Education* 94: 427–46.

Clifford, Geraldine Joncich, and James W. Guthrie. 1988. *Ed school: A brief for professional education.* Chicago: University of Chicago Press.

Cochran-Smith, Marilyn, and Susan L. Lytle. 1999. The teacher research movement: A decade later. *Educational Researcher* 28(7): 15–25.

————. 1990. Research on teaching and teacher research: The issues that divide. *Educational Researcher* 19(2): 2–11.

Cohen, David K. 1990. A revolution in one classroom: The case of Mrs. Oublier. *Educational Evaluation and Policy Analysis* 12(3): 311–29.

————. 1989. Willard Waller, on hating school and loving education. In D. J. Willower and W. L. Boyd, eds., *Willard Waller on education and schools.* San Francisco: McCutchan.

————. 1988. Teaching practice: Plus ça change. In Philip W. Jackson, ed., *Contributing to educational change: Perspectives on research and practice,* 27–84. Berkeley, Calif.: McCutchan.

Cohen, David K., and Michael S. Garet. 1975. Reforming educational policy with applied social research. *Harvard Educational Review* 45: 17–43.

Collins, Randall. 1979. *The Credential Society: An Historical Sociology of Educational Stratification.* New York: Academic Press.

Commission on the Reorganization of Secondary Education. 1918. *Cardinal principles of secondary education.* Bulletin no. 35, U.S. Department of Interior, Bureau of Education. Washington, D.C.: U.S. Government Printing Office.

Cook, K. M. 1927. *State laws and regulations governing teachers' certificates.* Bulletin no. 19. Washington, D.C.: Bureau of Education.

Counelis, James Steve, ed. 1969. *To be a phoenix: The education professoriate.* Bloomington, Ind.: Phi Delta Kappa.

Cremin, Lawrence A. 1961. *The transformation of the school: Progressivism in American education, 1957–1976.* New York: Vintage.

Cronbach, Lee J., and Patrick Suppes, eds. 1969. *Research for tomorrow's schools: Disciplined inquiry for education.* Report of the Committee on Educational Research of the National Academy of Education. New York: Macmillan.

Cuban, Larry. 1993. *How teachers taught: Constancy and change in American classrooms, 1890–1980.* 2d ed. New York: Teachers College Press.

Cusick, Philip A. 1992. *The educational system: Its nature and logic.* New York: McGraw-Hill.

Damrosch, David. 1995. *We scholars: Changing the culture of the university.* Cambridge, Mass.: Harvard University Press.

Dewey, John. 1933. *How we think.* Lexington, Mass.: D.C. Heath.

————. 1904/1964. The relation of theory to practice in education. In Reginald D. Archambault, ed., *John Dewey on education,* 314–38. Chicago: University of Chicago Press.

————. 1902/1990. "The child and the curriculum." In *The school and society and the child and the curriculum.* Chicago: University of Chicago Press.

Donmoyer, Robert. 1985. The rescue from relativism: Two failed attempts and an alternative strategy. *Educational Researcher* 14: 13–20.

Ducharme, Edward R. 1993. *The lives of teacher educators.* New York: Teachers College Press.

Ducharme, Edward R., and Russell M. Agne. 1989. Professors of education: Uneasy residents of academe. In Richard Wisniewski and Edward R. Ducharme, eds., *The professors of teaching: An inquiry,* 67–86. Albany: State University of New York Press.

————. 1982. The educational professoriate: A research-based perspective. *Journal of Teacher Education* 33(6): 30–36.

Eisenmann, Linda. 1990. The influence of bureaucracy and markets: Teacher education in Pennsylvania. In J. I. Goodlad, R. Soder, and K. A. Sirotnik, eds., *Places where teachers are taught,* 287–329. San Francisco: Jossey-Bass.

Elmore, Richard F., and Milbrey W. McLaughlin. 1988. *Steady work.* Santa Monica, Calif.: Rand.

Elsbree, Willard S. 1939. *The American teacher: Evolution of a profession in a democracy.* New York: American Book Company.

Erickson, Frederick. 1986. Qualitative methods in research on teaching. In Merlin C. Wittrock, ed., *Handbook of research on teaching,* 3d ed., 119–61. New York: Macmillan.

Fairweather, James S. 2002. The mythologies of faculty productivity. *Journal of Higher Education* 73: 25–48.

———. 1996. *Faculty work and public trust: Restoring the value of teaching and public service in American academic life.* Boston: Allyn and Bacon.

———. 1994. The value of teaching, research, and service. In National Education Association, *The NEA 1994 almanac of higher education,* 39–58. Washington, D.C.: NEA.

Fenstermacher, Gary D. 2002. A commentary on research that serves teacher education. *Journal of Teacher Education* 53(3): 242–47.

———. 1990. Some moral considerations on teaching as a profession. In John I. Goodlad, Roger Soder, and Kenneth A. Sirotnik, eds., *The moral dimensions of teaching,* 130–51. San Francisco: Jossey-Bass.

Feuer, Michael J., Lisa Towne, and Richard J. Shavelson. 2002. Scientific culture and educational research. *Educational Researcher* 31(8): 4–14.

Finn, Chester E., Jr. 2002. Introduction. In Chester E. Finn Jr., ed., *September 11: What our children need to know,* 4–11. Washington, D.C.: Thomas B. Fordham Foundation.

Floden, Robert E. 2001. "Research on effects of teaching: A continuing model for research on teaching." In Virginia Richardson, ed., *Handbook of research on teaching,* 4th ed., 3–16. Washington, D.C.: American Educational Research Association.

Floden, Robert E., and Christopher M. Clark. 1988. Preparing teachers for uncertainty. *Teachers College Record* 89: 505–24.

Florio-Ruane, Susan. 2002. More light: An argument for complexity in studies of teaching and teacher education. *Journal of Teacher Education* 53(3): 205–15.

Freedman, Samuel G. 1990. *Small victories: The real world of a teacher, her students, and their high school.* New York: HarperCollins.

Gage, Nathaniel. L. 1996. Confronting counsels of despair for the behavioral sciences. *Educational Researcher* 25(3): 5–15, 22.

———. 1989. The paradigm wars and their aftermath: A "historical" sketch of research on teaching since 1989. *Teachers College Record* 91(2): 135–50.

———. 1963. *Handbook of research on teaching.* Chicago: Rand McNally.

Gardner, Howard. 2002. "The study of the humanities." *Daedalus* 131(3): 22–25.

Gideonse, Henrick D., ed. 1992. *Teacher education policy: Narratives, stories, and cases.* Albany: State University of New York Press.

Ginsburg, Mark B. 1988. *Contradictions in teacher education and society: A critical analysis.* New York: Falmer.

Glazer, Nathan. 1974. The schools of the minor professions. *Minerva* 12(3): 346–64.

Goldman, Robert, and Ann Tickamyer. 1984. Status attainment and the commodity form: Stratification in historical perspective. *American Sociological Review* 49: 196–209.

Goodlad, John I. 1990. *Teachers of our nation's schools.* San Francisco: Jossey-Bass.

———. 1983. *A place called school.* New York: McGraw-Hill.

Goodlad, John I., Roger Soder, and Kenneth A. Sirotnik, eds. 1990a. *Places where teachers are taught.* San Francisco: Jossey-Bass.

———. 1990b. *The moral dimensions of teaching.* San Francisco: Jossey-Bass.

Graduate Record Examination Board. 1999. *Guide to the use of scores, 1999–2000.* Princeton, N.J.: Educational Testing Service.

Green, Thomas F. (with the assistance of David P. Ericson and Robert H. Seidman). 1980. *Predicting the behavior of the educational system.* Syracuse, N.Y.: Syracuse University Press.

Guba, Egon, and David L. Clark. 1978. Levels of R & D productivity in schools of education. *Educational Researcher* 7: 3–9.

Hamilton, David, and Erica McWilliam. 2001. Ex-centric voices that frame research on teaching. In Virginia Richardson, ed., *Handbook of research on teaching,* 4th ed., 17–43. Washington, D.C.: American Educational Research Association.

Hartz, Louis. 1955. *The liberal tradition in America.* New York: Harcourt, Brace and World.

Herbst, Jurgen. 1989a. *And sadly teach: Teacher education and professionalization in American culture.* Madison: University of Wisconsin Press.

———. 1989b. Teacher preparation in the nineteenth century: Institutions and purposes. In Donald Warren, ed., *American teachers: Histories of a profession at work,* 213–36. New York: Macmillan.

———. 1980. Nineteenth-century normal schools in the United States: A fresh look. *History of Education* 9: 219–27.

Hirsch, E. D., Jr. 1996. *The schools we need and why we don't have them.* New York: Doubleday.

———. 1988. *Cultural literacy: What every American needs to know.* New York: Vintage.

Hochschild, Arlie. 1983. *The managed heart: Commercialization of human feeling.* Berkeley: University of California Press.

Hofstadter, Richard. 1962. *Anti-intellectualism in American life.* New York: Vintage.

Holmes Group. 1995. *Tomorrow's Schools of Education.* East Lansing, Mich.: author.

———. 1990. *Tomorrow's Schools.* East Lansing, Mich.: author.

———. 1986. *Tomorrow's Teachers.* East Lansing, Mich.: author.

Holmes Partnership. 2003. About the Holmes Partnership. http://www.holmespartnership.org/about.html, accessed February 20, 2003.

Houston, W. Robert, ed. 1990. *Handbook of research on teacher education.* New York: Macmillan.

Howe, Kenneth R. 1985. Two dogmas of educational research. *Educational Researcher* 14: 10–18.

Howe, Kenneth, and M. Eisenhart. 1990. Standards for qualitative (and quantitative) research: A prolegomenon. *Educational Researcher* 19(4): 2–9.

Howey, Kenneth R., and Nancy L. Zimpher. 1990. Professors and deans of education. In W. Robert Houston, ed., *Handbook of research on teacher education,* 349–70. New York: Macmillan.

Huberman, Michael. 1996. Moving mainstream: Taking a closer look at teacher research. *Language Arts* 73:124–40.

INTASC (Interstate New Teacher Assessment and Support Consortium). 1992. Model standards for beginning teacher licensing and development: A resource for state dialogue. http://www.ccsso.org/intasc.html; accessed November, 2002.

Jackson, Philip W. 1986. *The practice of teaching.* New York: Teachers College Press.

Jencks, Christopher, and David Riesman. 1968. *The academic revolution.* Chicago: University of Chicago Press.

Johnson, William R. 1989. Teachers and teacher training in the twentieth century. In Donald Warren, ed., *American teachers: Histories of a profession at work,* 237–56. New York: Macmillan.

———. 1987. Empowering practitioners: Holmes, Carnegie, and the lessons of history. *History of Education Quarterly* 27: 221–40.

Judge, Harry. 1982. *American graduate schools of education: A view from abroad.* New York: Ford Foundation.

Katz, Michael B. 1975. *Class, bureaucracy, and schools* (expanded edition). New York: Praeger.

———. 1966. From theory to survey in graduate schools of education. *Journal of Higher Education* 36: 325–34.

Kennedy, Mary M. 1990. Choosing a goal for professional education. In W. Robert Houston, ed., *Handbook of research on teacher education.* New York: Macmillan.

Kilpatrick, William H. 1918. The project method. *Teachers College Record* 19(4): 319–35; www.tcrecord.org; accessed December 2002.

Kliebard, Herbert. 1986. *The struggle for the American curriculum, 1893–1958.* New York: Routledge.

Koerner, James. 1963. *The Miseducation of American Teachers.* Boston: Houghton Mifflin.

Kramer, Rita. 1991. *Ed School Follies: The Miseducation of America's Teachers.* New York: Free Press.

Krug, Edward A. 1972. *The American high school, 1920–1941.* Madison: University of Wisconsin Press.

———. 1964. *The American high school, 1880–1920.* Madison: University of Wisconsin Press.

Kuhn, Thomas S. 1970. *The structure of scientific revolutions,* 2d ed., enlarged. Chicago: University of Chicago Press.

Labaree, David F. (In press, 2004.) The ed school's romance with progressivism. In Diane Ravitch, ed., *Brookings Papers on Education Policy, 2004.* Washington, D.C.: Brookings Institution Press.

———. 2003. The peculiar problems of preparing and becoming educational researchers. *Educational Researcher* 32(4): 13-22.

———. 2000a. On the nature of teaching and teacher education: Difficult practices that look easy. *Journal of Teacher Education* 51(3): 228–33.

———. 2000b. Resisting educational standards. *Phi Delta Kappan* 82(1): 28–33.

———. 1998. Educational researchers: Living with a lesser form of knowledge. *Educational Researcher* 27(8): 4–12.

————. 1997a. *How to succeed in school without really learning: The credentials race in American education.* New Haven: Yale University Press.

————. 1997b. Public goods, private goods: The American struggle over educational goals. *American Educational Research Journal* 34(1): 39–81.

————. 1995a. The lowly status of teacher education in the U.S.: The impact of markets and the implications for reform. In N. K. Shimihara and I. V. Holowinsky, eds., *Teacher education in industrialized nations: Issues in changing social contexts,* 41–85. New York: Garland Publishing.

————. 1995b. A disabling vision: Rhetoric and reality in *Tomorrow's Schools of Education. Teachers College Record* 97(2): 166–205.

————. 1992. Power, knowledge, and the rationalization of teaching: A genealogy of the movement to professionalize teaching. *Harvard Educational Review* 62: 123–54.

————. 1990. From comprehensive high school to community college: Politics, markets, and the evolution of educational opportunity. In R. Corwin, ed., *Research in sociology of education and socialization,* vol. 9, pp. 203–40. Greenwich, Conn.: JAI Press.

————. 1988. *The making of an American high school: The credentials market and the Central High School of Philadelphia, 1838–1939.* New Haven: Yale University Press.

Lagemann, Ellen Condliffe. 2000. *An elusive science: The troubling history of educational research.* Chicago: University of Chicago Press.

————. 1989. The plural worlds of educational research. *History of Education Quarterly* 29(2): 185–214.

Lanier, Judith E., and Judith Warren Little. 1986. Research on teacher education. In Merlin C. Wittrock, ed., *Handbook of research on teaching,* 3d ed., 527–69. New York: Macmillan.

Larson, Magali S. 1977. *The rise of professionalism.* Berkeley: University of California Press.

Lasley, T. 1986. Editorial. *Journal of Teacher Education* 37, inside cover.

Lensmire, Timothy J. 1994. *When children write: Critical re-visions of the writing workshop.* New York: Teachers College Press.

Levin, Robert A. 1994. *Educating elementary school teachers: The struggle for coherent visions, 1909–1978.* Lanham, Md.: University Press of America.

Lindblom, Charles E., and David K. Cohen. 1979. *Usable knowledge: Social science and social problem solving.* New Haven, Conn.: Yale University Press.

Liston, Daniel P., and Kenneth M. Zeichner. 1991. *Teacher education and the social conditions of schooling.* New York: Routledge.

Lortie, Dan C. 1975. *Schoolteacher: A sociological study.* Chicago: University of Chicago.

Marx, Karl. 1867–94/1967. *Capital.* New York: International Publishers.

Mathews, Jay. 2002a. Understanding what teachers teach. *Washington Post,* September 24. www.Washingtonpost.com, accessed December 2002.

————. 2002b. A champion in the fight against testing standards. *Washington Post,* December 17. www.Washingtonpost.com, accessed December 2002.

————. 1998. *Class struggle: What's wrong (and right) with America's best public high schools.* New York: Times Books.

Merton, Robert K. 1968. Patterns of influence: Local and cosmopolitan influentials. In *Social theory and social structure,* enlarged ed., 441–74. New York: Free Press.

Metz, Mary Haywood. 2001. Intellectual border crossing in graduate education: A report from the field. *Educational Researcher* 30(5): 12–18.

Metz, Mary Haywood, and Reba N. Page. 2002. The uses of practitioner research and status issues in educational research: Reply to Gary Anderson. *Educational Researcher* 31(7): 26–27.

Mills, Geoffrey E. 2002. *Action research: A guide for the teacher researcher,* 2d ed. Englewood Cliffs, N.J.: Prentice-Hall.

National Center for Educational Statistics. 2002. *Digest of education statistics, 2001.* Washington, D.C.: Government Printing Office.

———. 1998. *Digest of education statistics, 1997.* Washington, D.C.: U.S. Dept. of Education.

———. 1991. *Digest of education statistics, 1992.* Washington, D.C.: Government Printing Office.

National Commission on Teaching and America's Future. 1996. *What matters most: Teaching for America's future.* New York: National Commission.

National Research Council. 2002. *Scientific research in education.* Edited by R. J. Shavelson and L. Towne, Committee on Scientific Principles for Education Research. Washington, D.C.: National Academy Press.

Neumann, Anna, Aaron Pallas, and Penelope Peterson. 1999. Preparing education practitioners to practice education research. In Ellen Condliffe Lagemann and Lee S. Shulman, eds., *Issues in education research: Problems and possibilities,* 247–88. San Francisco: Jossey-Bass.

Neumann, Anna, and Penelope Peterson, eds. 1997. *Learning from our lives: Women, research, and autobiography in education.* New York: Teachers College Press.

Newsam, Peter. 1999. Teaching and learning. *Microsoft Encarta Encyclopedia 2000.*

Oakes, Jeannie. 1985. *Keeping track: How schools structure inequality.* New Haven, Conn.: Yale University Press.

Page, Reba N. 2001. Reshaping graduate preparation in education research methods: One school's experience. *Educational Researcher* 30(5): 19–25.

Pallas, Aaron M. 2001. Preparing education doctoral students for epistemological diversity. *Educational Researcher* 30(5): 6–11.

Parsons, Talcott. 1951. *The social system.* New York: Free Press.

Paul, James L., and Kofi Marfo. 2001. Preparation of educational researchers in philosophical foundations of inquiry. *Review of Educational Research* 71(4): 525–47.

Peshkin, Alan. 1993. The goodness of qualitative research. *Educational Researcher* 22(2): 24–30.

Popkewitz, Thomas S. 2002. How the alchemy makes inquiry, evidence, and exclusion. *Journal of Teacher Education* 53(3): 262–67.

———, ed. 1987. *Critical studies in teacher education: Its folklore, theory, and practice.* New York: Falmer.

Powell, Arthur G. 1980. *The uncertain profession: Harvard and the search for educational authority.* Cambridge, Mass.: Harvard University Press.

———. 1976. University schools of education in the twentieth century. *Peabody Journal of Education* 54(1): 3–20.

Powell, Arthur, Eleanor Farrar, and David K. Cohen. 1985. *The shopping mall high school: Winners and losers in the educational marketplace.* Boston: Houghton-Mifflin.

Public Agenda. 1997a. *Getting by: What American teenagers really think about their schools.* New York: Public Agenda.

———. 1997b. *Different drummers: How teachers of teachers view public education.* New York: Public Agenda.

———. 1994. *First things first: What Americans expect from the public schools.* New York: Public Agenda.

Ravitch, Diane. 2002. Education after the culture wars. *Daedalus* 131(3): 5–21.

———. 2000. *Left back: A century of failed school reforms.* New York: Simon and Schuster.

Reese, William J. 2001. The origins of progressive education. *History of Education Quarterly* 41(1): 1–24.

Rhoades, Gary. 1990. Change in an unanchored enterprise: Colleges of education. *Review of Higher Education* 13: 187–214.

Richardson, Virginia, ed. 2001. *Handbook of research on teaching,* 4th ed. Washington, D.C.: American Educational Research Association.

Richardson, Virginia, and Peggy Placier. 2002. Teacher change. In Virginia Richardson, ed., *Handbook of research on teaching,* 4th ed., 905–47. Washington, D.C.: American Educational Research Association.

Rose, Lowell C., and Alec M. Gallup. 2001. The thirty-third annual Phi Delta Kappa / Gallup poll of the public's attitudes toward the public schools. *Phi Delta Kappan* 83(1): 41–58.

Rury, John L. 2002. *Education and social change: Themes in the history of American education.* Mahwah, N.J.: Lawrence Erlbaum.

Schön, Donald A. 1983. *The Reflective Practitioner: How Professionals Think in Action.* New York: Basic.

School of Education, Grand Valley State University. N.d., ca. 1998. *Professional development partnerships.* Grand Rapids, Mich.: Grand Valley State University.

Schwab, Joseph J. 1978. *Science, curriculum, and liberal education: Selected essays.* Chicago: University of Chicago Press.

Sedlak, Michael W. 1989. Let us go and buy a schoolmaster. In Donald Warren, ed., *American teachers: Histories of a profession at work,* 257–90. New York: Macmillan.

Sedlak, Michael W., et al. 1986. *Selling students short: Classroom bargains and academic reform in the American high school.* New York: Teachers College Press.

Sedlak, Michael W., and Steven Schlossman. 1986. *Who will teach?* Santa Monica, Calif.: Rand.

Sfard, Anna. 1998. On two metaphors for learning and the dangers of choosing just one. *Educational Researcher* 27(2): 4–13.

Shen, Jianping. 1999. *The school of education: Its mission, faculty, and reward structure.* New York: Peter Lang.

Shulman, Lee S. 1987. Knowledge and teaching: Foundations of the new reform. *Harvard Educational Review* 57(1): 1–22.

———. 1986a. Paradigms and research programs in the study of teaching: A contemporary perspective. In Merlin C. Wittrock, ed., *Handbook of research on teaching,* 3d ed., 3–36. New York: Macmillan.

———. 1986b. Those who understand: Knowledge growth in teaching. *Educational Researcher* 15(1): 4–14.

Sikula, John, ed. 1996. *Handbook of research on teacher education,* 2d ed. New York: Macmillan.

Silberman, Charles. 1970. *Crisis in the classroom.* New York: Vintage.

Sizer, Theodore, and Arthur G. Powell. 1969. Changing conceptions of the professor of education. In James Steve Counelis, ed., *To be a phoenix: The education professoriate,* 61–76. Bloomington, Ind.: Phi Delta Kappa.

Sowell, Thomas. 1993. *Inside American education: The decline, the deception, the dogmas.* New York: Free Press.

Stevenson, Harold W., and J. W. Stigler. 1992. *The learning gap: Why our schools are failing and what we can learn from Japanese and Chinese education.* New York: Summit Books.

Stone, J. E. 1999. The National Council for Accreditation of Teacher Education: Whose standards? In Marci Kanstoroom and Chester E. Finn Jr., eds., *Better teachers, better schools,* 199–214. Washington, D.C.: Thomas B. Fordham Foundation.

Stringer, Ernest T., and Egon G. Guba. 1999. *Action research,* 2d ed. New York: Corwin.

Sykes, Charles J. 1988. *Profscam: Professors and the demise of higher education.* New York: St. Martin's.

Tom, Alan R. 1984. *Teaching as a moral craft.* New York: Longman.

Toulmin, Stephen. 1972. *Human understanding.* Princeton, N.J.: Princeton University Press.

Travers, Robert M. W., ed. 1973. *Handbook of research on teaching,* 2d ed. Chicago: Rand McNally.

Trow, Martin. 1988. American higher education: Past, present, and future. *Educational Researcher* 17(3): 13–23.

Turner, Ralph. 1960. Sponsored and contest mobility and the school system. *American Sociological Review* 25: 855–67.

Tyack, David. 1974. *The one best system.* Cambridge, Mass.: Harvard University Press.

Tyack, David, and Larry Cuban. 1995. *Tinkering toward utopia: Reflections on a century of public school reform.* Cambridge, Mass.: Harvard University Press.

Urban, Wayne J. 1990. Historical studies of teacher education. In W. Robert Houston, ed., *Handbook of research on teacher education,* 59–82. New York: Macmillan.

U.S. Department of Education. 1986. *What works: Research about teaching and learning.* Washington, D.C.

U.S. News and World Report. 2000. Best graduate schools in education. Accessed June 22, 2000, from http://www.usnews.com/usnews/edu/beyond/gradrank/edu/gdedu1.htm.

———. 2001. Best graduate schools in education. Accessed August 11, 2001, from http://www.usnews.com/usnews/edu/beyond/gradrank/edu/gdedu1.htm.

Waller, Willard. 1932/1965. *The sociology of teaching.* New York: Wiley.

Warren, Donald. 1985. Learning from experience: History and teacher education. *Educational Researcher* 14(10): 5–12.

———, ed. 1989. *American teachers: Histories of a profession at work.* New York: Macmillan.

Weber, Max. 1968. *Economy and society.* Berkeley: University of California Press.

What Works Clearinghouse. U.S. Department of Education. http://w-w-c.org, accessed March 2003.

Wilson, Suzanne M., Robert E. Floden, and Joan Ferrini-Mundy. 2002. Teacher preparation research: An insider's view from the outside. *Journal of Teacher Education* 53(3): 190–204.

Wilson, Suzanne M., A. E. Richert, and Lee S. Shulman. 1987. 150 way of knowing: Representations of knowledge in teaching. In J. Calderhead, ed., *Exploring teachers' thinking*, 104–24. London: Cassell.

Wisniewski, Richard, and Edward R. Ducharme, eds., 1989, *The professors of teaching: An inquiry*. Albany: State University of New York Press.

Wittrock, Merlin C., ed. 1986. *Handbook of research on teaching*. 3d ed. New York: Macmillan.

Witz, Anne. 1992. *Professions and patriarchy*. New York: Routledge.

Young, Lauren Jones. 2001. Border crossings and other journeys: Re-envisioning the doctoral preparation of educational researchers. *Educational Researcher* 30(5): 3–5.

Zilversmit, Arthur. 1993. *Changing schools: Progressive education theory and practice, 1930–1960*. Chicago: University of Chicago Press.

Index